T0165339

——PARRIS——
ELECTORAL CONJECTURES
AND GOVERNANCE
IN GUYANA

HASLYN PARRIS

Order this book online at www.trafford.com
or email orders@trafford.com

Most Trafford titles are also available at major online book retailers.

Printed in the United States of America.

ISBN: 978-1-4269-6466-4 (sc)
ISBN: 978-1-4269-6465-7 (e)

Trafford rev. 08/18/2011

 www.trafford.com

North America & international
toll-free: 1 888 232 4444 (USA & Canada)
phone: 250 383 6864 ♦ fax: 812 355 4082

Contents

Overture

In 1767 Christoph Gluck, in the dedication of his opera *Alceste*, established the modern form of the opera overture by declaring that the overture should prepare the audience for the plot of the play. Accordingly, in *Alceste*, the overture, instead of closing before the curtain rises, merges into the mood of the opening act. This technique was later adopted by Richard Wagner in his operas such as Tristan and Isolde; and by Mozart (cf. Don Giovanni and The Magic Flute) in his overtures to set the emotional tones of the drama to follow. The works of Beethoven and Carl Maria von Weber have been described as showing similar thematic anticipation.

In the matter of the governance of The Co-operative Republic of Guyana I have succumbed to the temptation to alert readers to the tenor of the main text of this book by using the device of this type of 'Overture'. Maybe, what has worked for great pieces of musical drama will serve well for dealing with Guyana's great problem of governance.

In the foreword to *Alceste*, Gluck described his aims with the words **'simplicity, truth, and naturalness'.** This book is based mainly on the assumption that a governance system for a country, to be effective, must satisfy at least three necessary conditions.

The first condition is that there should be strict observance of whatever laws have been promulgated. This condition derives from acceptance of the principle of **'the rule of law'.** In this context, especially if the Constitution has been declared to be the supreme law, no deviations must be encouraged or permitted prior to effecting changes in the laws themselves; and such changes should be in accordance with the processes and procedures for change laid out in the Constitution.

The second necessary condition is that policies and practices should not be based on myths, or on other internally illogical or false statements or asseverations.

The third is that it should be presumed that there does **not** exist any perfect type of solution to problems of governance, good for all time and for all possible circumstances internal or external to the country being governed. This non-existence axiom ensures that appropriate revision could be made in a structured, systematic, and timely manner to policies and practices as a response to changes in the milieu in which the country finds itself.

An example of non-satisfaction of each of these necessary conditions is given below.

Even though my passport says so, I cannot be a citizen of the Republic of Guyana. The fact is that the 1980 Constitution states that it is the Constitution of the country named **'The Co-operative Republic of Guyana'**. Article 1 of the 1980 Constitution states: *'Guyana is an indivisible, secular, democratic, sovereign state in the course of transition from capitalism to socialism and shall be known as the Co-operative Republic of Guyana'*. That clause has not yet been changed in the current Constitution (although there is a proposed new Article 1 deriving from the Constitution Reform Commission Report of 1999)[1]. Re-naming the country requires a referendum, and none has been held on this matter! So much for the rule of law with respect to the very **first** Article of our Constitution! However, with gay and almost puerile abandon, we have persisted for at least a decade in asserting officially that our country is named **'The Republic of Guyana'**[2]. The difference between 'Cooperative' as an adjective and 'Cooperative' as a noun (with little faith in it as an effective form of economic organisation) has been ignored, **despite the clear intention of Article 13 of the Constitution**.

This is an interesting state of affairs, since in the 1974 publication *("A Primer for National Commitment")* by the then Ministry of National Development, the following two questions and answers were given, as Items 16 and 17 in the section entitled *"From a colony to a Nation"*:

---

1   The book: *'An Annotated Handbook of the 17 July 1999 Report of the Constitution Reform Commission Guyana'* contains all the recommended changes. It can be obtained by visiting Trafford Publishing at **www.trafford.com**

2   Guyana's ignoring of the Constitution in its consideration of a matter that is politically or technically difficult has the precedent of the behaviour of the US Congress in 1921, when Congressmen were constitutionally required to deal with the reapportionment of seats to States on the basis of the 1920 population census. Congress snubbed the Constitution (because of the political and technical difficulties associated with reapportionment) and stayed with the results that had been determined on the basis of the 1910 census, and so continued for at least the next thirty years!

"16.   WHY DID WE CHOOSE TO BECOME A 'CO-OPERATIVE REPUBLIC'?

We chose to become a Co-operative Republic because the system to be used for the all-round progress of the Republic is based on the idea of Guyanese pooling their skills, money and other resources and working together for the common good. The co-operative way of thinking and doing is promoted and supported by Government."

"17.   WHY DO WE CALL OUR COUNTRY THE CO-OPERATIVE REPUBLIC OF GUYANA?

We call our country the Co-operative Republic of Guyana for these reasons:

a.   We will build Guyana through our work in co-operatives.

b.   We will build Guyana by working in co-operation with each other as proud and loyal Guyanese.

c.   Even before Guyana became a Republic, the Guyanese people knew that working together was best for them."

My recollection of the discussions on this matter at the Constitution Reform Commission is that great emphasis was placed on the unsuitability of the form of economic organisation called 'co-operative'.

I was born in the village of Friendship, which adjoins the village of Buxton, on the East Coast of Demerara; and have the audacity to consider myself 'Buxtonian', having been delivered by the Buxtonian midwife, Nurse French. Buxton/Friendship is one of the main areas in Guyana in which 'false names' are so prevalent and accepted that many persons have official names on their Birth Certificates that bear no relation to what the members of the village normally call them and know them as[3]. Thus **'Badap'** may be Mr Ifill; **'Oyo'** may be Ms Vaulda Robinson; and **'Mala'** may be Mr Anthony Gonsalves. Few people know the officially registered names, and the majority refer to each person by their **'false'** or **'call'** name. In the case of Guyana, the **country's** 'false' name is routinely used by even the

---

3   My understanding is that apart from *'false names'*, Buxton also has a reputation for **steatopygous females**. See Appendix #0 to this overture for some greater insights into the matter.

persons in the highest levels of political leadership; and it appears on legal documents, e.g Passports![4]

As a general rule, people behave in accordance with their beliefs, even when there is ample evidence that contradicts those beliefs. Thus, in accordance with the belief that God exists, cares, and is responsive to the pleas called 'prayer', persons will pray for success even in competitive situations; and when those prayers appear to go unanswered, as from time to time they must do, then the explanation that *'God knows best'* suffices and the belief persists. This persistence of the belief occurs even when scientific evidence indicates that the belief is incorrect. Indeed, the belief may even be enshrined in our language. For example, the term *'waving a red rag to a bull'* has not lost its place in our use of the English language as a result of the emergence of the scientifically proven fact that bulls are colour blind. Indeed, it is the 'waving' and not the 'colour' that generates the irritating effect on the bull. A rag with any other of the seven colours of the rainbow (or indeed a colour resulting from mixing any number of those colours) will suffice to produce the same effect if waved. In relation to bulls, the concept *'Is so red rags stay'* is indeed bull.

This reference to colours of the rainbow is coincidentally apposite since the ethnic categories of Guyana are allegedly, according to the 1991 Population and Housing Census of Guyana as supplied by Guyana's Bureau of Statistics, the following nine mutually exclusive categories: African/Black; East Indian; Amerindian; Chinese; White; Portuguese; Mixed Race; Others; and Not Stated. We do not hesitate to endow with truth the concept *"Is so 'x' people stay"* where *'x'* is any of the ethnic categories other than 'Others' or 'Not Stated'. This should be of more than passing interest, since the characteristics of the ethnic categories were not determined by members of the categories themselves, but by allegedly eminent and knowledgeable members of the group of colonisers - a group that, in accordance with the upsidedowness of human affairs, has been deemed by a large proportion of the colonised, enslaved, indentured, and their progeny, to be wise and worthy of emulation! In Guyana, it appears that ideas about 'ethnicity' have been stuck in 19th century thinking, with the conceptual support of many allegedly important international institutions. This thinking is not

---

4   Another breach of the Constitution relevant to the Electoral System is the one dealing with not allowing Guyanese resident overseas to vote in Guyana's national elections. Ralph Ramkarran, one of the Presidential nominees for candidate at the 2011 elections has highlighted this unconstitutionality (cf. his letter on Page 6 of Stabroek News 13 Feb, 2010 entitled **'Under the constitution Guyanese resident overseas have a right to vote'**).

unrelated to linguistic usage that has enshrined the presumption that in any endeavour, there is a correlation between degree of desirability and pigmentation. Thus, in general, things angelic and desirable are associated with 'white' while things demonic and undesirable are associated with 'black'.

With respect to the third necessary condition, for decades, leading politicians and the political Party that each has claimed to lead, have boldly asserted that there is some *'ismic'* solution to Guyana's governance and economic development problems. Thus, serious study with a view to adaptation has been focused from time to time on, for example: Capitalism, Socialism, Leninism, Marxism, Cooperativism, Maoism, Scientism, Freemasonry, Yugoslavia and its Basic organisations of Associated Labour (BOAL), and The Juche Idea, to name only a few of the alleged roads to Nirvana that have been proffered in Guyana[5]. This book asserts that **there is no *'ismic'*** solution to Guyana's governance and economic development problems. My claim that there is no ismic solution to Guyana's governance and economic development problems includes the rejection not only of individual isms, but also of yard-fowlism[6], and of all attempts to produce an appropriate ism through syncretism. This assertion, almost certainly true, thus justifies a certain forlornness since the author believes that La Rochefoucauld was correct when he stated in Maxim #318 that *'There are ways of curing madness, but none of righting the wrong-headed'*.

---

5   Readers should note that I have placed in the category *'ism'* various conceptual/philosophical approaches to governance even though they do not have names ending with the syllable '**ism**'. Also, it is interesting to note that the concept of *'Nirvana'* for the society has varied over time, and will continue to so do; and accordingly it may not be reasonable to expect to find any *'ism'* that will satisfy all versions of *'Nirvana'*.

6   See Page 618 of the **Dictionary of Caribbean English Useage** by Richard Allsopp. There, the explanation of yard-fowl-ism is given as *'The political practice of giving or receiving favours in return for toadying; sycophancy in politics.'*

Appendix # 0

1. The anecdote has been told about a somewhat steatopygous female[7], popular in Buxton, who had entered a beauty contest outside of Buxton (In common Guyanese parlance, she had 'a tear-a-brass of a rass'). She did not win, and when she returned she allegedly gave the following explanation to her supporters for her not winning:

> "In face and waist, ah didn't place;
> An dat is how ah lost the race;
> But in bubby and arse, ah bus dey rass.!"*(So much for the effectiveness of steatopygia)*

Article 13 of the Constitution makes it clear that even those persons who have the kinds of views reflected in this bit of doggerel cannot be excluded from participation in the decision-making processes of the State. Steatopygous adult females apparently have a constitutional right to express opinions, and have Article 13 backing for those opinions to be considered seriously in areas of decision-making that directly affect their well-being, including stopping railway trains with dignitaries aboard. Their paramours are well aware of the dangers of ignoring such rights.

2. The following is a list of some fifty Buxtonian **'False Names'**:

Baccoo	Crapaud	Lyrics	Smokey
Badingdingding	Danny Kaye	Mantool	Soorah and Doorah
Bag o Lotay	Darkie	Mojo	Spirit
Ballicks	Demon	Monkey	Sweet Willie
Bassel	Donkey Belly	Mud Fish	Timber
Big ooman Patta	Double Ugly	Nockka	Toast Oil
Black Anancy	Dye Pokey Norma	Oyo	Took
Born Paper	Foot Flap	Powerless	Tullah
Bubbles	Footabumbum	Saga	Typee
Budso	God Bird	Sardine	Wallababy
Bull	Iron Man	Secret	Zap
Convict	Juice Cup	Sexy Kitten	
Crab	Lullah	Skoja	

---

7   Allegedly the result of a (favourable?) genetic trait in Buxtonian women?

The trouble with Official names (on Birth / Baptismal Certificates, or on Independence Proclamations for Countries) is that they derive from **aspirations** or **asseverations** (e.g. concerning paternity) while 'false' names, at least in the case of Buxtonians, derive from the **truths of actual experience**! 'False' names are earned. Birth Certificate names are officially given, often by those who couldn't know better. They are expressions of hope, and in the case of surnames, they are not infrequently paternal acts of faith - *thanks be to God for the visual loophole provided by the vagaries of genetics*. Officialdom poses problems by not admitting the realism of the 'false' names and by insisting that documents, e.g. transports certifying ownership of land, use the names on Birth Certificates, thus ignoring the glaring facts, such as for instance, that everyone knows that a particular house and land belong to Budso.

3. The practice of attributing 'false names' is clearly not uniquely Buxtonian. For instance, the man who allegedly changed the approach to medical diagnosis had the 'false name' **Paracelsus**. This was the nickname of:**Theophrastus Philippus Aureolus Bombastus von Hohenheim** (1493-1541) ; and **Molière** (1622-1673), allegedly the greatest of all writers of French comedy had the original name **Jean-Baptiste Paquelin,** while **Voltaire** was the false name of **Francois-Marie Arouet**; and, perhaps understandably, **Mozart** (1756-1791), whose baptismal name was **Johannes Chrysostomus Wolfgangus Theophilus Mozart**, referred to himself as **Wolfgang Amadè**. **Plato** (probably because the word meant broad/wide forehead) allegedly was the 'false name' of **Aristocles** (427 - 347 BC).

PREFACE - Why this Book?

I suspect strongly that human beings are driven primarily by two consuming passions - the passion to fornicate, and the passion to communicate. Of the two, the first is by far the stronger, with both literal and figurative manifestations.

The literal manifestation pushes in the direction of the preservation of our species through the propagation of genes. In that mode, the usually unconscious objective is to pass on genes for individual bodies to cause those genes to reproduce and survive. The best exposition I know of this aspect of things is in Richard Dawkins' book *River Out of Eden*[8], perhaps best read in conjunction with his *The Selfish Gene*.

The figurative manifestation moves us in the direction of the destruction of 'weaker' individuals, and groups of individuals, thereby paradoxically supporting preservation of the species, and the evolution of memes. This destructive feature, a kind of winnowing, derives from the figurative manifestation of fornication in the activity of competition ("fucking up" your competitors and their supporters). Competition, which is frequently not benign, is a persistent state among human beings. Often, during competition we attempt to best each other, with the winner enjoying rewards and the loser paying penalties of one kind or another, including 'death' - permanent removal as a whole organism from the competitive arena. It is in this milieu of competition (where we metaphorically fornicate with each other) that our predispositions to seek the *frisson* of *schadenfreude*, and also paradoxically to pursue cooperation[9] in all the games of life, manifest themselves.

To facilitate the pursuit of the objectives of fornication in both senses, it has been found necessary for living agents to communicate. Thus, for example, the development of an embryo is made possible by individual cells sending out chemical messengers to trigger the development of other cells to produce a self-consistent network leading to a coherent organism. In response to this need for agents to communicate, there has been the corresponding evolution of appropriate means of communication - particularly language among humans. Thus we seek to influence the thoughts and actions of others - often through the use of written language

---

8   The Science Masters Series, Basic Books, http://www.harpercollins.com
9   See Robert Axelrod's 1984 book The *Evolution of Cooperation*.

(memos, poems, standing orders, rules and regulations, etc.), and often through writing whole books.

Taken all together, the mix of literal fornication, metaphorical fornication, and communication varies in an extremely complex manner with age, gender, education, and sexual orientation (among other things) in a turbulent cauldron of genes and memes. It is some version of this mix that I perceive has stimulated me to write this book.

Yet, this book is like all other books. It is intended to influence the thoughts and actions of some subset of human beings. However, it differs from most other books in many senses. One area of difference is that the subset which the author hopes to influence is the narrow set of human beings that comprise the Guyanese public. Another is that the matter on which he seeks to wield influence is how Guyanese should choose Guyana's leadership cadres to form a Government.

It is in this context that we need to note that a major difficulty in effectively influencing anyone, or any group, is the difficulty of getting persons to accept proposals that conflict with their beliefs. If those beliefs are myths, the difficulty is greatest when those myths have already become entrenched as truths in the belief systems of the society. Stereotypes about ethnicity are prime examples of such myths[10].

It is this kind of difficulty to which Leo Tolstoy must have been referring when he wrote:

> *'I know most men, including those at ease with problems of the greatest complexity, can seldom accept even the simplest and most obvious truth if it be such as would oblige them to admit the falsity of conclusions which they have delighted in explaining to colleagues, which they have proudly taught to others, and which they have woven, thread by thread, into the fabric of their lives.'*

There are thus three main myths with which this book will have to contend. They comprise beliefs that conflict with reason, but that are generally accepted nevertheless by many Guyanese; regardless of their levels of intelligence.

---

10 This category includes the assumption that 'brown' or 'red' women are more lascivious than others of different hues.

These myths[11] may be stated as follows:

(1)   Guyana has a Westminster model Constitution and system of Government;

(2)   Voting in Guyana is along ethnic lines, so that elections very much represent something of an ethnic census; and

(3)   Leaders need to be visionaries, intellectually blessed, and thereby capable of giving guidance to the people on a broad range of issues.

Each of these myths, particularly the last two, is dealt with in this book. The first has, in my view, already been adequately dealt with in Professor Ralph Carnegie's paper **"Floreat the Westminster Model? A West Indian Perspective."** Professor A. R. Carnegie, then Professor of Law and Deputy Principal, University of the West Indies, Cave Hill Campus, Barbados, had presented this paper at a meeting of the Commonwealth Secretariat in Hamilton, Bermuda, 5-9 December, 1988. That meeting was entitled *'Meeting of Law Officers of Small Commonwealth Jurisdictions'*. The first paragraph of that paper states:

> *'No statement could surely be more trite and elementary in relation to the Constitutions of the twelve Caribbean and circum-Caribbean States which are full members of the Commonwealth than the statement that they are all, with the exception of Guyana, Westminster model Constitutions.'*

The States being referred to are: *Antigua and Barbuda, The Bahamas, Belize, Barbados, Dominica, Grenada, Guyana, Jamaica, St. Christopher and Nevis, St. Lucia, St. Vincent and the Grenadines, Trinidad and Tobago.* Guyana's exception was clearly based on the fact that in Guyana in 1988, the Headship of State was not effectively separated from the Headship of Government - a separation that is a necessary condition for a Westminster model. Accordingly, the issue with which Professor Carnegie's paper dealt was the inappropriateness of applying the terminology *'Westminster*

---

11 Two recent examples of highly intelligent persons subscribing to these myths are to be found in the Stabroek News of Friday, April 17, 2009 in the section 'Letters to the Editor'. On page 19, Eric M. Phillips allegedly authored the letter captioned 'The Westminster system imprisons Guyana'; and on pages 6&7, Emile Mervin contributed the letter captioned 'What other surprises await us around the corner?' Both letters assume the truth of these myths.

model' to the remaining eleven, even though they had separated Headships of State and of Government.

In that matter, the paper concluded:

> *'......when we speak of our Westminster model Constitutions, we are not being lawyers or even political scientists. We are at best being poets.'*

Clearly there are persons in Guyana (and employees / representatives of prestigious and powerful international institutions) whose perceptions / preferences refuse to allow even Guyana to be excluded from the group of Caribbean States that allegedly have *'Westminster Model Constitutions'*. Many of such persons boldly state, and treat as a self-evident truth (without even the benefit of poetic licence), that Guyana has a Westminster Model Government system. They even boldly attribute some of Guyana's practices, and problems related to its electoral processes, to this Westminster Model. To these persons I recommend Professor Carnegie's Article; and invite them to note that there have been several formal changes made to the Westminster type constitution imposed by the British Government in 1966, the year Guyana attained political independence. Chapters 1 and 2 of the 2006 publication (Transition, Special Issue 35-36) by the Institute of Development Studies and Faculty of Social Sciences of the University of Guyana, entitled 'The Constitution of Guyana- A Study of its Dysfunctional Application' authored by Professor of Law R. W. James are very informative about this concept of Westminster Model Constitutions.

In dealing with the last two myths, I cannot avoid repeating material that I have already published, much from the book[12] '1992-2003 Heretical Musings about Guyana'. I have deemed this to be acceptable since, taken by itself as a whole construct, **this** book is heretical, and aims at influencing its readers to accept, support, and lobby for, a shift of a specific paradigm in the matter of how Guyana is governed. I have long been convinced that such a transfiguration is a necessary condition for Guyana to pursue successfully material progress and prosperity in an atmosphere of persistent peace. Indeed, there is the need to consider the matters with which we have to deal as issues of what the American mathematician Warren Weaver in his 1948 paper calls problems of *organized complexity.*

---

12   The book can be obtained from Trafford Publishing at **www.trafford.com**

It would however be insufficient to deal with only the myths mentioned above. Indeed what is required is appropriate treatment of a complex of: Uncertainties, Myths, and Intuitively stimulated Presumptions. The following haphazard listing of four additional categories just about covers the areas that need to be addressed:

(i)   The uncertainties related to the issue of how to derive a societal consensus from clearly expressed individual opinions - a matter that often impinges on the very meaning of 'democracy';

(ii)   Power Sharing in the process of Governance;

(iii)   The Role of Political Parties in the process of Governance;

(iv)   The meaning of 'Ethnicity'-The definition by Guyana's Bureau of Statistics, and some of its implications;

This book has therefore been constructed to have two Parts. Part I deals with the last two myths cited above and also addresses the four additional categories just listed. Part II gives the additional analytical basis for, and ends by proposing, a new electoral system called PEC (The Parris Electoral Process Conjectures). The liberty is taken of adding Appendices to each Part to help point readers away from directions of mere conjecture, and to bring them face to face with some real problems that the author has confronted during the exploration of **his** conjectures. Many of these Appendices comprise dated essays previously published in the book '1992 - 2003 Heretical Musings About Guyana'. They comprise background necessary for a clear understanding of the issues on which a new electoral system should be based; and therefore occupy a pivotal position in making the case for PEC.

I hope that the book, taken as a whole, will be deemed to have provided an adequate basis for the transfiguration that it recommends.

INTRODUCTION

The Preface to this book ends with a sentence that almost certainly is an expression of a forlorn hope. I experienced that phenomenon of a forlorn hope in 1993 when I published the book BUNARO. 'BUNARO' is an Arawak word, an intransitive verb, one of whose meanings is *'a change from darkness to light'*. In 1993 I chose to use that word in the title of a book about the emergence of new ways of looking at Guyana and its development. During the ensuing decade and a half, evidence accumulated that convinced me that at least one of the following had happened: few people had read the book; those who had read it were unmoved, perhaps because they were bemused by its argumentation (or poverty thereof), or both; the author's words carried little weight, regardless of the truth of what he had said, perhaps because he was not sufficiently prestigious. Nevertheless, I had become very hopeful about the book attaining its stated objectives when, in 1997, I acquired and read the quartet of books - *Complexity* (published 1993 by M. Mitchell Waldrop); *The Selfish Gene* (published 1989 by Richard Dawkins); *The Blind Watchmaker* (published 1996 by Richard Dawkins); and *The Economy as an Evolving Complex System* (A Proceedings Volume in The Santa Fe Institute Studies in the Sciences of Complexity -Volume V- published 1988, Edited by Philip W. Anderson, Kenneth J. Arrow, and David Pines)[13]. The rise in my level of hope had derived from my perception that the books quoted had strengthened the concerns, supported the conjectures, and confirmed many of the conclusions that I had written about in BUNARO.

I had long ago developed what I think of as the 'cush-cush' habit of reading. After one has grated 'dry' coconuts, and got the coconut 'milk' out of the grated kernel of the coconut by squeezing it, more coconut milk could be acquired if water were poured onto the cush-cush[14] and it were squeezed again. You could add water to the twice squeezed cush-cush and get yet more milk; and continue this leaching sequence until you have got practically all the milk out of the kernel of the coconut. Rarely could you get all out of one (the first) squeezing. Similarly, with written material that an author had put a lot of thought into writing, each revisit and re-read produces clarifications of ideas/concepts that previous readings may not have adequately revealed. Such inadequacies occur partly because

13 The ease of reading this Volume is directly related to the reader's comfortableness with non-trivial mathematical formulations.
14 See the Dictionary of Caribbean English Usage by Richard Allsopp, published 1996 by Oxford University Press.

imprecision is a characteristic of human thought and action. Also, if re-reads take place long enough after the first read, the circumstance of the reader's own maturing affords the opportunity of a matured vantage point, almost certainly not previously available. New insights can thereby then arise.

My cush-cush approach to the four books successively entrenched the BUNARO type ideas and concepts in my mind. Nevertheless, the passage of time, the more than ten years since 1997, has seen confirmation of the imperviousness of the Guyanese public, and its leadership cadres, to the ideas expressed in BUNARO. Unfortunately, I have not seen the error of my writing ways; and the emerging circumstances of Guyana in 2008 have stimulated me to author **this** book. None of this means that I have resiled from my belief that the greater the deviation of a new paradigm from an existing one, the longer it takes for the new paradigm to be generally accepted.

The focus this time is narrower than that of BUNARO. It is a focus primarily on the processes (mainly the electoral processes and their implications for decision-making) that we persist in using to determine by whom, and how, Guyana should be governed. To the extent that those processes are based on internally contradictory and otherwise inadequate concepts, then we should not be surprised if the governance of Guyana is from time to time poor; and not clearly poised to improve monotonically over time. This book argues that if the Guyana Economy were to be considered as a Complex Adaptive System, then its capacity to evolve into a *'better?'* state through adaptation, and through creative problem solving and opportunity finding, is severely limited by the entrenchment of some concepts in the minds of the body politic, of its alleged leaders, and of various advisors including those from international institutions. It is also limited by the **absence** of some concepts.

In this book, some of these main inhibiting concepts that are present, and some necessary ones that are absent, are highlighted, alternative concepts are proposed, and amended concepts and processes based on them are offered. Hopefully, the proposals will not be deemed to be too outlandish, and be deemed to be too much at variance with what passes for established wisdom. They might therefore be treated as at least worthy of mature consideration. How can one dare ask for anything more?

Two paragraphs ago, I casually threw out the phrase *'complex adaptive system'* as though anyone familiar with the English language would be bound to understand fully the significance of that characterisation of Guyana. That act was manifestly unfair since the science of Complexity is still emerging. I am myself unclear about many aspects of how a multivariate interconnected system, such as the Guyana economy is, might behave dynamically as it adapts in the context of feedback and increasing returns to the changing circumstances of its own and the world environment. Happily for my ego and my sanity, I am aware that I am not alone in my ignorance; but there exist those who deny the existence and the importance of their own ignorance, and the inappropriateness of their models. Most worrying of all, there are those who know enough, who have their own agendas (their own self-interests) not necessarily 'in the best interests' of Guyana, and who deliberately and systematically seek to persuade both leaders and the led in Guyana to adopt and implement policies supportive of those non-Guyanese agendas.

Thus there are 21st century missionaries who claim to be privy to the 'truth' about how to practise democracy, how to secure peace and progress, and how to ensure that we Guyanese are on the right road to becoming 'developed' like the countries and institutions from which they have come as emissaries. This is not a new phenomenon. It existed before, during, and after slavery in Guyana. Indeed, the historical records are replete with examples of the non-native powers that were defining stereotypes and prescribing for their 'civilization' in pursuit of the country's 'betterment'.

As the author of this book, I freely admit to having a bias that underpins my belief (and therefore influences the tenor of this book) that it is time for us to stop being a nation that eagerly and uncritically imports clichés, catchwords, and catchphrases, in which the new colonisers are not the missionaries bringing Christianity to the heathens, but ID card bearing visitors from soi-disant international institutions who purport to bring the secrets of democracy and development to 'third world' countries like Guyana. They pronounce on whether our governance practices are adequately democratic, on whether our elections are appropriately free and fair, and generally on whether our governance of ourselves is acceptable to them. This book does not hesitate to depart from acceptance of their views when logic/rationality/arithmetic suggests that such departures may be eminently sensible, or adherence to the proffered views eminently otiose.

In all these circumstances, I do not despair since I take heart from the failure of Jean-Antoine Dubois in his many attempts to convert the Hindus in parts of South India to Roman Catholicism. As an ordained priest, it took him more than 30 years, from 1792 to 1822 when he returned from India to Paris, to become convinced that that conversion of Hindus was impossible.

However, readers should not interpret my freely admitted bias as being synonymous with xenophobia. Instead, the bias should be understood to represent a form of scepticism that I recommend highly to persons concerned with matters of governance, and of development. Particularly with respect to predictions about, and prognoses of, development, scepticism may be our only protection from being misled by the mouthings of the knowledgeable and experienced, especially when they enjoy reputations of success. They, by virtue of being human, are nevertheless fallible; and there may well be great merit in Jean Jacques Rousseau's reported assertion that what we think we know, but do not, harms us far more than what we do not know.

I offer the following cautionary examples (for the accuracy of which I cannot vouch) that I have come across[15]. They are statements allegedly made by knowledgeable people, or prestigious institutions, clearly experienced in the field about which they are reported to have allegedly spoken.

c. 1895 by Lord Kelvin (British mathematician, physicist and President of the British Royal Society)[16]
Heavier -than-air flying machines are impossible.....

1902 *by the astronomer Simon Newcomb.*
Flight by machines heavier than air is unpractical and insignificant, if not utterly impossible.

---

15 This information was allegedly published by Decision Strategies International.

16 Around 1876, the Russian scientist Dmitry Ivanovich Mendeleyev had been led by his interest in aeronautics to make balloon ascents for scientific observations. The activity also led him to encourage his colleagues to pursue the possibilities of heavier-than-air flights.

1913 *by the American Railroad Congress.*
It is an idle dream to imagine that....automobiles will take the place of railways in the long distance movement of....passengers.

1920, *by Robert Andrew Millikan, the 1923 Nobel prize winner in physics, 1921 director of the Norman Bridge Laboratory of Physics at California Institute of Technology, Pasadena, and subsequent chairman of that Institute until his retirement in 1945.*
There is no likelihood man can ever tap the power of the atom.[17]

1929, *November 16, Harvard Economic Society.*
A severe depression like that of 1920-1921 is outside the range of probability.

1943, Thomas J. Watson, Chairman of IBM.
I think there is a world market for about five computers.

1968, August 2 Business Week.
With over 50 foreign cars already on sale here, the Japanese auto industry isn't likely to carve out a big slice of the U.S. market for itself.

1977 *by Ken Olson, the President of Digital Equipment Corporation.*
There is no reason for any individual to have a computer in their home.

To this list one might add the comment made by **President Rutherford B. Hayes** of the USA as his response to Alexander Graham Bell's telephone which was exhibited on 25 June, 1876, at the International Centennial Exhibition in Philadelphia celebrating the hundredth birthday of the United States. The comment allegedly was: *"That's an amazing invention, but who would ever want to use one of them?"*

Apart from needing to avoid tragedies like Hiroshima and Nagasaki, there are deeper reasons than the one already given (i.e. human fallibility even in the presence of knowledge and undoubted experience) for my strong

---

17 *On Aug 6, 1945 the USA dropped an atomic bomb on Hiroshima, pulverizing by the combined heat and blast 4.4 square miles, killing 70,000 to 80,000 people, besides injuring more than 70,000 others. On Aug 9,1945 a second bomb was dropped, on Nagasaki, devastating 1.8 square miles, killing 35,000 to 40,000 people, and injuring a similar number.* A possibly interesting historical coincidence is that exactly forty years after Hiroshima, LFS Burnham died.

Haslyn Parris

recommendation for scepticism, meticulous checking, and reliance on one's own reasoning and creativity. Those reasons relate to what has been called *'the reductionist hypothesis'*; and to what has been called *'lock-in'*.

Simply and perhaps simplistically put, the reductionist hypothesis asserts that the workings of all economies obey the same fundamental laws. Research, find, study, and apply those laws to your economy, and you'll get the results you desire through the acts of rational governance applied to the interacting economic, social, and political forces. On the face of it, what could sound more reasonable? Assume otherwise, and the very rationale for studying things like economics threatens to disappear. Yet, there **is** evidence that, in the environment of an interconnected world, the fundamental laws (or the results of their application) are not immutable. They vary over changes in scale, time, stage of development, and the state of world development. More perplexingly, those 'laws' also appear to manifest themselves differently in the context of occurrences that are accidents of history (happenstance).

Nevertheless, if an individual has a body of laws he/she considers fundamental, and a track record of 'success' in applying actions based on those laws, then it is to be expected that a certain confidence of correctness will be built up in the individual. That confidence of correctness will be manifested in the individual's dealings with anyone to whom he/she gives advice.

I suspect that it is this phenomenon to which the commentator Akio Morita was referring when he said:
> *'If you go through life convinced that your way is always best, all the new ideas in the world will pass you by.'*

Akio Morita continued:
> *'Americans tend to think that the American system is the way things should work all around the world, but they should not be blind and deaf to how things are done in other countries.'*

There do appear to be different strokes required for different folks at different times and in different places. However, I perceive that in Guyana there is a certain predisposition to imitate, almost blindly, both the objectives and the alleged means of achieving those objectives; and therefore a tendency to swallow hook, line, and sinker, the mouthings of foreign consultants from developed countries or from prestigious international institutions. It does not help that many among our leaders are intellectually eminently competent persons who choose to not apply that competence persistently to considering that each of the various current ideologies and associated theories of development has severe deficiencies in relation to Guyana's circumstances. Their willing bemusement by the reputations of leading thinkers in prestigious academic institutions in which they may have been trained, and therefore their own mis-education, prohibits their assuming such heretical stances.

Lock-in has to do with our willingness to accept a number of things without question, purely because that's the way we found them, that's just the way they are, even when they are indeed simply the results of historical accidents - happenstance. One of the most celebrated examples of lock-in is the arrangement of the keyboard of a typewriter. The traditional QWERTY typewriter keyboard, the usual arrangement of whose letters of the alphabet begins with those six letters on the top left hand corner of the second row, was designed by Christopher Scholes in 1873. It allegedly was a response to the need to slow down typists, since the typewriters of that period tended to jam if the typists went too fast. From as far back as the 1920s, several alternative keyboard layouts were demonstrated to be superior in the senses that they were easier to learn, created less operator fatigue, and permitted faster typing.[18] However, the accident of history that the Remington Sewing Machine Company mass-produced typewriters with the QWERTY keyboard meant that many typists learnt to use the system, and other companies producing typewriters began to offer that kind of keyboard. Consequently, even more typists learnt to use the QWERTY keyboard, and this trend fed on itself. The net result is that the traditional QWERTY layout has persisted and is associated with millions of personal computers, and with other devices requiring keyboard type data entry, despite its known ergonomic inefficiency.

A not dissimilar story can be told about the concept *'clockwise'*. It appears that there is no reason other than the accident of history which says that non-digital clocks should run in a clockwise direction. An *'anti-clockwise'* clock can be used to tell time accurately, and would be no

18   There are, for instance, the Dvorak keyboard, a scientifically designed keyboard layout requiring, in pursuit of speed and ease, less finger reaching and stretching to reach commonly used keys; and keyboards for one handed *(left-handed)* and for one handed *(right-handed)* persons *(See Appendix #10)*.

harder to manufacture or to learn to read than a *'clockwise'* one. In fact, in 1443 Paolo Uccello designed the Florence Cathedral clock which ran anti-clockwise, and showed all 24 hours.

These are only two examples of what I refer to as 'lock-in'. The progress of horology does not appear to have been inhibited by the convention 'clockwise' any more than car manufacture has been by traditional preferences for driving on the left hand or the right hand side of the road. The point here is that these accidents of history (and there are many more) have led to situations in which people tend to accept *'what is'* as *'how it is meant to be'*; and jettison all thoughts about how it might better be different. This type of mental inertia is what I am suggesting be replaced by a kind of selective scepticism as part of the basis for creativity and problem solving. It is interesting (and almost certainly beneficial) to have a sceptical and undogmatic cast of mind in at least some areas of one's life. Actually, I am simply supporting the idea expressed by Goethe in the following words: *'Daring ideas are like chessmen moved forward, they may be beaten, but they may start a winning game.'*

Other reasons for the mental inertia relate to the seamier issues of economic growth: issues such as alliances among major international corporate entities, powerful governments supportive of those corporations, prestigious academic institutions, and international-aid institutions generating conditionalities that ensure that nations lose control over their national resources, and that the rich get richer and the poor get poorer, while democracy is relegated to backstage. Here I refer to what the Argentinean investigative journalist Rodolfo Walsh, in an open letter dated 24 March 1977, characterised as 'planned misery'. With this plea for reliance on your native curiosity and creativity, the way you were when you were about 5 years old, full of expressions of intelligent curiosity and clear-eyed scepticism, I invite you to read on. Once again I admit to being influenced by Johann von Goethe: *'Unlike grownups, children have little need to deceive themselves';* and I disregard my suspicion that the innumeracy of Guyana's citizenry will prevail.

PART I

SOME ENTRENCHED MYTHS

SOME ENTRENCHED MYTHS

One of the prices we pay for not being omniscient is that, under the pressure to act in response to some stimulus, we often make assumptions that are just best guesses with varying degrees of irrationality. These guesses cover the spectrum from *'wild'* to *'carefully pondered intuitive'*. Often, the guesses are based on what we perceive to be our experience in the context of what we understand to be accepted wisdom; but perhaps more often they are pivotally influenced by those who purport to know - the *soi-disant* experts often with international institutional anointment.

There are at least three observations that are almost certainly useful in dealing cautiously with all guesses. Two have been mentioned in the Introduction to this book. One is the assertion by Jean-Jacques Rousseau[19] that what we think we know but do not, harms us far more than what we do not know. The other is that imprecision is frequently a characteristic of human thought and action.

To this duo I suggest that we add a third. It is based on the 1931 publication of a revolutionary paper[20] by Kurt Gödel, then a 25 year old Austrian-born mathematician at the University of Vienna. That paper has been described in a citation by Harvard University as one of the most important advances in logic in modern times. Its title, translated from German into English, is *'On Formally Undecidable Propositions of Principia Mathematica and Related Systems'*[21]. Essentially, the proof states that within any rigidly logical mathematical system there are propositions that cannot be proved or disproved (or questions that cannot be resolved) on the basis of the axioms within that system.

A question to which Gödel's concept of formally undecidable propositions appears to me to be relevant may be phrased as follows:

---

19 The French philosopher, writer, and political theorist *(28 June 1712 - 2 July 1778)* whose treatises and novels inspired the leaders of the French Revolution. The history of medicine and cures for diseases is replete with examples of the truth of this observation.

20 The article first appeared in Monatshefte fur Mathematik und Physik, vol 38 (1931).

21 See Appendix # 8 (the essay "The Upsidedowness of Power Sharing) for insights into the likely importance of Gödel's work in consideration of our electoral system.

> *Are the alleged conclusions about Governance of a multi-ethnic society in fact the 'necessary logical consequences' of the initial assumptions of ethnic voting for political parties in national elections to select a government of that multi-ethnic society?*

Further, have the traditional beliefs about ethnic voting and its consequences not been undermined by the ambiguities peculiar to ethnicity, including the definitional ambiguity[22] about to what ethnic category does an individual uniquely belong?

Against this background, I am reminded of Bertrand Russell's epigram, viz.: *'Pure Mathematics is the subject in which we do not know what we are talking about or whether what we are saying is true.'* I support the view that ethnic voting is a myth entrenched in the society by a number of conceptual errors and difficulties. Appendix #9 (the essay "Ethnic Voting - a Myth?" written in 2004) treats with some of these errors and difficulties. However, before one plunges into the details dealt with in Appendix #9, it is perhaps useful to pause and consider the following comments about 'myths'.

I suggest that a **myth** can be considered as a **meme** that is characterised by one or more of: **untruth, fuzziness, internal contradiction**, or **undecidability.** The undecidability to which I refer is that of Gödel's concept of formally undecidable propositions. Accordingly, any attempt to analyse reality on the basis of a myth is almost certainly bound to produce contestable conclusions.

If you look at an object through a lens, then, unless the lens has special features such as those an optometrist determines to correct vision using spectacles, the object will be seen as a distorted construct. If you have no idea of what the object **should** look like, then the distorted image will be deemed by you to be the reality. That distorted reality will be perceived to be reality whenever the object is looked at through that lens.

I suggest that 'Ethnicity' is an inappropriately constructed lens since it is based on fuzziness and has too many internal contradictions. Accordingly, any analysis of reality as observed through the lens of ethnicity is bound to be a distorted analysis. Decisions made on the basis of such analyses

---

22 We appear to be quite comfortable ignoring a precept expressed by Descartes as follows: *"When transcendental questions are under discussion be transcendentally clear."*

are therefore very likely to be un-useful, and possibly even misleading and dangerous as bases for action/policy making. The situation is akin to looking at the real world through an inappropriate lens, and, as any qualified optometrist can attest, inevitably seeing distorted images of reality. Further, if one considers communicating those distorted images to persons dealing with reality, and who have varying versions of the myth underpinning the analysis, confusion compounded is assured.

The situation may be demonstrated by the following example which relies on the message sender being a victim of 'lock-in', where the conviction is that all worthwhile computers have QWERTY keyboards. If the message someone wishes to communicate to me is typed into my computer using the assumption that a QWERTY keyboard is the keyboard of my computer, then the following message:

> **"A fundamental problem with Guyana is that it is a multi-ethnic society that has not learnt how to manage the juxtaposition of its composite ethnicities in a manner that avoids prejudice and preference based on ethnicity."**

will be seen by me on my computer's screen as:

> **_A ugam.byan lprxn.m ,cyd Igfaba co yday cy co a mgnyc[.ydbcj orjc.yf yday dao bry n.apby dr, yr mabai. Yd. Hgqyalrocycrb ru cyo jrmlrocy. .ydbcjcyc.o cb a mabb.p yday akrceo lp.hgecj. Abe lp.u.p.bj. Xao.e rb .ydbcjcyfv_**

if my keyboard is in fact **DVORAK** style[23].

If my keyboard is **RIGHT (One Hand)**, i.e. to facilitate me in the circumstance that I am right-handed and type with only one hand (indeed I may have lost my left hand or never had one), then the same message would appear as:

> **_& asn97w6no7c b.yic6w 5uoh Esr7n7 u8 oh7o uo u8 7 wscou[6ohnux 8yxu6or oh7o h78 nyo c67.no hy5 oy w7n7e6 oh6 tszo7by8uouyn ya uo8 xywby8uo6**

---

23   See Appendix # 10: *Computer keyboard Layouts*

**6ohnuxuou68 un 7 w7nn6. Oh7o 7,yu98 b.6ts9ux6 7n9
b.6a6.6nx6 i7869 yn 6ohnuxuorg_**

and if my keyboard were **LEFT (One Hand)**, then the same message
would be seen by me as:

**&_ dsnc-ibnu-z 6y.wzbi qouh Tsr-- ok uh-u ou ok -
iszuo2buhnog k.gobur uh-u h-k n.u zb-ynu h.q u. I-n-
tb uhb esxu-6.kouo.n .d ouk g.i6.koub buhnogouobk
on- i-nnby uh-ur -v.ock 6ybescogb -nc 6ybdbybngb
w-kbc .n buhnogour0&**

This apparent gobbledegook would **not** have been the result of faulty analysis
or of typographical errors, but rather the result of miscommunication based
on the presumption that the keyboard layout I happen to be locked into is
QWERTY. That erroneous assumption is the source of **all** of the problem;
and no matter how accurate / correct the message is, it will be of no use to
me because of the miscommunication. The twin jeopardies of a conclusion
being otiose, because it is based on myths, or because its communication
mechanism is inappropriate, are firmly with us (inescapable) in the matter
of how we might best govern ourselves as a society. Let us summarise
along the dimensions mentioned above (i.e. **untruth, fuzziness, internal
contradiction**, and **undecidability**) some of the major myths we use
axiomatically for guidance in the matter of governance. The appendices
of this book, comprising various essays (many previously published as the
analyses underpinning the derivation of PEC[24]) provide the information in
a more detailed manner.

Re **ETHNICITY**
(1)   Untruth
The ethnic categories applied to the Guyanese population have an interesting
history. More than 170 years ago, the population of Guyana comprised
indigenous tribes, slaves, and subsequently indentured labourers, overseen
by a much smaller number of colonisers of mainly Dutch and British origin.
The countries of origin of the bulk of the non-indigenous population
comprised mainly Africa, India, China, Madeira, the Azores, Cape Verde,
and Malta. It was the colonisers and their Government personnel (of the
colony, and of the parent country) who determined the conditions under
which that population came to, and existed in, Guyana. It was that same
group of colonisers and their Government personnel who devised the

24 The Parris Electoral Conjectures

taxonomy of that population, surrounded conceptually by uncertainties such as whether the imports from Africa were fully human or a sub-species of humans[25].

The taxonomy was also devised in an atmosphere of political realities and ambitions that required the colonisers and their Governments to be at the top of the social pile, and to manage the populace by 'divide-and-rule' tactics as deemed necessary. These requirements determined, for instance, that while the colonisers and their Government personnel were to be classified as 'European', there should be a category called 'Portuguese' that was accorded a lower social status than 'European' even though their countries of origin were geographically in Europe. Also, for instance, there were the requirements for Amerindians to hunt down runaway slaves; and for different ethnic categories to have different laws and practices applied to various economic activities and the access to credit[26] Their categorisation called 'ethnicity' was determined in these circumstances, and race (often determined by physical characteristics such as skin colour or hair texture) turned out to be the criterion closest to hand.

The approach that was taken was not peculiar to Guyana. Slavery had been justified by the planters' belief that black slaves were a separately created animal species. This pernicious planter lore led, for instance, to the apologists for Jamaican slavery even in the 1770s categorising 'Negroes' as a different species of human. Planter literature embraced the notion of the 'contamination' of racially pure white blood. Nevertheless, respected institutions of learning such as the University of Cambridge, had persons such as the Revd Peter Peckard whose pamphlet *"Am I Not a Man and a Brother?"* cogently made the case that 'Black and White men, though different in *Sort* are the same in *Kind*, and consequently .... Negroes are Men'. Indeed, this was part of the vibrant debate about whether black men were brothers of Cambridge dons.

25 At the time of the practice of the capture and importation of slaves from parts of Africa, Darwin had the suspicion that black humans and white humans were not different species (cf. the book *"Darwin's Sacred Cause"* by Adrian Desmond and James Moore, published 2009). The idea of different species supported the presumption of the inherent superiority of whites over blacks; and slave owners, not usually near the pinnacle of intellectual achievement, but influenced by many who were, eagerly subscribed to the view being challenged by Darwin. Where ignorance was bliss, prejudice and economic avarice ruled.

26 This, for instance, is how ownership of rum shops primarily by Portuguese came about.

It was in this conceptual milieu that tribal differences, e.g. among indigenous peoples or among African tribes, did not deter the classifiers from labelling all in the same ethnic category[27]. The stereotypes associated with each of the ethnic categories were simultaneously defined by the ruling elite, all of whom had derogatory views of other peoples, particularly the slaves of African origin. Thus, in Guyana, the inventors of officially recognised ethnicities and their associated stereotypes were the colonisers and their Government personnel. Each individual (slave, indentured labourer, indigenous person) had to learn that it belonged to that ethnic group into which it had been placed, and that it had those characteristics associated with the defined stereotype.

Thus, for example, Africans learnt that they were **'black'** and that they harboured innate characteristics of tendencies to indolence, insolence, aggression, physical strength, petty thievery, and childish predispositions in relation to the pursuit of pleasure and the avoidance of entrepreneurship. They also learnt the associated terminology such as 'nigger'. The net result has been a categorisation of a pseudo-scientific character. A main characteristic of the act of classification was that the objects classified were not required to subscribe to the accuracy of the classification. But though domestic animals - dogs, cats, chickens, pigs, cows, for example - are not required to accept the stereotypes associated with their classification, members of the ethnic groups defined are, and linguistic practices reinforce this phenomenon, e.g. the phrase *'take it like a chinee'*.

The unacceptability of stereotypes as a basis for making decisions is well understood by students of the so-called 'hard' sciences (e.g. number theory in mathematics as opposed to sociology); and so can give rise to conjectures but are not accepted as proofs. It is simply that *'Extrapolating from the pattern so far'* is accepted as a most unreliable mechanism for establishing truth. A few examples from number theory may help reinforce the point.

27   This practice survives. The 1993 populations of the nine 'Amerindian' tribes *[cf. Macmillan Guyana Atlas]* were estimated as: Arecuna (562), Arawak (15,500), Akawaio (5,000), Carib (3,000), Macushi (7,750), Patamona (5,000), Warau (5,000), Wapishana (6,900), and Wai-Wai (200) - but despite their wide geographical distribution over coastal, upland, and savannah areas, and their distinct languages, they were nevertheless lumped together in the ethnic category 'Amerindian'; as indeed were all from Africa regardless of their tribe of origin - e.g. Igbo, Fulani, or (Kgoi, San, or !Kung women with their steatopygia) -at the point of their capture into slavery.

The following numbers are all prime (i.e. they have no factors other than themselves and 1):
31; 331; 3,331; 33,331; 333,331; 3,333,331; 33,333,331.

However 333,333,331 is **not** prime! 333,333,331 = 17 x 19,607,843

Nevertheless, if you note that:
1 x 1 = 1
11 x 11 = 121
111 x 111 = 12321
1111 x 1111 = 1234321
then you may be tempted to conclude that 111,111,111 x 111,111,111 = 12345678987654321.
If you did, it would turn out that your conclusion is correct!

What is more worrying is that when one thinks that a pattern has established the truth of a conjecture based on accumulated evidence from that pattern, the conjecture may nevertheless turn out to be untrue. The best example I can think of is referred to as ***Euler's conjecture***. It states that there are no solutions to the equation: $x^4 + y^4 + z^4 = w^4$
where x, y, z, and w are positive integers.

Nobody could prove Euler's conjecture for two hundred years; but nobody could disprove it by finding a solution, i.e. finding a counter example, so the conjecture continued to stand as very probably true. However, in 1988, Naom Elkies of Harvard University found the following solution:
x = 2,682,440 ; y = 15,365,639; z = 18,796,760; w = 20,615,673.

The conjecture thus turned out to be false, despite the 200 years of evidence of not finding a solution after tries involving probably more than a million numbers. What is more, Elkies proved that there are infinitely many solutions!

In the face of these examples, it is not unreasonable to distrust the principle of stereotypes based on 'race' *(i.e. extrapolating from the alleged pattern so far)* in the realm of human behavioural variation in Guyana.

Yet, as far as I recall, **all** our political leaders, and our official institutions, such as the Statistics Bureau, have **not rejected** and **not insisted on not using** the ethnic groupings that have had these unsavoury and conceptually inadequate origins. Among the most recent examples of this conceptual inadequacy was that which occurred when a newspaper reporter had asked the late President, Dr. Cheddi Jagan, about what his views were about the matter of Africans being at the 'bottom of the ladder' in Guyana. The brief dialogue that followed did not highlight the inadequacy of the 'ladder' concept or the inappropriateness of the 'ethnic categorisation' concept, that together made the inquiry a nonsense question. The fuzziness of the ethnic categorisation 'African' is mentioned below; and also I do not recall that the reporter was cautioned that if the 'ladder' concept was relevant, then the implication must have been that some group other than African should occupy the bottom rung!

(2)   **Fuzziness, Internal contradiction,** and **Undecidability**
Unlike the situation with dogs, cats, chickens, pigs, cows, for example, among the categories of objects to which the classification of ethnicity applies, miscegenation **is** possible (even with the preferred suspicion that blacks are a sub-human species). Over 170 years of cheek by jowl existence, given the powerful attraction of curiosity and fornication, there was bound[28] to arise the problem of how to classify the results of miscegenation, if individuals are to belong to one and only one ethnic category - avoidance of 'fuzziness'[29] of the set.

In the USA, for instance, there were attempts to resolve the issue by defining rules that depended on the percentage of 'black' that the individual genetically had. Logically, such attempts were internally contradictory, unless 'black' were treated as a contamination. Thus if the individual had more than x % black they were to be classified as 'black', but if they were more than x % 'non-black' they were not whatever 'non-black' was. Accordingly, uniqueness of classification would have been lost unless the asymmetry of the contamination of pure ethnicities by blackness was preserved. Thus any admixture that genetically contained enough 'black' would be classified ethnically as 'black' - and some purists defined 'enough' to be synonymous with 'any'[30].

---

28   The gender mix of imports for indentureship encouraged miscegenation.
29   Fuzziness is used in the strict mathematical sense of fuzzy sets associated with degrees of belonging.
30   The United States Bureau of the Census has ruled: "A person of mixed white and Negro blood should be returned as a Negro, no matter how small the

These types of definitional difficulties have persisted in the US government circles in the collecting of vital statistics, especially data on disease incidence. The confusion is illustrated by the rules that have been used to record the race or ethnic group of individuals. Thus, for instance, in collecting statistics about infant mortality, the following rules have been used (cf. Monthly Vital Statistics Supplement 1989) to classify infants of 'mixed' parents:

"(1) if one parent is white, the fetus or infant is assigned to the other parent's race;
(2) when neither parent is white, the fetus or infant is assigned to the father's race."

There is however an exception - *if the mother is Hawaiian the infant is classified as Hawaiian.*
Apparently, the tradition followed is that offspring of ethnically mixed unions are deemed to possess traits, especially behavioural traits, of the parent that is from the more socially disadvantaged ethnic group.

The case of Cy Grant is an interesting example of the results of 'fuzziness' in the matter of classification. According to Gus John, writing the obituary of Cy Grant (born 8 November 1919, died 13 February 2010) for the Guardian newspaper in England, Cy Grant was born in the village of Berterverwagting in British Guiana. Cy joined the RAF in 1941, trained as a navigator, and in 1943 was shot down in the Battle of the Ruhr, and landed in Holland. The Gestapo, defeated by the 'fuzziness' of Cy's racial origins, identified Cy as "a member of the Royal Air Force of indeterminate race". He was held as a prisoner of war for two years; but the Gestapo were not provided with appropriate rules to determine his 'race'.

In Guyana, the users of creole language met the challenge of illogicality by coining terms - e.g. **'Dougla'** to mean *'a person of mixed African and Indian (or sometimes Chinese) parentage';* and **'San-tan-tone'** to mean *'a person of mixed African and Portuguese ancestry'.* Of course, the official ethnic classification did not contain these categories, or indeed any category defining specific mixed ethnicities! The unwieldiness of defining the population by naming ethnic categories that allowed for **all** possible results of miscegenation was avoided by staying with: 'pure' ethnicities;

---

percentage of Negro blood. Both black and mulatto persons are to be returned as Negroes, without distinction."

the internal contradiction of 'black' contamination; and sometimes the device of a category called 'mixed'[31].

---

31 Guyana's current (2009) ethnic classification process as used officially by the Statistics Bureau has preserved this illogicality.

Some (many?) news releases had taken to citing President Obama as the first Black President of the United States of America. Interestingly, there are persons that are informed by the ideas expressed in the previous paragraphs, who claim that in fact there were seven black Presidents before Barack Obama. These are listed as:

1.   **John Hanson** (a Moor), 1781 - 1782, the 1st President.
2.   **Thomas Jefferson**, 1801 -1809, the 3rd President. The allegation is that his mother was a half-breed Indian squaw and his father a mulatto (half white and half black) from Virginia.
3.   **Andrew Jackson**, 1829 - 1837, the 7th President. The allegation is that his mother was a white woman from Ireland, and that his father was black.
4.   **Abraham Lincoln**, 1861 - 1865, the 16th President. Allegedly his mother was from an Ethiopian tribe and his father was an African American. His nickname was allegedly 'Abraham Africanus the First'.
5.   **Warren Harding**, 1921 - 1923, the 29th President.
6.   **Calvin Coolidge**, 1923 - 1929, the 30th President.
7.   **Dwight E. Eisenhower**, 1953 - 1961, the 34th President. Allegedly his mother, Elizabeth Stover Eisenhower was half black.

All this derives from the 'fuzziness' of the concept 'ethnicity' based on race. In the case of Guyana (and maybe in others), the words of the 14th century Arab historian, **ibn Khaldün**[32] (born in Tunis, May 27, 1332; died in Cairo, March 17, 1406) are appropriate to describe the group who defined the ethnic categories and their stereotypes: they were feeding *'in the pasture of stupidity'*.

It does appear that the colonisers and the Government personnel who were the architects of the ethnic categories and stereotypes were familiar with the concept highlighted by the following Swahili proverb: *'The beginning of Wisdom is knowing who you are'.* Accordingly, it was important to apprise the slaves, their descendants, the indentured labourers and their descendants, and the indigenous peoples of who they are, by providing

---

32   The 20th-century English historian Arnold Toynbee has described the work of **ibn Khaldün** as "a philosophy of history which is undoubtedly the greatest work of its kind that has ever yet been created by any mind in any time or place".

the respective stereotypes[33] - lest they revert to using their own ethnic groupings[34]!

As with all myths in a complex adaptive system, the reactions of the target populations included creating their own counter-myths. Thus, for instance, the white colonisers were categorised as *'backra'*,[35] and stereotyping produced statements like *'When blackman tief he tief half-a-bit, when backra tief he tief whole estate.'* Also, the term **'Backra Nigger'** was coined to refer to a person more nearly white than black in physical appearance, especially one who despises black people - a quadroon, octoroon, devil-whip, etc.; and the sentiment was expressed that: *'These backra people feel they white but little do they know that 'whiteness' is more than skin-colour!'* This phenomenon of "Passing" as 'not black' was not peculiar to Guyana. Thus the Cuban mulatto poet, Nicolas Guillen wrote:

> "Yesterday they called me "nigger"
> so I should get mad;
> but he who called me thus
> was as Black as I am.
> You pretend to be so white-
> but I know your grandmother!"

It is interesting to note that the ethnic categories in Guyana have not been invariant over time. There was a period during which'Lebanese' and 'Syrian' were officially recognised as ethnic categories, because a significant number of persons in these categories engaged in trade involving, for instance, the selling of suit/pants lengths (cloth for making English style clothing). Some, now classified as Portuguese, have Lebanese links.

In all these circumstances of fuzziness, internal contradictoriness, and undecidability, it would appear that if ethnicity and stereotypes based on race were to be used statistically as a framework for analysing societal behaviour, then the *complete* array of ethnicities and stereotypes ought to have been used - those supplied by the colonisers and Government

33 Dr. Robert Moore's *'Colonial Images of Blacks and Indians in 19th century Guyana'* gives useful insights into what those stereotypes were. Also, see Appendix # 2 for some further comments on ethnicity and race..
34 What would have happened had slaves been allowed to see themselves exclusively as ethnically Yoruba, Fulani, Hausa, etc. is an extremely interesting question.
35 See Dictionary of Caribbean Usage by Richard Allsopp.

personnel, and those supplied as a reaction in the workings of the complex adaptive system. To do otherwise is to apply only a portion of the meme of ethnicity and stereotypes! In considering voting behaviour, the question could be put as follows:

> **"If we wish to test the hypothesis that voting behaviour is ethnically determined, what categorisation of ethnic groups should we consider as the one appropriate for the analysis, given the realities of more than a century of miscegenation?"**

I find it difficult, indeed almost impossible, to resist the following conclusion:

> *Any attempt to define the human variation in Guyana by an ethnic group classification based on race, as part of an attempt to understand the diversity of behaviour, including voting behaviour, is certainly interesting; but equally certainly* **useless***.*

Frankly, however, I fear that the meme 'ethnicity based on race' will have the resilience of proverbial 'cockroaches' - capable of surviving even a nuclear blast! A large part of the reason for this resilience is that various consultants from, or trained in, foreign lands where the practice of utilizing the inadequate concept of 'ethnic groupings based on race' persists[36], preach to us with financial backing of prestigious foreign aid institutions. In these circumstances, we tend to swallow their ideas, hook, line, and sinker. If we insist on perceiving Guyana as a pot-pourri of ethnic groups masquerading as categories with well-defined characteristics determined and endowed by slavers and colonisers through more than a century of history, then we will have condemned ourselves to trying to resolve an unresolvable problem born of our own inept conceptualisation.

Among the most recent examples of the difficulties and contention that arise, are the responses to the *'Report of the independent expert on minority issues'*. The independent expert on minority issues, Ms Gay McDougall, visited Guyana between 28 July and 1 August 2008. Her 26 page report focuses in large part on the ethnic groupings popularly labelled as 'Afro-Guyanese' and 'Indo-Guyanese'. It was presented and discussed as the Annex to Agenda Item 3 of the tenth session of the Human Rights Council

---

36 See Appendix #11 for a brief exposition of the matter of Ethnicity and Race.

of the General Assembly of the United Nations, 27 February 2009[37]. The report is recommended reading for anyone who wishes to familiarize themselves with the difficulties that this section highlights. As reported on Page 21 of the Stabroek News of Thursday, May28, 2009, Bishop Juan Edghill, the then Chairman of Guyana's Ethnic Relations Commission (the ERC) deemed the report to be unbalanced and unfair. Bishop Edghill is right for the wrong reasons, reasons which would make the functioning of the ERC under his chairmanship equally misleading and un-useful. Confusion compounded has once again been assured. I am reminded of the comment by Johann von Goethe that *'There is nothing more frightening than ignorance in action'.* Having lived and observed matters in Guyana for more than two-thirds of a century, I concur.

Re **Voting** (Free and Fair) as a mechanism to determine societal opinion from individual opinions.

(1)   Untruth and Undecidability
There is a popularly believed concept which states that 'free and fair' voting by individuals should be a fundamental part of the electoral process that determines what societal opinion is. However, that is only a small part of the story. In deriving societal opinion from the free, unadulterated, expression of individual views, the **process** of derivation is of pivotal importance. This matter is dealt with in Appendix #5, the 1996 essay entitled 'Who shall Govern us?' In particular, we should refer here to the startling thesis of the co-winner of the 1972 Nobel prize for economics (Kenneth J. Arrow won with Sir John R. Hicks). That thesis is known as the *"Impossibility Theorem"* or *"Arrow's theorem"*. In summary, it states that under certain conditions of rationality and equality, it is impossible to guarantee that a ranking of societal preferences will correspond to rankings of individual preferences when more than two individuals and alternative choices are involved.

The complexities introduced in the preceding paragraph are compounded when we consider the issue of whose individual opinions one is attempting to use as a basis for determining the society's opinion. Eligibility to vote

---

37   The study *'The political Culture of Democracy in Guyana, 2009: The Impact of Governance'* conducted under the Latin American Public Opinion Project (LAPOP)is another study misguided by logically unsupportable definitions of the ethnic groups comprising Guyana; but its reported results have been accepted by USAID and are used to 'prioritise funding allocations and guide programme design'. *[cf. Sunday Stabroek, Feb 20, 2011, Page 9]*

has been constrained at various times by variables such as age, ownership of property/assets, and the then philosophically acceptable meaning and practice of 'democracy'. One has to deal with issues such as whether the views of a well formally- educated 17 year old are less important than those of an illiterate 30 year old; whether a 16 year old female single parent should have her views count at all, or the same as, her 25 year old lover. The example provided by the Roman Catholic Church is not helpful. There has been the rule, sanctioned by God speaking through the Pope, that 7 years is the lower limit of the age of reason in the matter of administering first communion[38]. This leads to the question of what age an individual needs to achieve before their views on any important societal issue be considered seriously - the issue of participation in a supposedly inclusionary democratic process. Consider, for instance, matters like child abuse determined without the input of the potentially abused!

It is against the background given above that I contend that **'Ethnic Voting'** falls in the category of myth. Indeed, the previously quoted epigram by Bertrand Russell about Pure Mathematics, i.e. it *'is the subject in which we do not know what we are talking about or whether what we are saying is true'* should now be clearly seen to be applicable to Ethnic Voting. The concept is therefore an inappropriate basis for conducting the analysis of elections in Guyana; or indeed for inclusion among concepts for proper analyses of Guyana's problems of governance. However, 'myths' are associated with 'believers', and 'belief' underpins behaviour. Indeed, as asserted by the Yale surgeon Dr Bernie S Siegel, author of the best-selling book "Love, Medicine, and Miracles", **'We are addicted to our beliefs and we do act like addicts when someone tries to wrest from us the powerful opium of our dogmas.'** Accordingly, whatever systemic reorganisation we propose ought to take account of the myths that underpin behaviour, especially the ones about ethnicity and ethnic voting to which we have been subjected for decades.

In this regard, I am reminded of two pronouncements attributed to the Greek sophist Protagoras of Abdera. One deals with the matter of what is real - the relativity to the individual of all perceptions and of all judgments. That pronouncement is: *"Man is the measure of all things, of those which are that they are and of those which are not that they are not."* It makes

---

38 This aberration should not be confused with its companion aberration based on anthropophagy, that declares wafer and wine to be 'the body and blood of Christ' as a kind of ritual cannibalism that absorbs the spiritual essence of the deceased.

no sense to tell someone in Guyana that he belongs to an ethnic group to which he is convinced he does not belong; or that ethnic groups do not exist, when he knows for sure that they do exist. No man who thinks he is a *coolie man* can be convinced that he is a *black man*; and vice versa. A man who knows he is a *buck man* will never agree that he is a *putagee*; and vice versa. Indeed, the situation with 'ethnicity' in Guyana is very similar to that of 'swing' in the arena of jazz. When Louis Armstrong[39] was asked what *'swing'* meant, he allegedly replied *"If you have to ask, you'll never know."* If you have to ask what is a *coolie* man, or a *putagee* man, or a *black* man, or a *buck* man, or a *white* man, or a *chinee* man, you'll never know!

The other pronouncement of Protagoras laid the foundation for agnosticism. It is the one referred to as *"Concerning the Gods".* It states: *'About the gods I am not able to know either that they are, or that they are not, or what they are like in shape, the things preventing knowledge being many, such as the obscurity of the subject and that life of man is short.'*

With appropriate adjustments, this quotation can be made to apply to the concepts of ethnicity and of ethnic voting in Guyana.

Re Visionaries - the need for their leadership of the society.

In the Guyanese vernacular the term 'visionary' is easily associated with the term 'obeah man', since the focus is on 'seeing far' into the future and on having the intuitive insights to do so persistently. It is not unreasonable to assume that visionaries do not exist in profusion, and it should follow that the task of finding a person with visionary qualities is quite formidable. Accordingly, finding astute leadership for the society is by definition an elusive objective of any system of the society (including free and fair voting) for choosing its leadership personnel if it is a requirement that those personnel must have visionary qualities.

I suspect that our feeling that there is the necessity for visionaries in governance of the society, derives from our emphasis on individuals as opposed to groups[40] in decision-making. Thus there is a tendency to think in terms of an individual (e.g. President, Prime Minister, Minister, Leader of a Political Party) wielding power, and for the requirement that

---

39 Armstrong taught the whole world about 'swing' in music.
40 This is particularly so if the individual has supernatural access to some omnipotent being.

the individual be visionary if good governance of the society is to be achieved. The notion of collective intelligence in action, derived from the body politic through mechanisms for consultation and conjoint decision-making facilitated by communication (as by honeybee swarms in their choice of a nest site[41]) is apparently not accepted as an appropriate basis of governance. Accordingly, mechanisms for routinely using collective intelligence to identify and resolve community problems have not tended to be devised, tested, and revised in an unending stepwise manner. Indeed, the Constitution Reform Commission of 1999 recommended that 'Co-operative' be **deleted** from the name of the country and the country be named simply 'The Republic of Guyana'. This change requires a referendum to give effect to it, but no such referendum has as yet been held. However, I have reasons to believe that the mindset of the change has occurred and persists.

Given the frequency/pace of the requirement of good decision -making, it is hardly surprising that there is pressure to find individuals willing to assume responsibility for making decisions; and there is hope, however forlorn, that a continual search will throw up competent individuals from time to time. Also, given the perks of political power, there is a conviction that various individuals will crave and offer themselves for the positions, having convinced themselves of their suitability and that "goat ent bite them". But by definition visionaries must be scarce; and love of political power is neither a necessary nor a sufficient condition for identification of members of the subset from which visionaries might be chosen.

Also, in terms of the history of the world and its peoples, visionaries are more associated with paradigm shifts than with the day to day aspects of governance. These individuals tend to engage in conceptual battles of their view against then current popularly accepted opinion; and are often generally recognised as having been correct only long after they are dead. In any event the battleground is often the very complex one of aetiology, and the most perspicacious individuals are difficult to identify with foresight rather than hindsight. Thus, for example, non-understanding of the causes of bubonic plague led in 1348 to persecution of Jews who, in Basel, were all locked inside wooden buildings and burned alive. Not

---

41 cf. The Article 'Independence and Interdependence in collective decision-making: an agent-based model of nest-site choice by honeybee swarms' published in Philosophical Transactions of the Royal Society B, Biological Sciences, available to download at **rstb.royalsocietypublishing.org/ content/364/1518.toc**

dissimilar 'inhuman' treatment of isolation and peremptory extermination was meted out to Jews in many other parts of Europe on the basis of the then popular conviction that they were the cause of the bubonic plague.

The best example that comes to my mind about a visionary and an important paradigm shift has to do with the theory and practice of medicine. Paracelsus[42] had the perspicacity, the audacity, and the bombast to reject the then widely supported Theory that there were four 'cardinal humours' *(blood, phlegm, choler, and melancholy)* in each person, that good health comprised the proper balance of these four humours, and that disease resulted from an excess or an insufficiency of one or another of them. Paracelsus insisted that disease was not the maladjustment of bodily humours within a person, but had a specific cause outside the body. The path to the concepts of modern medicine was thus established by a person, a visionary who had a radically different concept of what disease was about.

It is also true that in the matters of governance of a society there is the reality of multi-dimensionality; and a person would have to be a polymath to command an understanding of a sufficient number of these dimensions to be a reliable source of conceptual leadership and advice on the majority of these matters. For each matter/issue, there is almost certainly great merit in selecting a group of persons knowledgeable about the matter/issue, and trying to get that group to consult and thereby arrive at a consensual decision about the society's possible best response. In constructing the group to be consulted, we must be careful to not exclude persons of no learning but of profound wisdom! The shortage of visionaries would then be less of a difficulty. I am reminded of a statement by CLR James in 'Nkrumah and the Ghana Revolution': *"The countries known as underdeveloped have produced the greatest statesmen of the twentieth century, men who have substantially altered the shape and direction of world civilisation in the last fifty years. They are four in number: Lenin, Gandhi, Mao Tse-tung and Nkrumah."*

If James is reflecting the availability of such visionaries, even approximately, then we would be well advised to treat a national search for them as pursuit of a chimera. It is against this background that I argue that the following statement be treated as a myth (a romantic harking back to the oracle at Delphi):

42 Paracelsus (1493 - 1541) was the nickname of Theophrastus Philippus Aureolus Bombastus von Hohenheim.

'Leaders need to be visionaries, intellectually blessed,
and thereby capable of giving guidance to the people on
a broad range of issues.'

Interestingly, if we accept the notion of the necessity of a visionary for good governance, and also accept the idea that visionaries are scarce, then it should follow that when we think we have found a visionary, our own commonsense would persuade us not to change that individual as a political leader, thereby establishing a prolonged period of non-change in our political leadership. We would therefore be in conflict with our own ideas of the need for elections with a predetermined medium-term (5 years?) periodicity.

In the preface to this book, there were four areas listed as areas that need to be addressed. They were stated as:

(i)   The uncertainties related to the issue of how to derive a societal consensus from clearly expressed individual opinions - a matter that often impinges on the very meaning of democracy;

(ii)   Power Sharing in the process of Governance;

(iii)   The Role of Political Parties in the process of Governance;

(iv)   The meaning of 'Ethnicity' - the definition by the Bureau of Statistics, and some of its implications[43].

To these four we should add a fifth:

Determining the Term of a Government, whatever the
mechanism of choice that we choose to use.

As indicated in various footnotes, the Appendices of this Part1 address these issues. They represent thoughts assembled on these issues, and most were published as essays in the book 'Heretical Musings 1992-2003'. They thus represent a stepwise construction over time of the views that eventually led to the conjecture for a new electoral process. The essays and their years of construction are:

---

43   See Appendix # 11.

Red Balls, Blue Balls, and Ethnic Voting Patterns [1992]	Appendix # 1
The Ethnic Problem (More Interesting Insights) [1995]	Appendix # 2
with Address by D. Hoyte at 150ᵗʰ Anniversary of Abolition of Slavery	
Tourism - A Counter-Intuitive Conjecture [1995]	Appendix # 3
The Term of Government *(or What's so special about 5?)* [1995]	Appendix # 4
Who shall Govern Us? [1996]	Appendix # 5
Whither goest we? [1996]	Appendix # 6
Some further Comments on Guyana's Electoral System [1998]	Appendix # 7
The Upsidedowness of Power Sharing [2002]	Appendix # 8
Ethnic Voting - a Myth [2004]	Appendix # 9
Computer Keyboard Layouts	Appendix# 10
Ethnicity and Race	Appendix# 11

Reading these Appendices, in whatever order the reader deems convenient, and absorbing their content is a necessary condition for understanding PEC which is presented in Part 2 of this book.

I am perhaps overwhelmingly, but not inordinately, concerned about the myths that underpin the concept and practice of governance in Guyana. These concerns relate to my general perception that all myths are associated with believers, and beliefs underpin the actions of believers. Humans do perceive the world through the lenses of their beliefs; and as intelligent beings they often do tend to act in accordance with those beliefs.

Among the most unsavoury myths that I have encountered is the one that asserts that a male lover's fidelity can be secured by giving him 'tea' made with water that has been strained through the crotch of his paramour's recently worn panties[44]. Accordingly, if I were attracted to a female whom I suspected believed that myth, I would be more than likely to refuse an offer of 'tea' from her. However, the world abounds in myths of all sorts, both benign and maleficent. In this cornucopia of myths are ones not discussed in the Appendices of Part 1, but which do impact on some aspects of governance systems in Guyana. That cornucopia includes misperceptions such as that at Independence all ethnic groupings would <u>have been accorded</u> equal treatment.

44 This belongs to the same class of beliefs as **'Channel Eggs'** promoting **'tabanca'**.

Unfortunately, the various ethnic groups would have each had as their legacy the remnants of pre-Independence (including pre and post abolition of slavery) myths. In this mix, Africans had the unique place of being the only ethnic group about which there was serious doubt about whether they belonged to the human species[45]. For instance, in the 1820s, in both Jamaica and Brazil, there was the common opinion that black was merely an intermediate step between man and the brute creation. There were claims that 'The native inhabitants of Africa are not of the Human Species; that they are Animals of an inferior class; or if they have any relationship to the human race, they are some spurious blood'. Out of pernicious planter literature of the kind that spread these views came the notion of the 'contamination of racially pure white blood'. The outlawing in 1807, of the trading in slaves in the British dominions owed more to economics than to moral suasion, as law makers and entrepreneurs compared the costly tariffs propping up West Indian sugar imports with imports from the free-labour East Indies. Slavery, described as 'the black agony brought on by white greed', left imprints on ethnic characterisation that abolition did not erase.

Re: Political Parties - Necessary entities for effective governance?

For at least the past 50 years the presumptions have been that the governance of the territory currently known as Guyana should take place in a framework that includes:

(1)   Political Parties competing for power;

(2)   Competing 'isms', or versions thereof, favoured by those competing Political Parties as the preferred basis for the exercise of power and the pursuit of the country's development strategies; and

(3)   Competing individuals attempting to demonstrate, within and across Political Parties, that they have charisma.

---

45   This comment may not be quite accurate! For instance, as mentioned on Page 63 of the book: 'A New System of Slavery The Export of Indian Labour Overseas 1830-1920', John Gladstone, the then proprietor of the estates Vreedenhoop and Vriedenstein in Demerara, in correspondence (4 Jan 1836) with Gillanders, Arbuthnot and Co. asking them to provide a hundred coolies for five to seven years, received a letter containing the following: *"The Dhangurs are always spoken of as more akin to the monkey than the man. They have no religion, no education, and in their present state no wants beyond eating, drinking and sleeping; and to procure which they are willing to labour."*

The isms that have been favoured are of rather old vintage - communism, socialism, capitalism - and a few of perhaps rather more recent vintage like cooperativism. Mainly, the isms were those of the vintage of the student days (mainly student days in some European metropolis, or in the USA or Canada) of the contesting leaders; and the political parties they founded / headed sought to teach those isms to their younger members in colleges set up for that purpose (e.g Accrebe college on the East Bank Demerara, and Cuffy Ideological Institute off the Soesdyke/Linden Highway)[46]. Accordingly, the isms were old established ideologically justified memes (a prime example of the impact of mainly European ethnocentric ideas on Guyana's choice of ideology to underpin development), as opposed to well researched systems governance techniques, such as those currently emerging from the science of complexity applied to Complex Adaptive Systems; or those related to game theoretical analyses such as those investigated by Robert Axelrod[47] using the mathematical model of 'the iterated Prisoner's dilemma'. They were also heavily influenced by the parameters of the ideological battle among the countries of the capitalist west and the socialist / communist east, with that battle for minds being spiced up with the blandishments of financial assistance to parties that favoured one camp as opposed to the other in the pursuit of political power in national and international fora.

As a result, three key questions have emerged. One is: *Can an electoral process that is focused on individuality and charisma, lay an adequate basis for consensual governance?* A second, more disturbing one, is: *Can the practice of consensual governance be inhibited by the process for choosing in whose hands the responsibility for governance is placed?* The third, and perhaps most worrying of all, is: *Can the electoral process determine whether consensual governance practices can be established?*

The continual focus on 'consensual' derives from the thinking that was eventually formally expressed in Article 13 of the Guyana Constitution which states:

---

46 It was recognised, as former Minister Hubert Jack once noted, that for instance one could not build socialism in Guyana without socialists - so local and foreign education / indoctrination activities for party cadres, trade unionists, etc. had to be established. Ranji Chandisingh, Member of the Central Executive Committee of the People's National Congress was appointed Director of Studies, Cuffy Ideological Institute.

47 The reference is to Robert Axelrod's 1984 publication 'The Evolution of Cooperation'.

'The principal objective of the political system of the State is to establish an inclusionary democracy by providing increasing opportunities for the participation of citizens, and their organizations in the management and decision-making processes of the State, with particular emphasis on those areas of decision-making that directly affect their well-being.'

The three questions mentioned above ought to be considered within the context of Articles 8, 9, and 10 of the Constitution of Guyana. These state as follows:

Article 8
This Constitution is the supreme law of Guyana and, if any other law is inconsistent with it, that other law shall, to the extent of the inconsistency, be void.

Article 9
Sovereignty belongs to the people, who exercise it through their representatives and the democratic organs established by or under this Constitution.

Article 10
The right to form political parties and their freedom of action are guaranteed. Political parties must respect the principles of national sovereignty and of democracy.

In this context, the three questions have the answers respectively of: *Perhaps; Yes; Yes.*

Near the beginning of this Part I, the following was offered: "a **myth** is a **meme** characterised by one or more of: **untruth, fuzziness, internal contradiction**, or **undecidability**." It has also been noted that people's behaviour is strongly influenced by their beliefs; and those beliefs include the entrenched myths mentioned above. If we take account simultaneously of the three questions, of the answers proffered, and of the focus of the Constitution, then the process we choose to use to elect a government ought to:

(i)   be treated as a conjecture that we commit to re-evaluate continually in the light of our experience with its functioning;

(ii)   be amended on the basis of that re-evaluation, and in the context of then current beliefs as they may have been amended by experience; and

(iii)   be continually appraised to ensure that Articles 8, 9, and 10 of the Constitution are not breached.

I suspect that if practices based on these principles are established, then the role of political parties in the pursuit of good governance will change drastically over time. What changes should take place is a matter that ought to be considered in a different publication from this one, and in any event will be partly determined by the experience of trying to implement PEC. Accordingly, it is probably best to study the following Appendices which attempt to establish the main details of the conceptual framework necessary for the recommended foray on governance.

Appendix # 1
Red Balls, Blue Balls, and Ethnic Voting Patterns [1992]

The Problem

For the past three decades I have heard it asserted repeatedly that voting behaviour in Guyana is ethnically determined. There appears to have been a consensus arrived at that makes the assertion be treated as a self-evident truth; and if anyone sceptically asks for the empirical evidence, the cognoscenti dismissively assert: "Just look at the results of the national elections that were not rigged" - the most recent being that of October 5, 1992.

The underlying assertion is that the results of the secret ballot called elections are an indicator of the truth of the statement that voting is ethnically determined. Put another way, the allegation is that if voting behaviour were not ethnically determined, the results of the election would have been significantly different from what they actually were. There is also the companion implication that if one knows the ethnic composition of the community of voters, then the results of voting that is purely ethnically determined are predictable.

I have introduced the qualifier "purely" in juxtaposition with "ethnically determined" because there has always been the suggestion that the phenomenon being dealt with is one of predominant behaviour of the major ethnic groups, as opposed to one in which there is absolutely no variation from the ethnic stereotype. Here begins my sense of disquiet about the precision of the whole concept of "predominantly ethnic voting behaviour" and its manifestation in election results.

Three sets of related questions may be posed.

First, for a community with a known ethnic mix, is there some index based on the results of elections which might be used to measure whether the phenomenon of ethnic voting is getting weaker or getting stronger?

Second, for a community with a known ethnic mix, and assumed levels of ethnic bias for each important ethnic group in that community, can the results of an election be predicted?

Third, for a community with a known ethnic mix, whose voting results are known, do these results uniquely indicate the levels of ethnic bias for each important ethnic group in the community?

The first question is important because it is consensually agreed on moral and philosophical grounds that ethnic voting is "undesirable". Against that background it must be important to know whether we are improving or deteriorating in the matter of how ethnic bias is impinging on the results of free and fair democratically conducted elections. Here, the following ethical question: *"Is it not "democracy" in action that gives me the right to prefer one Party to the other on whatever basis I choose, including ethnicity?"* is not being dealt with. We are simply going with the popular tide that says that there is something undesirable about having voters' preferences in elections, especially national elections, ethnically determined.

The choice of "undesirability" is being made as a facilitating device, even though it remains unclear why it is acceptable to have ethnic predispositions operate in important areas such as "whom one marries"; or "whom one sleeps with"; or "who are one's close friends"; but not acceptable to have them operate in the matter of "who shall govern us", where that is a societal choice derived from individual preferences.

The second question in some ways derives its importance from the first. If the answer is "no", then we can have no statistical yardstick (based on the parameters of ethnic mix, ethnic bias, and results) applicable for telling us whether the results indicate greater or lesser ethnic bias among the community's ethnic groups. A similar comment holds good for the third question. In all this one is deliberately excluding anecdotal evidence.

For the purposes of this initial tilt at the problem, I further suggest that the fundamentally important differences between ethnicity and race be ignored. I also suggest that we admit as a workable concept the idea that **ethnic bias** means **the predisposition of a person to vote for the Party whose leadership by reputation allegedly favours the ethnic group to which the voter perceives the voter belongs.**

To avoid the crudities and the emotional trauma likely to arise in talking about *"black people voting for the PNC as a known black people's Party"* and *"coolie people voting for the PPP as a known coolie people's Party"*, the next section of this discourse will be conducted in terms of choosing

Red balls and Blue balls on the basis of various predispositions. Only when we have derived answers to the questions posed at the beginning of this section will we revert to the more traumatic terrain.

Hopefully this device will avoid emotion from interfering with good judgement, and simultaneously provide us with insights into the issues through the use of an emotionally neutral decision-making model.

THE FACILITATING MODEL
(Choosing Red balls and Blue balls)

Assume that there is a community in which there are **NALL** people. **NR** of them always wear red shirts or blouses. **NB** of them always wear blue shirts or blouses. The remaining **NO** people always wear some colour other than red or blue.

Assume further that the group of NR people is characterised by the fact that if any one of them is asked to choose between a red ball and a blue ball, where the two balls look identical except for colour, then the probability that the red ball is chosen is denoted by p_r. The number of times a red ball is expected to be chosen by the NR group is then p_r**NR**; and the number of times a blue ball is expected to be chosen is **(1-p_r)NR**.

Thus, for instance, assigning the value **1** to p_r for the **NR** group is equivalent to saying that the members of this group are so enamoured of the colour "red" that they will always choose a red ball; and the number of times a red ball is expected to be chosen is **NR**. If, however, there is an **80%** chance that an **NR** type will choose a red ball, p_r assumes the value **0.8** and the number of times a red ball is expected to be chosen is **0.8NR**; while the number times a blue ball is expected to be chosen is **0.2NR**.

We can deem the NR group to be perfectly unbiased in the matter of colour if each member is just as likely to choose a red ball as they are likely to choose a blue ball. This corresponds to assigning the value **0.5** to p_r. Then we would expect a red ball to be chosen a half of the time, and a blue ball the other half, with the expected results of **0.5NR** red choices and **0.5NR** blue choices.

The arguments in the preceding three paragraphs can be repeated for each of the groups of the **NB** and the **NO** people; and we can assign appropriate values of p_r to each group to derive expected results.

To complete this framework, let us assume a community mix of numbers of NR, NB, and NO people as follows:

NR people	300	53% of total community
NB people	175	41% of total community
NO people	90	16% of total community
NALL people	565	100% of total community

Now we use the simple arithmetic based on the principles set out above to derive the results we would expect for varying levels of $\mathbf{p}_r$ for each group in the community. The results are instructive, despite the simplicity of the model.

CASE 1
Perfect bias within the NR and NB groups and perfect lack of bias among NOs.

NR=300	$p_r=1$	RED Balls= 300	BLUE Balls= 0
NB=175	$p_r=0$	RED Balls= 0	BLUE Balls=175
NO= 90	$p_r=0.5$	RED Balls= 45	BLUE Balls= 45
NALL=565		RED Balls= 345	BLUE Balls=220
(100%)		**(61%)**	**(39%)**

CASE 2
Less than perfect but equal reciprocal bias within the NR and NB groups and perfect lack of bias among NOs.

NR=300	$p_r=0.6$	RED Balls= 180	BLUE Balls=120
NB=175	$p_r=0.4$	RED Balls= 70	BLUE Balls=105
NO= 90	$p_r=0.5$	RED Balls= 45	BLUE Balls= 45
NALL=565		RED Balls= 295	BLUE Balls=270
(100%)		**(52%)**	**(48%)**

CASE 3
Less than perfect but unequal reciprocal bias within the NR and NB groups and perfect lack of bias among NOs.

NR=300	$p_r=0.6$	RED Balls= 180	BLUE Balls=120
NB=175	$p_r=0.2$	RED Balls= 35	BLUE Balls=140
NO= 90	$p_r=0.5$	RED Balls= 45	BLUE Balls= 45
NALL=565		RED Balls= 260	BLUE Balls=305
(100%)		**(46%)**	**(54%)**

CASE 4
Less than perfect but unequal reciprocal bias within the NR and NB groups and some bias among NOs.

NR=300	$p_r=0.65$	RED Balls= 195	BLUE Balls=105
NB=175	$p_r=0.2$	RED Balls= 35	BLUE Balls=140
NO= 90	$p_r=0.33$	RED Balls= 30	BLUE Balls= 60
NALL=565		RED Balls= 260	BLUE Balls=305
(100%)		**(46%)**	**(54%)**

CASE 5
Less than perfect but unequal reciprocal bias within the NR and NB groups and some bias among NOs.

NR=300	$p_r=0.6$	RED Balls= 180	BLUE Balls=120
NB=175	$p_r=0.3$	RED Balls= 53	BLUE Balls=122
NO= 90	$p_r=0.5$	RED Balls= 50	BLUE Balls= 40
NALL=565		RED Balls= 283	BLUE Balls=282
(100%)		**(50%)**	**(50%)**

CASE 6
All groups unbiased (i.e. all p_r = 0.5)
Then the overall expected result will be as in Case 5.
The following characteristics can be gleaned from the arithmetic of these six cases:

(1)   If the composition of the community of ball choosers (i.e. the percentages of **NR**s, **NB**s, and **NO**s) is known, and the respective probabilities that characterise each group (the levels of p_r for each group) are also known, then it is possible to calculate the expected results of colours of balls chosen (provided no other decision-making parameters are introduced).

(2)   If the composition of the community of ball choosers is known, and the expected results of colours of balls chosen is given, then it is impossible to uniquely determine the levels of respective probabilities that characterise each group. Cases 3 and 4, and 5 and 6 are pairs which indicate this characteristic.

(3)   If unbiasedness is deemed to be a desirable trait, then Cases 5 and 6 indicate that the expected result for overall unbiased community (i.e. 50% Red balls and 50% Blue balls) does not emanate uniquely from unbiased choice behaviour in each of the community' groups.

(4)   The levels of the p_r s in Cases 3 and 4, and in Cases 5 and 6 indicate that even when the same overall expected results occur, it becomes difficult to say which ball choosing predispositions are more desirable when unbiasedness is set as a criterion of perfection. Even if one is to assert that the Case 6 configuration of p_r s is "perfection", that still does not automatically allow us to rank the configurations of Cases 3, 4, and 5.

These characteristics put us on notice that being given the expected results of colour choosing of balls, and the composition of the community of ball choosers, may well be woefully insufficient information for us to conclude anything about the levels of colour choice bias that characterise the constituent groups of our ball choosing community. And even if we did settle on some estimated likely levels of bias for each of the constituent groups, we would have great difficulty in applying the criterion of unbiasedness to say which behaviour was an improvement on which.

It is even more instructive to complicate our model a little. Assume that the choice of ball is not entirely dependent on colour prejudice. Let us introduce the concept of the weight of the ball, and introduce the idea that for all members of the community, given what they wish to do with the balls, there is a view of acceptability of the ball based on its weight. Let all red balls be the same weight, significantly different from the weight of all blue balls which all weigh the same.

Now let the probability of a red ball being acceptable to anyone in the community on the basis of its weight be denoted by v_r, and that of a blue ball be v_b. The decision-making steps that now apply for each individual chooser will conform to the following sequence:

Step 1: Allow your colour prejudice to operate and pick a ball of your preferred colour.

Step 2: Test the weight of the ball picked. If its weight is acceptable, choose it. If not, do not choose it.

Step 3: If you did not choose a ball of your preferred colour, examine a ball of the other colour. If its weight is acceptable, choose it. If not, do not choose it.

These three steps impose a paramountcy of "rationality" over colour prejudice in the choice of ball, since if a ball of your preferred colour cannot do the job because its weight is inappropriate you will not choose it. And if a ball of the colour you do not like **can** do the job because its weight is appropriate, you **will** choose it, even though you do not like its colour. And if no ball has the appropriate weight you will choose neither. The slightly more complicated algebra gives the following configuration of probabilities for each group in the community:

Probability that a **Red** ball is **chosen:**	$v_r - (1 - p_r) v_b v_r$
Probability that a **Blue** ball is **chosen:**	$v_b - p_r v_b v_r$
Probability that **Neither** a Red nor a Blue ball is **chosen:**	$1 - v_b - v_r + v_b v_r$

Some of the illuminating results that may be derived are given below:

CASE 7 (cf. CASE 1)
Perfect colour bias within the NR and NB groups and perfect lack of bias among the NOs.

$v_r = 0.7$ and $v_b = 0.8$ for all groups, indicating the view that the Blue balls are agreed as more appropriate for the Job when colour prejudice is ignored.

	RED BALLS	BLUE BALLS	NEITHER
NR =300 (100%) $p_r = 1$	210 (70%)	72(24%)	18(6%)
NB =175 (100%) $p_r = 0$	25 (14%)	140(80%)	11(6%)
NO = 90 (100%) $p_r = 0.5$	38 (42%)	47(52%)	5(6%)
NALL=565(100%)	272 **(48%)**	259**(46%)**	34**(6%)**

When "rationality" intervenes, the perfect colour prejudice has its effect significantly watered down (cf. Case 1) but the agreed "better" blue balls still lose out to the agreed "inferior" red balls by 2 percentage points. Also, though only 31% of the community favour Blue balls for their colour, Blue balls are chosen 46% of the time. **It would be erroneous to conclude that this result shows a decline in the colour prejudice of the Red ball or Blue ball supporters!**

CASE 8 (cf. CASE 7)
Colour bias within the NR and NB groups **is reduced to 90%** ,and there is perfect lack of bias among the NOs.
$v_r = 0.7$ and $v_b = 0.8$ for all groups, indicating the view that the Blue balls are agreed as more appropriate for the Job when colour prejudice is ignored.

		RED BALLS	BLUE BALLS	NEITHER
NR =300 (100%)	$p_r = 0.9$	194 (65%)	88(29%)	18(6%)
NB =175 (100%)	$p_r = 0.1$	34 (19%)	131(75%)	11(6%)
NO = 90 (100%)	$p_r = 0.5$	38 (42%)	47(52%)	5(6%)
NALL=565(100%)		266 **(47%)**	266**(47%)**	34**(6%)**

When "rationality" intervenes, even though colour prejudice is still significantly equally high in the NR and NB groups, the expected results show equal percentages of Red balls and Blue balls being chosen. **It would be erroneous to claim that these results indicate a significant non-operation of colour prejudice!**

Varying the parameters in this model gives a feel for how the expected results of choice vary with levels of colour prejudice and assessment of the appropriateness of the weight of the balls. The sensitivity of the results to these variations is remarkable. For instance, if we keep the assumption of perfect bias for the NR and the NB groups and unbiasedness for the NO group, keep the probability of the weight of the red balls being deemed appropriate at 70%, **but change the probability of the weight of the blue balls being deemed appropriate to 91%**, the expected overall result becomes: Red balls - 45%; Blue balls -52%; Neither Red nor Blue balls - 3%. **The Blue balls could be expected to enjoy a simple majority of 52%, even though there is perfect colour prejudice in a community in which 535 of the people prefer Red balls on the basis of colour alone; and only 31% of the people prefer Blue balls on the basis of colour alone.**

BACK TO THE REAL WORLD

This is a good point at which to leave the facilitating model and all its algebra. It has served its purpose to put us on notice that "rationality" can quite startlingly overcome the results of prejudice, even when prejudice is operating in an otherwise unbridled fashion. Also, it indicates the impossibility, or at least the great hazard, of deducing support for assumed prejudices on the basis of observed results.

If democracy is to persist with the manifestation of a secret ballot in free and fair elections, with choices free from fear, it is a waste of time trying to deduce from the results of such an election and the ethnic mix of the voting community, statistically justifiable statements about ethnic bias in voting. Not only does one not know what to expect when ethnic bias is present, given the other factors operating (such as views about the appropriateness of policies to be followed), but also one is not in a position on the basis of the results to say whether there has been a diminution of the impact of ethnic bias.

Why individuals vote the way they vote is obviously a complex question and deserves a far more complex approach than simply looking at the ethnic mix of the voting community and rushing on to statistically insupportable conclusions.

A concluding set of remarks is appropriate. First, the model indicates clearly that if a politician in the minority ethnic group perceives that there might be ethnic predispositions operating, the worst argument he could advance is that of saying that the other Party cannot but follow the policies he espouses! If he does so successfully, then in terms of the model he is making **vr** equal to **vb** and preparing the ground for "rationality" in terms of the inefficiency of his competitor's policies to not operate. If he is disadvantaged in ethnic terms, that's among the worst arguments for him to use, for then in policy terms it really does not matter which Party is chosen. A voter can then comfortably fall back simply on his/her ethnic prejudice.

Second, for those who insist on asserting that they are clear about what they mean by voting along ethnic lines, here is a conundrum. At what stage will you conclude that a community which is predominantly (near 100%) one ethnic group, that traditionally votes predominantly for the Party allegedly supporting its ethnic group, is no longer voting ethnically? Is it only when they vote predominantly for the Party allegedly supporting the other ethnic group?

Third, none of the arguments presented above is intended to indicate that voter decision-making is not significantly ethnically determined. However, it is intended to indicate that if voter behaviour is ethnically determined it may be well nigh impossible to estimate the extent to which that behaviour is so determined from the results and knowledge of the ethnic mix of the community of voters. Indeed, the arguments support the following conjectures:

(i)   Ethnic predispositions impact on the results of elections far less than is consensually assumed, and become rapidly less important the more other "rational" choice parameters operate.

(ii)   A community in which ethnic predispositions underpin main societal decisions may indeed constitute a morally "undesirable" situation; but of all the areas of decision-making, voting behaviour is perhaps among the least worthy of worry. Other areas such as discrimination of one group against another may be far more important, e.g. East Indian owned taxis refusing to take "Black" passengers, or vice versa; or East Indian vendors selling at higher prices to "Black" customers, or vice versa; or East Indian owned businesses tending to not hire "Black" employees, or vice versa; or ethnic considerations determining whether you abscond from the scene of a motor vehicle accident by comparing your ethnicity with that of the accident victim and of the neighbourhood in which the accident occurred. Perhaps the most important of all classes of issues has to do with the perception that depending on the Government in power, one main ethnic group is deliberately given a systematic advantage over the others in matters of competition for a share of the economic cake!

END (1992)

Appendix # 2
The Ethnic Problem (More Interesting Insights) [1995]

THE ETHNIC PROBLEM
(More Interesting Insights - 1995)

In the first volume of essays entitled *"some of My Favourite Heresies"* there is the essay *"Red Balls, Blue Balls & Ethnic Voting Patterns"*. That essay indicated some of the difficulties which arise in trying to decide whether the ethnic element in voting decisions was getting stronger or weaker over time; but also made the point that nothing said in the essay was ***"intended to indicate that voter decision-making is not significantly ethnically determined."*** Perhaps a good starting point for this tilt at the ethnic problem in Guyana is that of putting the question in a little better perspective by providing some evidence about the impact of ethnicity on voting patterns.

What follows should be an amateur psephologist's delight. The basic data provided in the ten-page appendix to this essay comes from the official voting results of the 1992 General Elections as they relate to Georgetown. The ethnic distributions quoted were acquired informally from the initial voter registration data listings (which **did** garner ethnic information, although this was never officially published - perhaps quite understandably?).

Obviously Georgetown is not the whole of Guyana, and may well be argued to be not representative of national voting behaviour. However, the ethnic variation within Georgetown makes it statistically interesting, in a manner that a more ethnically homogeneous area would not be. The following is a listing of ten salient statistical statements that emerge from the statistical analyses detailed in the appendix. The first two statements deal with the ethnic mix of the 1992 Georgetown voter population, and the remaining eight note some of the interesting correlations and other relationships.

TEN SALIENT STATISTICAL STATEMENTS[1]

1. *The polling divisions comprising Georgetown were characterised by an ethnic predominance of persons who describe themselves either as East Indians or as Africans. The two groups together accounted for a **minimum** of **64%**, a **maximum** of **97%**, and an **average** of **83%** of the voter populations in the individual polling divisions.*

2. *The percentages of voters of African ethnicity and voters of East Indian ethnicity were **highly negatively correlated (a correlation of -0.954)**; and for every percentage point increase in the percentage of voters of East Indian ethnicity there was a 0.920 percentage point decrease in the percentage of voters of African ethnicity.*

3. *There was a significantly **large positive correlation (0.941) between the percentage of pro-PPP votes and the percentage of voters of East Indian ethnicity.** [Put another way, the variation in the percentage of voters of East Indian ethnicity explains **88.56%** of the variation in pro-PPP votes.]*

4. *There was a significantly **large negative correlation (-0.899) between the percentage of pro-PPP votes and the percentage of voters of African ethnicity.***

5. *There was a significantly **large positive correlation (0.913) between the percentage of pro-PNC votes and the percentage of voters of African ethnicity.** [Put another way, the variation in the percentage of voters of African ethnicity explains **83.38%** of the variation in pro-PNC votes.]*

---

1. *These statements should be interpreted in the context of **"voters"** meaning **"registered voters"** rather than **"persons who actually voted."** The ethnic distribution of the latter category is the same as the former only if voting or not voting was not related to ethnicity!*

6.   *There was a significantly **large negative correlation (-0.927) between the percentage of pro-PNC votes and the percentage of voters of East Indian ethnicity.***

7.   *The rate at which the percentage of pro-PPP votes increased with increases in the percentage of voters of East Indian ethnicity was 0.968 percentage point for every 1 percentage point increase in East Indian ethnic composition.*

8.   *The rate at which the percentage of pro-PNC votes increased with increases in the percentage of voters of African ethnicity was 0.975 percentage point for every 1 percentage point increase in African ethnic composition.*

9.   *The rate at which the percentage of pro-PPP votes decreased with increases in the percentage of voters of African ethnicity was 0.959 percentage point decrease for every 1 percentage point increase in African ethnic composition.*

10. *The rate at which the percentage of pro-PNC votes decreased with increases in the percentage of voters of East Indian ethnicity was 0.955 percentage point decrease for every 1 percentage point increase in East Indian ethnic composition.*

The question of what these statistical facts imply as true statements of voting behaviour is quite complex.   Essentially, the complexities arise from at least two sources. First, there are the well known difficulties that inhere in going from correlation to causation as one interprets statistics.   High correlation quite often does not properly imply causation; and when it does, by itself it gives no clue to the direction of cause and effect. Secondly, there is the reality of the "null hypothesis", where by this I allude to the fact that at best the statistics will say that they provide insufficient evidence to support rejection of the specific hypothesis being considered. Never do the statistics say that the hypothesis is true - they only say that you can be confident that there is too little statistical reason to treat it as false, i.e. reject it.

The reader needs to bear the two caveats of the previous paragraph in mind as the immediately following paragraphs are perused.

A. Given that a "perfect" statistical relationship between two variables is associated with a correlation of 1 or -1, statements 3 and 5 above highlight the fact that people of East Indian ethnicity very strongly supported the PPP (a correlation of 0.941) while people of African ethnicity very strongly supported the PNC (a correlation of 0.913). But was East Indian support for the PPP indeed stronger than African support for the PNC as the correlations seem to suggest? One approach to this question could be to calculate whether the two correlations are not approximately equal in statistical terms. However, a perhaps more interesting approach might be to take on board the fact that in 30 of the 59 Polling Divisions the percentage pro PPP vote was less than the percentage of East Indians in the Division; while in only 3 of the 59 Polling Divisions was the percentage of pro PNC vote less than the percentage of people of declared African ethnicity! I suggest that the proper interpretation may include the idea that when the PPP got votes it was mainly East Indians who voted for them; but several East Indians (probably at least about 8%) did not vote for the PPP!

B. Statements 1 and 2, taken together with statements 3 and 5, imply that statements 4 and 6 should be expected as the obverse side of statements 3 and 5; including the appearance that East Indian rejection of the PNC (a negative correlation of -0.927) was stronger than African rejection of the PPP (a negative correlation of -0.899).

C. Statements 7, 8, 9, and 10 are associated respectively with the following mathematical relationships:

PPP% = 0.570 + 0.968 East Indian %
PNC% =14.328 + 0.975 African %

PPP% = 80.246 - 0.959 African %
PNC% = 94.494 - 0.955 East Indian %

The absolute values of the slopes of the lines represented by the four equations (i.e. 0.968, 0.975, 0.959, 0.955) are all approximately equal, signalling that the percentage votes for the PPP and the PNC were about equally affected, positively and negatively on almost a one for one basis, by every one percentage point increase or decrease in the ethnic grouping. The approximate one-for-oneness represented by the coefficients (i.e. the slopes of the lines) probably can be interpreted as an indication of the degree of ethnic bias in voting decisions - the lower the degree of ethnic bias, the further away from 1 will the absolute value of the coefficient be.

The constants in the equations, with particular reference to the approximately zero constant in the first equation dealing with the PPP%, might well be interpreted as evidence in favour of the hypothesis that support for the PPP was almost purely ethnic while that for the PNC was not!

For the statistically more sophisticated reader, the ten-page appendix to this essay provides a useful basis for their own further ruminations. Those ruminations may with great interest include the following three questions. None of them is dealt with directly in this essay, partly because I have not yet made up my own mind about their answers; but I am convinced of their philosophical and practical importance, and therefore recommend them for consideration.

Question (1)
In a society in which the voting behaviour described above is a systemic trait, what strategies and tactics might the two major political parties that are the foci of this polarised but non-symmetric ethnic support be expected to employ, both overtly and covertly, in the serious game of pursuing a Parliamentary majority of seats under our current electoral system?

Question (2)
Under what conditions are the strategies and tactics identified in the answers to Question (1) viable over time, in the sense that they will persist in being the best for pursuing a Parliamentary majority of seats under our current electoral system?

Question (3)
Assuming that we have philosophical or other reasons for objecting to the determination of which Party governs being substantially influenced by ethnic considerations, does there exist a set of changes to the current electoral system that could nullify or at least make minimal the effect of ethnicity?

Whatever lack of clarity attends the derivation of answers to these three questions (and their derivatives), it does appear clear that if there is to be the opportunity for interested persons to consider the questions of ethnic impact on voting behaviour, **officialdom will have to make the ethnic distribution of polling divisions available.** This is a matter than can easily be addressed in terms of collecting base data at the time of national voter registration. If something of this kind **is not** done, we will continue to be without any reliable statistical yardstick for attempting to answer the question of how ethnicity impinges on our voting behaviour. If it **is** done, it may well be opportune to revisit the categorisations we traditionally use for ethnicity. For instance, there is no need to embrace the presumption that "East Indian" is a homogeneous ethnic category. Instead, we could collect data in a manner which allows the categorisations: East Indian- Hindu; East Indian - Muslim; East Indian - Christian; East Indian - Other (i.e. none of Hindu, Muslim, or Christian); to be statistically investigated as though they represent different ethnicities, as they may well do. Of course, on reflection it may well be decided by officialdom not to exacerbate the ethnic problem by allowing an empirical spotlight to be beamed on it. Then, most of us could each retire to our favourite dark conjectural corner with degrees of comfort or discomfort determined by our imaginings unchallenged by empiricism, and bolstered by our favourite anecdotal evidence[2].

This whole approach of trying to understand our behaviour from the vantage point of ethnicity is quite interesting.   It requires the courage to grasp the nettle of ethnic predispositions without fear of being deemed racist.   It is not racist behaviour to try to estimate how strong our predispositions are to choose or reject those who would govern us by picking or rejecting persons, or groups of persons, who are or are not of our own image and likeness in terms of physical and cultural characteristics.   But such an attempt does raise uncomfortable questions.   Foremost among these questions is that of the Guyanese version of the stereotypes which inform us.

That Guyanese ethnic stereotypes exist is a presumption this essay makes. Further, it is assumed that each individual is aware of the stereotype that attaches to each ethnic group.   In particular he/she is presumed to be aware of the stereotype that attaches to his /her own ethnic group.   Awareness of the stereotype does not presuppose acceptance of its accuracy, nor pride in its content by the members of the ethnic group it purports to characterise. Indeed, this awareness may often be associated with anger and embarrassment about aspects of the content of the stereotype by members of the ethnic group to which the stereotype is attached.   Lastly, it is assumed that there is a one-to-one correspondence between stereotypes and ethnic groups.   Thus, for instance, the stereotype attached to the ethnic group "African" is assumed to be the same whatever the ethnicity of the perceiving person.   A Chinese person's understanding of what is the African stereotype is assumed to be the

---

2. *After this was written I discovered that the Elections Commission had in fact decided (around 4 March, 1996) not to garner information about the ethnicity of the voters, with the exception of Amerindians, during the voter registration exercise.   This was deemed by the commissioners to be a "progressive" step having something to do with going into the 21st century!   In fact that decision simply reflected and entrenched our preference for innumeracy and cant in important matters.   More specifically, it is a reflection of a certain lack of appreciation of the importance of data gathering in the process of creative problem solving.*

same as an East Indian' s understanding, and indeed the same as that of a person of any ethnic group (including those of the African group).

These assumptions are entirely that - assumptions, made in pursuit of simplicity. In theory there could be 25 different stereotypes related to 5 ethnic groupings - 1 for the stereotype that each of the 5 ethnic groups has of itself, and 4 for the stereotypes that each of the 5 ethnic groups has of each of the other 4. No "scientific" or other non-anecdotal evidence underpins the assumption that there are only 5 stereotypes. The assumptions are purely intuitively plausible presumptions, themselves based on the presumption that over many years a kind of convergence of popular views has occurred across and within ethnic groups[3] to make the assumptions adequately reflective of reality. In summary, I am blatantly accepting the conventional wisdom inherent in the colloquialisms: *"Is so X people stay"* where the parameter *"X"* ranges over **"Black"**, **"Coolie"**, **"Chinee"**, **"Putagee"**, and **"Buck"** - with a possibly unwarranted ignoring of the jeopardy of inaccuracy[4].

It is against this background of assumptions that I asked a few adults, chosen quite haphazardly and unscientifically in a survey methodology sense, to write down for me two or three paragraphs stating what their understandings are of the stereotypes associated with each of the five main ethnic groups - East Indian; African; Chinese; Portuguese; and Amerindian. Each person was assured of the anonymity that their name would not be associated with their views; and was apprised of the fact that what was required was not what they personally believed about each ethnic group, but rather what they understood the popularly held view to be, even if it conflicted with their own experience. *(I was quite intrigued by the fact that none of the persons I asked objected*

---

3. *In some ways this is the analogue of the gastronomic convergence represented by East Indians liking Low Mein, Africans liking Roti and Curry, Amerindians liking Garlic Pork and bacelhau, and all liking pepperpot.*

4. *We have for the longest while subscribed to this way of thinking, as is exemplified by our treatment of the Signs of the Zodiac. Pisces people are supposedly different from Taurus or Cancer people, and newspapers routinely publish daily prognoses and advice based on these categorisations of the Zodiac. Horoscopes **are** popular!*

that there might be more than one stereotype for any ethnic group. So much for the power of suggestion and convention.)

The summaries of the results of this truly haphazard "experiment" - a set of gossipy *on-dits* - are listed below[5].   They are summarised as comments about the following five dimensions: sexuality, attitude to members of the same ethnic group, attitude to members of other ethnic groups, entrepreneurship, attitude to work and play.

It is well nigh impossible for each reader not to form his/her own judgement about whether the descriptions are accurate; but perception rather than truth is the important thing here. The vantage point which readers are invited to use as they read the summaries is that implied by the following question: ***"How likely is it that groups which believe these things about themselves and other ethnicities will cooperate and collaborate in accord with the Guyanese motto - One People, One Nation, One Destiny; and what might be done to pursue such an objective?"***   Always, however, the reader is invited to restrain any sense of outrage, since what is being written is not fact but alleged perceptions.

---

5. *This essay does not comment in the body of the text on the fact that the persons who were asked to provide the stereotype descriptions found it a difficult task, not so much because of embarrassment but more because it apparently required considerable mental effort to dredge up the views from their minds and systematically lay them out on paper. This may well be a significant indicator of how deeply embedded and how surreptitiously entrenched these views are; or simply that the persons recognised that unique stereotypes do not exist but decided to humour me anyway!*

Haslyn Parris

African Stereotype

Sexuality
Males are sexual predators, reputedly generously endowed genitally for the activity, and proud of it. They harbour strong preferences for promiscuous relationships with non-African partners, particularly East Indians, Amerindians, and Mixed Race persons of light skin colour. Females are more stable than males, but they can be sexually demanding sexual partners prone to intense jealousy expressed as strong and possibly violent verbal and physical reactions when faced with a partner's infidelity. Males see females mainly as sex objects rather than as potential life partners. The net result is a large number of black single family homes run by mothers.

Attitude to Members of Same Ethnic Group
Respect is grudgingly given to members of the same ethnic group, and leadership types often face the query: "Is what he/she playing?" Typically, members easily and frequently indulge in denigrating[6] others, particularly those who appear to be achieving success and prominence in the society. In money matters this attitude manifests itself in an unwillingness to repay debts or to support one another in business ventures, or to express goodwill towards those who appear to be making progress in terms of accumulating material wealth, or improving their social status. Members who are in positions of authority or influence often are unhelpful, particularly to less fortunate ones.

Attitude to Members of Other Ethnic Groups.
In many ways this set of attitudes is the opposite of the attitudes adopted towards members of the same ethnic group; and there is a certain pride apparent in the inclusion of individual members in the activities of other ethnic groups. There is a fascination inherent in close liaison with other ethnic groups, and not a little pride in being chosen for inclusion in such

---

6. *The linguistic origins of this word appear to fit in remarkably with the stereotype.*

associations. Yet, there is an innate superiority presumed over all other ethnic groups in terms of ability to provide sexual pleasure, fight, dance, play popular music, or excel in activities that require physical strength and aggression.

Entrepreneurship

Generally, they have poor business acumen. They are generally foolish or naive in financial matters. They have a predisposition to prefer cash flow to profitability, and a compulsion to exhibit wealth through extravagant conspicuous consumption patterns of dress, entertainment, and acquisition of material possessions. Even those with formal academic training in business-related disciplines do not tend to become success stories on their own behalf, although they can perform excellently as valuable employees when working for business owned by other ethnic groups. They make good bureaucrats and professionals rather than successful entrepreneurs, and are more likely to establish churches than businesses.

Attitude to Work and Play

Work is an activity determined by the need to earn money, and the objective is to do as little as possible for as much money or material benefits as possible. Work is therefore to be shirked and not to be treated as an end in itself associated with pride, professionalism, and self-fulfillment. Life is really about fun, fetes, alcohol, dressing fashionably, and womanising or flirting, so that Play is the paramount thing desired. All the parameters associated with work - e.g. the disciplines of timeliness, quality, cost control, waste reduction, tidiness - are impositions to be avoided if possible, or minimally observed. Utopia would have no requirement to face the responsibilities of work.

East Indian Stereotype

Sexuality

Members of the group possess strong libidos, but the subservient and cloistered niche into which young women have been placed has generated typical male behaviour best described as frequent copulators but poor lovers insensitive to the sexual gratification of their female partners. This male attitude to sex forces male concentration on females of the same ethnicity since females of other ethnic groups often demand more in matters sexual. The attitude also lends itself to male promiscuity, including incest, confined within the ethnic group; but also to the women surreptitiously indulging in liaisons (including adulterous ones) with males of other ethnic groups - mainly the African group. The male's predisposition to become easily intoxicated simply reinforces these behaviour patterns.

Attitude to Members of Same Ethnic Group

There is a very highly developed ethnic group consciousness and group loyalty. This manifests itself in mutual support mechanisms and behaviour patterns within the ethnic group in all areas, but particularly in business and employment practices vis-a-vis other ethnicities. Such patterns do not however rule out cut-throat and often dishonest competition within the group, frequently manifested for example in land ownership or other property disputes with inter and intra family physical violence and conflict. A kind of ethnic herd instinct operates in the context of multi-ethnic gatherings, where members of the ethnic group will gravitate towards each other and form an easily identified sub-group, with women tending to separate out from men in a sub-sub-group. The women are extremely supportive of their men.

Attitude to Members of Other Ethnic Groups

Other ethnic groups are seen as competitors in all dimensions. In true game-theoretic fashion, collaboration is pursued only when material advantage could be gained. Members of this group regularly seek advantageous alliances with people whom they can exploit; and stooping to conquer is as integral a part of their competitive armoury, as is arrogance when they perceive they are "on top". Both on an individual and a group level, the attitude (cultivation, fawning, collaboration, deferring, bribing) to members of other ethnic groups is determined by the perceived balance of material advantage in the context of perceptions of political, economic, or intellectual power. Not infrequently sexual favours from close relations (e.g. daughters, wives) are offered to members of other ethnic groups as inducement to action that would further the material welfare of an individual. Once the objective is achieved, the favours are withdrawn and the attitude reverts to one of ethnic polarisation.

Entrepreneurship

Cunning, acquisitive, money-grabbing, thrifty, opportunistic, hard-working, not averse to dishonest and illegal practices - all these terms describe aspects of the group's attitude towards the unrelenting pursuit of material wealth. Their desire to acquire material possessions seems unbounded, with particular reference to real estate and money, and most means (fair and foul) would be used towards satisfaction of this desire. Particularly among the older group, accumulation of wealth does not tend to lead to conspicuous, Western style consumption patterns, but instead towards education of the younger members of the family or contributions towards their establishment in business.

Attitude to Work and Play

Extremely earnest and hard working, seizing every opportunity to learn new skills for their eventual personal material benefit. Even in workplaces there is evidence of ethnic clannishness. Loyalty to institutions for which they work is often really self-serving in pursuit of personal advancement. Males are far more outgoing in matters of partying than females, the gender disparity being wider than for other ethnic groups, but the ability to absorb alcohol without rapid deterioration into an embarrassingly inebriated state is quite low. In such a state their ethnic parody of dancing to Caribbean rhythms can be a considerable source of amusement, no less amusing than dancing to their own preferred ethnic music. Their preferences for bilious gaudy colours in personal and other decoration, for their own ethnic music, and for their own ethnic cuisine as their staple diet, are all evidence of the resilience of their culture in the face of opposing cultural influences. They are the only group which has maintained a strong cultural link (e.g. in religion, music, cinema) with the land of their ancestors, and often give the impression (e.g. during cricket competitions between the West Indies and India or Pakistan) that their allegiance really lies with that land rather than with Guyana or the Caribbean.

Chinese Stereotype

Sexuality

Many a myth has arisen as a result of members of this group having a preference for restricting their sexual activity within their ethnic group. Allegations by members of other ethnic groups lend credence to the ideas that male members of this group have small genitals; females have a non-standard geometry to theirs - the "crossway" assertion; males make use of aphrodisiac potions and salves; and high frequency of copulation is used to compensate for the shortness of time in which intercourse is completed. Intense privacy is a preferred characteristic of their sexual activity, and they do not have a reputation for being promiscuous.

Attitude to Members of Same Ethnic Group

There is great group cohesion and mutual support. The frequent utilisation of some version of Chinese language among themselves facilitates and preserves the privacy of their affairs, even when disagreements occur. Cultural practices such as the observance and celebration of Chinese New Year, the vibrancy of the Chinese Association, and the predisposition to participate in ownership and operation of ethnic restaurant business activity, all reinforce the image of apartness of the group from other ethnic groups.

Attitude to Members of Other Ethnic Groups

Their inscrutability - allegedly one never knows what their real thoughts are - militates against close involvement with other ethnic groups; and there is more than a suggestion that they consider themselves in many ways superior to other ethnic groups. Pleasant, polite, modest, quiet non-involvement and independence, mixed with severely selective associations outside their ethnic group characterise their relationships with members of other ethnic groups.

Entrepreneurship
Traditionally members of the group are prominent in restaurant, laundry, and grocery and other shopkeeping businesses, running them profitably and contributing to the maintenance of their ethnic dominance in these areas through family and other cooperation within the group, bolstered from time to time by immigrants of the same ethnicity. Theirs is a reputation for frugality and good investment, combined with avoidance of conspicuous consumption, and an insistence on educating their young for entry into business and the accounting and medical professions.

Attitude to Work and Play
As employees they are dedicated workers who bring to bear all the skills of quiet efficiency, willingness to learn, attention to detail, honesty, and severely muted reactions to perceived insults or injustices in industrial relations matters. Their ethnic apartness is maintained without giving offence. Participation in revelry is also muted, and "rambunctious Chinese" would be a contradiction in terms.

Portuguese Stereotype

Sexuality
The dominant influences appear to be religion (Roman Catholic), the perception that they are "like white", their level of formal education, and how much money they have. Depending on the mix of these influences, members of this group satisfy one of two stereotypes - the type that sees sexual activity primarily as an activity for producing progeny respectably within marriage; and the type (colloquially described as "ignar trellis") that sees it in a manner not dissimilar to the view of members of the African stereotype. This latter type is often described as "wutless putagee people" indicating in some way

that they are an aberration of true portuguese, and a bit of an embarrassment to the true portuguese.

Attitude to Members of Same Ethnic Group
There is a group consciousness that preserves the distinctions drawn in the previous section, with "wutless" ones being treated almost as though they belong to the African stereotype. Among the others there is a clannishness, supportiveness, group arrogance and soi-disant superiority that accords with thinking of themselves as being "like white". This often leads to behaviour that accords with the presumption that they have an automatic inalienable right to VIP status in all matters - whether it is sitting prominently up front in church, or access to the best jobs, or entree to the most fashionable and prepossessing clear-skinned partners.

Attitude to Members of Other Ethnic Groups
All other ethnic groups other than "white" are deemed to be somewhat inferior, with the African group being decidedly the least respectable. Rankings of the others correlate with clearness of skin colour and apparent wealth. Members of other ethnic groups have severely limited access to the group's socialising; and when they enter other groups they expect to do so on a special treatment, VIP basis.

Entrepreneurship
The production and sale of alcoholic beverages - e.g. rum, wines, and more recently beer; the establishment and management of grocery shops; jewelers; pawnbrokers; and commercial banking are considered the group's forte in business activity. There is also an apparent preference for keeping business ownership mainly in the family, and preferably in the ethnic group (e.g. Boards of Directors of many businesses do not include the African group). Generally, the group enjoys a reputation for being vibrant, astute, successful businessmen and businesswomen.

Attitude to Work and Play
Work preferences correlate with the predispositions to entrepreneurship and the pursuit of professions such as medicine, law, and accountancy in all of which the group enjoys a high reputation for skill, astuteness, and honest hard work. This penchant for disciplined, competitive endeavour, transfers into activities pursued for fun. It manifests itself particularly among the males who often occupy positions of noteworthy achievement in all sporting activities (cricket, football, cycling, hockey, to name a few) and in playing both classical and popular music as participants in bands. The co-existence of these traits with those described in the other sections of this pen picture of the stereotype constitutes an interesting paradox.

Amerindian Stereotype

Sexuality
These "children of the forest" have a delightfully amoral attitude to sex. Both sexes find the activity pleasant, and do not complicate its enjoyment by considerations that there is a responsibility to ensure that one's partner enjoys it; that promiscuity or incest is particularly undesirable; or that pregnancy, for which there are herbal contraceptives and abortifacients if necessary, is a worrisome likely consequence. Satisfaction of this primordial urge is supported in its simplicity by clear understandings about the subservient role of women, so that, subject only to taboos like avoidance of intercourse during menstruation and minimal concerns about privacy, the activity is not inhibited by time, place, age, or family relationships; but jealousies do arise, often with violent consequences particularly when alcohol is involved. The geometry of the female genitals is uniquely designed to facilitate both intercourse in any position and the easy delivery of babies.

Attitude to Members of Same Ethnic Group
Tribal ties and clannishness persist in hinterland communities, but outside of those communities no overwhelming preferences for dealing primarily with members of their own ethnic group appear to manifest themselves.

Attitude to Members of Other Ethnic Groups
A certain docility and shyness characterises relations with other ethnic groups. There appears to be a preference to follow and fit in with whatever is the existing activity, as opposed to the active pursuit of leadership roles. All this summarises into an attitude of wanting to be accepted, liked, and fairly treated, against a background of not assuming superiority - a stance that is often mistaken for an assumption of inferiority. When not influenced by alcohol, perceived unfair treatment usually generates the response of simply dissociating themselves from the offending source rather than generating confrontation. Under the influence of alcohol, old grudges may well surface as violent action against the source of offence.

Entrepreneurship
Though members of the group may be possessed of various skills, these skills are rarely utilised for the setting up of businesses except in the cases of the production and sale of ethnic products such as cassava bread, casareep, and so-called nibbi furniture and hammocks. Such business ventures remain small because members of the group exhibit little tendency for saving, a great tendency for satisfaction of mainly immediate material wants, and little desire to accumulate wealth.

Attitude to Work and Play
Work is a means to the end of satisfaction of immediate material wants. Leisure is the preferred state. The result is that if material wants are adequately satisfied before a work project is completed, then no reason exists for continued effort at work, and unless forced work activity will cease or substantially decrease. Nevertheless, work is undertaken willingly, conscientiously, and with a sense of pride and professionalism within this framework. A certain instability of place of employment, or reliability of turning up to work, often results from this approach to work as an employee; but there are few tasks of which they are capable that they will not undertake once the stimulus of satisfaction of material want exists. It is unusual for any job to be considered too menial. Leisure is avidly pursued, with the activities of dancing, feasting, drinking alcoholic beverages, and sex being the preferred ones, once the shackles of the need to work have been removed. Alcohol tolerance is as low as liking for it is high.

It would be fascinating to record the historical and other processes that have led to the generation of these stereotypes[7].   Unfortunately, though the accuracy of an assertion is not determined by the social rank of the assertor, its credence is.   Accordingly stereotypes, like fashions in dress, are often statements that belie both intelligence and professional training and frequently simply highlight prejudices.   They are however a part of the current conventional wisdom, and these perceptions cannot but continually inform our language[8], and our individual and collective actions[9].

The insights generated by this essay force me to sympathise with the goodly Bishop, whose task it is to chair a Committee to do the preparatory work for the establishment of the Race Relations Commission, in terms of the complexities with which he will have to deal.   It cannot be of help for him to have to deal also with the issue of the religious texts that enshrine the concept of *"chosen people"* where the preference is signalled by a deity.

Whatever the methodology of the Committee' s work, I cannot see that it can avoid dealing with both the problem of ethnicity in voting behaviour and the effects of the existence and acceptance of stereotypes.   In each of these two problem areas there exists the opportunity to attempt to measure levels of ethnic polarisation and divisiveness; and we will not know how we are progressing with our ethnic problems if such measuring instruments are not

---

7. *Such an investigation would reveal gems such as the following from William Hilhouse in Indian Notices:* **"united to the evils of constant poverty and want"** *as a description pertinent to the* **Mulatto, Mestize,** *and* **Amerindian;** *and* **"After 10 or 15 years of invalided ease, he dies of old age, having never known want"** *as a statement applicable to* **the Negro Slave;** *and* **"Dies at an advanced age from want"** *as a description of the state of* **the Free Negro.**

8. *The Warau phrase for* **East Indian** *is* **"hotomo howara"** *- a phrase which when translated literally means* **"buttocks wash";** *and the colloquialism* **"tek it like a Chinee"** *means* **"being stoic in the face of adversity or blatant injustice";** *while among rum drinkers a* **"buck man"** *is a half of a quarter bottle of rum - the amount required to get an Amerindian drunk?*

9. *Perhaps one of the most valuable contributions that the academic community can make to the deliberations of the Race Relations Committee would be an analysis of the existence , content, and significance of current stereotypes, based on proper survey methodology.*

derived and utilised, with the results of the measurements being made public. Cooperation and collaboration often require knowledge, understanding, trust, and respect among potential cooperators, but our nation' s current state seems to lack a sufficiency of all four! The stereotypes described above indicate the depth of the problem. It certainly doesn' t help when any of our leaders, flying in the face of historical fact, rely on the senescent predisposition to create visions of *"the good old days"* and *"the way we used to be"* to suggest that there was a time when there was ethnic ease of association and non-divisiveness in this country, and that we should be trying to revert to that state.

The following final set of comments derive initially from the difficulties to which I alluded earlier in relation to the nexus between correlation and causation. Political Parties derive from people; and individuals cannot but bring to the grouping called "Party", as part of their conceptual baggage, the stereotypical perceptions that they consciously and subconsciously harbour. Inherent therefore in the collective consciousness of the grouping called "Party" is the body of perceptions that comprise the stereotypes of the various ethnic groupings. But the real source of the perceptions is the body politic from which the Party membership was drawn. It should follow that what the Party thinks, as opposed to what its leadership mouths, about ethnic matters is unlikely to be different from what the body politic from which it was drawn thinks - especially since membership of the Party does not cut one off from the body politic. Certainly the subconscious compulsions remain the same. In such circumstances ethnic voting behaviour cannot properly be attributed in a causative sense to the urging of the Party, since all Party urgings on this matter themselves came from the body politic that is allegedly being urged.

Indeed, in one case of which I have some personal knowledge, ethnically neutral behaviour by a Party Leader led to the derisive amendment of his surname to "Persaud." He paid this price in relation to many ordinary members of his Party; and to many intelligent and influential members of the society who were Party supporters but not necessarily members. From all these categories, the criticism was essentially that he was not appropriately ethnically biased in his decision-making; and accordingly was less helpful to one ethnic group that he was expected to help, and more helpful than he should have been to the other major ethnic group. He lost out going and coming - winning little from the ethnic group that he was accused by his own Party of supporting, and losing quite a bit from the ethnic group from which he was alleged to be defecting. A good indicator of that Party Leader's empathy for, and depth of understanding, informedness, and feeling about the ethnic group from which he allegedly defected, is the speech he made on the occasion of the 150th anniversary of the formal abolition of slavery. That speech is reproduced in its entirety in the appendix to this essay. Party Leaders of our two major Parties are, and maybe cannot but be, prisoners of their putative ethnically sensitive supporters!

If this conjecture is correct, then no Party can be looked to as the **lead agent of change** in the matter of ethnic voting predispositions or behaviour! On this issue of ethnic divisiveness and polarisation, Political Parties, though decidedly capable of aggravation or exacerbation, are genetically incapable of taking the lead in the process of fusion implied by the vision *"One People, One Nation, One Destiny."* Indeed, Political Parties have a track record of utilising ethnic associations, organisations, and predispositions in the competitive power game of becoming the Party in Government[10]. Rhetoric has been their only effective positive contribution, and we have a case of the hypocritical child preaching to the hypocritical parent.

The issues are to a great extent moral and religious ones. Their resolution requires a change in vantage point, and a contribution to remedy through fundamental changes in the formal education system. The lead in appropriate action needs to be taken by an appropriate religious grouping. However, any religious grouping whose theosophy, rituals, and icons are Euro-centric must be inappropriate, since the issues demand images of perfection and harmony that do not themselves demand special mental effort for the majority of Guyanese to see themselves as being capable of achieving that perfection and harmony; and of their ancestry as not automatically denying them access to

---

10. *A revealing account of this aspect is provided by Dr. Ralph R. Premdas in the February, 1972 publication by the Department of Political Science - University of Guyana: "Occasional Papers No.2, Voluntary Associations and Political Parties in a Racially Fragmented State: The Case of Guyana.*

the perfect group in whose physical image and likeness they have not been made.[11]   This argument disqualifies all the major so-called Christian sects currently established in Guyana - a disqualification that should not be too worrying since the majority of Guyanese are not Christian anyhow.

An admittedly cursory examination of the religions currently established in Guyana as candidates for the job leads me unwaveringly to *Islam* as the one that best qualifies.   The majority of Guyanese (those of African and East Indian descent) have history on the side of them finding this religion most relevant to their ancestry.   In Guyana, Islam also appears to be the only religion that does not require severe modification of interpretation to claim applicability specifically to **both** Africans and East Indians.   But Islam is not historically without its own skeletons in the cupboard of atrocities against Africans; and then, what about the Hindus?

These conjectures constitute an appropriate set of thoughts on which to end this essay.   After all, the intention was only to provide *"More Interesting Insights!"*

END (1995)

---

11. *Consider for instance the impact on young minds created by providing Afro or Indo - Guyanese children with a picture of Jesus to colour, where the drawing of Jesus is clearly not that of a person of African or Indian descent!* ***"The Resurrection"*** *by Coypel,* ***"La Deploration Du Christ"*** *by Rubens,* ***"The Maries At The Sepulchre"*** *by an Imitator of Mantegna,* ***"Doubting Thomas"*** *by Caravaggio,* ***"The Ascension"*** *by Rembrandt,* ***"The Transfiguration"*** *by Raphael, and* ***"The Last Supper"*** *(**perhaps the most famous and popular rendition being the fresco by Leonardo da Vinci**) are just some of the more famous Euro-centric portrayals of Jesus to which traditionally "well educated" Guyanese are likely to have been exposed.*

APPENDIX
Georgetown - 1992 General Elections

Pol Div	Description	PNC%	PPP%	EI %	AFR %	Valid Vote
413111	Kingston (West)	57	40	38.22	38.59	400
413112	Kingston (East)	47	48	44.33	38.37	420
413121	Thomas Lands	59	37	13.71	70.16	73
413131	Queenstown	62	28	27.48	44.36	1,245
413132	Alberttown	67	26	28.19	48.33	1,656
413141	South Cummingsburgh	57	32	28.06	45.57	1,188
413142	North Cummingsburgh	45	45	46.67	30.28	951
413211	Kitty (North)	75	19	19.40	58.54	1,092
413212	Kitty (Central)	52	45	45.34	41.67	1,812
413213	Kitty (South)	33	64	59.95	27.77	1,875
413221	Subryanville / Bel Air Gardens	47	40	37.47	26.95	422
413222	Bel Air / Bel Air Springs	28	69	65.02	22.96	466
413231	Prashad Nagar	52	44	53.75	25.00	655
413232	North East Campbellville	42	54	34.15	53.25	1,055
413233	North West Campbellville	36	62	75.92	16.23	940
413241	Lamaha Gardens	48	40	21.99	50.60	420

APPENDIX
Georgetown - 1992 General Elections

Pol Div	Description	PNC%	PPP%	EI %	AFR %	Valid Vote
413242	Section K Campbellville	68	26	26.73	53.66	1,041
413251	Bel Air Park	70	24	36.75	30.26	402
413252	Newtown / Campbellville	53	42	39.11	43.87	2,766
413311	Sophia / Liliendaal (North)	45	51	56.47	34.27	360
413312	Pattensen/ Turkeyen	38	59	63.52	23.90	292
413321	Cummings Lodge North (Nth Rway)	65	33	22.55	65.11	299
413322	Cummings Lodge Central (Sth Rway)	11	87	83.78	9.33	630
413331	Cummings Lodge South	1	99	92.31	4.62	149
413333	Sophia / Liliendaal (South)	69	27	13.92	72.15	379
413342	Sophia / Pattensen (Central)	73	26	51.52	43.18	331
413411	Tucville	93	2	3.91	78.91	1,491
413412	Guyhoc Park Cum Annexes	95	3	2.88	89.30	509
413421	Festival City	95	3	2.16	86.21	564
413422	North Ruimveldt Housing Scheme	96	2	2.69	82.60	1,992

APPENDIX
Georgetown - 1992 General Elections

Pol Div	Description	PNC%	PPP%	EI %	AFR %	ValidVote
413431	South Ruimveldt Park (East)	93	3	4.79	77.46	1,095
413432	South Ruimveldt Park (West)	89	6	7.13	74.50	640
413441	South Ruimveldt Gardens (East)	82	10	10.77	64.77	809
413442	South Ruimveldt Gardens (West)	81	12	7.03	68.69	302
413451	Roxanne Burnham Gardens	94	4	5.86	79.28	536
413452	Guyhoc Gardens	95	4	1.22	85.37	388
413471	Riverview	47	48	43.16	36.32	308
413472	Alexander Village	26	72	64.03	24.07	1,308
413481	West Ruimveldt	88	10	14.24	71.04	2,857
413482	East Ruimveldt	95	3	5.61	82.26	2,037
413511	Agricola	80	17	18.25	71.09	1,129
413512	McDoom	57	40	42.45	44.06	571
413513	Houston / Meadowbank	30	64	62.75	27.35	568
413522	Rome (S/Cane Cult)	95	2	3.66	81.71	91
413611	Lodge (North) Botanical Gardens	94	3	5.00	78.84	1,179

APPENDIX
Georgetown - 1992 General Elections

Pol Div	Description	PNC%	PPP%	EI %	AFR %	Valid Vote
413612	Lodge (South)	92	4	7.13	80.63	2,433
413622	Meadowbrook Gardens	94	2	6.86	75.74	658
413641	North East / East La Penitence	89	7	7.57	76.99	1,037
413642	West La Penitence	61	35	40.60	47.77	1,691
413651	Albouystown	72	24	35.52	48.62	1,965
413652	Charlestown	73	23	28.19	54.35	1,931
413711	Bourda (West)	72	26	28.46	51.48	552
413712	Bourda (East)	68	25	25.42	45.21	946
413721	Stabroek / Wortmanville (East)	88	8	11.19	68.69	1,917
413722	Stabroek (Central) Wortmanville (West)	79	12	14.78	67.81	753
413731	Werk-en-rust (East) Newburg	78	16	17.54	58.27	1,313
413732	Werk-en-rust (West)	70	25	30.16	51.19	514
413741	Robbstown / Lacytown (West)	58	35	33.82	37.03	285
413742	Stabroek (Central) / Lacytown	78	18	35.65	42.69	1,081
ALL	59 Polling Divisions	70	26	28.17	54.43	56769

APPENDIX
Georgetown - 1992 General Elections

PPP% / EI % Regression Output:

Constant	0.570097
Std Err of Y Est	7.907311
R Squared	0.885559
No. of Observations	59
Degrees of Freedom	57

X Coefficient	0.968451
Std Err of Coeff.	0.046113

PPP% = 0.57 + 0.968 EI%

PNC% / AFR% Regression Output:

Constant	14.32769
Std Err of Y Est	9.54336
R Squared	0.833819
No. of Observations	59
Degrees of Freedom	57

X Coefficient	0.975198
Std Err of Coeff	0.057665

PNC% = 14.33 + 0.975 AFR%

AFR% / EI% Regression Output:

Constant	80.44111
Std Err of Y Est	6.6042
R Squared	0.909232
No. of Observations	59
Degrees of Freedom	57

X Coefficient	-0.92028
Std Err of Coeff.	0.038514

AFR% = 80.441 - 0.920 EI%

PPP% / AFR% Regression Output:

Constant	80.2462
Std Err of Y Est	10.24027
R Squared	0.808068
No. of Observations	59
Degrees of Freedom	57

X Coefficient	-0.95854
Std Err of Coeff	0.061876

PPP% = 80.246 - 0.959 AFR%

PNC% / EI% Regression Output:

Constant	94.49352
Std Err of Y Est	8.794992
R Squared	0.85886
No. of Observations	59
Degrees of Freedom	57

X Coefficient	-0.95522
Std Err of Coeff	0.05129

PNC% = 94.494 - 0.955 EI%

APPENDIX
Georgetown - 1992 General Elections

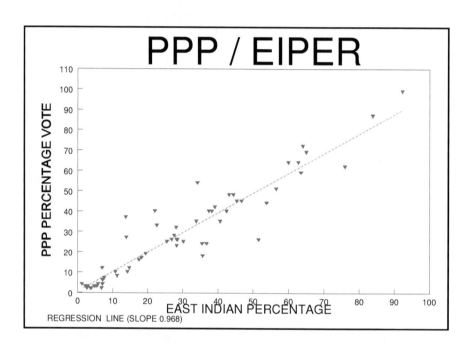

REGRESSION EQUATION

PPP% = 0.570 + 0.968 EI%

SQUARED CORRELATION = 0.8856

APPENDIX
Georgetown - 1992 General Elections

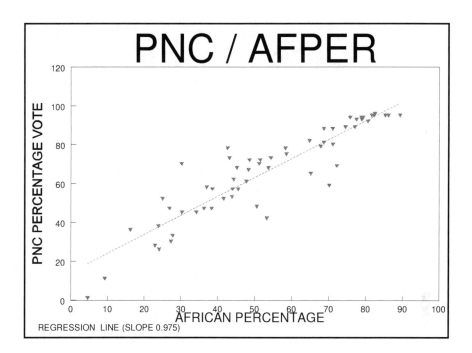

REGRESSION   EQUATION

PNC% = 14.33 + 0.975 AFR%

SQUARED CORRELATION = 0.8338

APPENDIX
Georgetown - 1992 General Elections

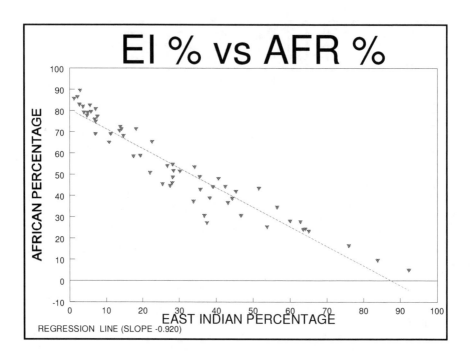

REGRESSION   EQUATION

AFR% = 80.441 - 0.920 EI%

SQUARED CORRELATION = 0.9092

APPENDIX
Georgetown - 1992 General Elections

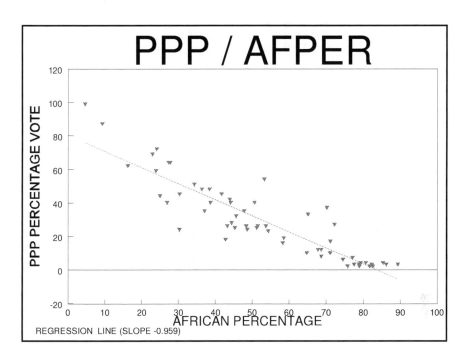

REGRESSION EQUATION

PPP% = 80.246 - 0.958 AFR%

SQUARED CORRELATION = 0.8081

APPENDIX
Georgetown - 1992 General Elections

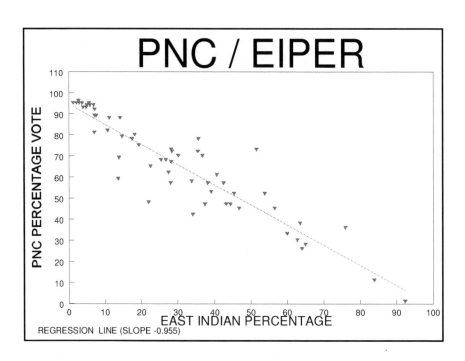

REGRESSION EQUATION

PNC% = 94.494 - 0.955 EI%

SQUARED CORRELATION = 0.8589

END (1995)

Address at 150th Anniversary of Abolition of Slavery

ADDRESS BY **HIS EXCELLENCY HUGH DESMOND HOYTE, S.C.**, PRESIDENT OF THE CO-OPERATIVE REPUBLIC OF GUYANA, AT THE COMMEMORATION ACTIVITIES OF THE 150th ANNIVERSARY OF THE FORMAL ABOLITION OF THE SYSTEM OF SLAVERY.

FREEDOM DAY! GUYANA AND THE AFRICAN EXPERIENCE

As I reflect on the 150th Anniversary of the formal dismantling of the institution of slavery in our country, some lines of Martin Carter's keep recurring in my mind:

And I bent down
Listening to the land
And all I heard was toungeless whispering
As if some buried slave wanted to speak again

And could he speak to us today, at this time of commemoration, what would he be saying to us? Would he talk of *Despair* or of *Courage*? Of *Submission* or of *Fortitude*? Of *Defeat* or of *Triumph*? Of *Stagnation* or of *Growth and Development*? His message, I think, would be provocative and challenging; for he would want to fire our imagination; imbue us with a sense of dignity, self-esteem and purpose; and strengthen our confidence in our own capacity to struggle and achieve.

In his concern about our future, he would want us to search our own hearts and be honest with ourselves. He would warn us that we could not secure that future unless we learnt the lessons of the past, for history is the key to the future. And for this purpose he would, I believe, invoke what Leo Frobenius described as *"the godlike strength of memory;"* and, recalling the seminal role of Africa in the evolution of mankind and the great cultures and civilisations which originated and flourished there, he would remind us of Africa's profound influence on the development of human civilisation in the course of its ancient and productive history.

Haslyn Parris

Address at 150th Anniversary of Abolition of Slavery

And he would tell us too, that an intelligent awareness of their history is the well-spring of a people's motivation to think and act creatively; to pursue intellectually and physically strenuous endeavours; to confidently challenge the unknown; to build unceasingly for the future; and to seek continuously to enlarge *"the bounds of human empire to the effecting of all things possible."*   In his effort to impress upon us the importance of such awareness he might perhaps leave with us, as a cautionary tale, this Sumarian legend:

> *"What became of the Black People of Sumer?" the traveller asked the old man, "For ancient records show that the people of Sumer were Black.   What happened to them?"   "Ah," the old man sighed, "They lost their History, so they died....."*

The self-knowledge which derives from a perceptive understanding of History is, if I may borrow a phrase from a German philosopher, *"Life-furthering, Life-preserving, Species-preserving."*   We Guyanese must therefore pay great attention to the study and correct interpretation of our own History, and use it as a necessary tool for promoting the development, well-being, cohesiveness and integrity of our Nation.

Our History will reveal brutal crimes and enormous wrongs commited against us in the past.   But it is, nevertheless, an inspiring story of courage and fortitude and of the triumph of the human spirit over apparently insuperable odds.   Its lessons have a supreme relevance for us today as we grapple with the problems of Nation-Building.   We must use those lessons creatively.   It would be a grievous mistake for us to brood over past wrongs and succumb to anger, bitterness and hatred.   This would be a sterile and unrewarding exercise that would inhibit the clear thinking, rational decisions and constructive actions that we need at this time to consolidate our gains and plan successfully for the future.

Three continents have played a major role in determining the course of our history: Europe, Africa and Asia.   We cannot fully comprehend our own history unless, against the background of the roles they played, we make

Address at 150ᵗʰ Anniversary of Abolition of Slavery

the relevant connections with the history of those continents. To grasp the real significance of the event we are commemorating today and its implications for the future, not only for those of African descent, but for all of our people, we have to turn to the history of Africa.

"Africa has history." With this terse sentence Professor Ki-Zerbo of Burkina Faso began his general introduction to Volume 1 of The General History of Africa commissioned by UNESCO. Remarkable though it might seem to us, it was necessary to make this statement. The clues evidencing that history were numerous; they dated back to very ancient times. Yet, particularly in the 19th and 20th centuries, European historians mutilated, distorted, and eventually denied the existence of that history; and the myth that Africa has no history passed into popular currency. Yet, there was always sufficient material to give proof of Africa's history. Ancient historians like Herodotus and Pliny the elder had recorded aspects of African civilisation. In later centuries, so had the historians of the Mediterranean world and of medieval Islamic civilisation. From the 16th century onward written records of African History increased. There were many accounts by Africans themselves written in Arabic and Swahili, and even by Europeans themselves who had visited Africa.

But, as the Europeans tightened their grip on Africa, abducted and deported into slavery millions of its people, and eventually seized the land itself to secure the cheap resources they needed to fuel their industrial revolution and their material prosperity, it became fashionable and politically expedient to claim that Africa had no history. In Europe, this view became accepted theology and its classic exposition was enunciated by **Hegel**, in his *"Philosophy of History"*. According to him, Africa was *"no historical part of the world;"* that it had shown no change or development, and its black people were incapable of education and improvement.

This comfortable doctrine served as the moral justification for the enslavement of the Africans and the plunder of their country. Its underpinnings were notions of racial superiority which found some of their

Address at 150th Anniversary of Abolition of Slavery

crudest expression in the writings of **Joseph de Goberneau, H.S. Chamberlain** and other members of their school of thought. We see here early origins of the nazi pseudo-philosophy of *"Herrenvolk,"* which was later to bring so much misery and destruction to Europe itself. Here, too, is the genesis of its monstrous offspring, the theory and practice of apartheid in Southern Africa today.

This unscholarly, unscientific and racist view of Africa and its history continued to have its adherents even in our own time. In the 1960s, **Trevor-Roper**, then regius professor of modern history at Oxford, denied that Africa had any history apart from the history of Europeans in Africa. For Trevor-Roper and those historians from whom he was lineally descended, Africa was the "dark continent". And yet, by the beginning of the 20th century, historians like Leo Frobenius with a more sensitive feel for human evolution were calling for light to be shed on the history of Africa.

Frobenius could not accept the smug, unscientific and unsupported verdict that Africa had no history. He had no doubt that its history was there for those who wished to see it; but, as he wrote, "learning to see" was the most difficult of things. Despite its many imperfections, his field-work in Africa produced evidence of Africa's civilisations and history that was incontrovertible. It must have been with great personal satisfaction that he wrote the following words:

"It required an unusual amount of fortitude and optimism to keep fast to the faith that time would supply material evidence of an intensive civilisation and thus afford an opportunity of linking up Africa with the history of the world at large. Time in its course justified this steadfast faith."

And time keeps justifying it in ample and ever-increasing measure. Today, rigorous research, careful archaeological work, the application of scientific techniques to ascertain dates of artifacts and other finds are uncovering complex and highly developed cultures and civilisations; and objective

Address at 150ᵗʰ Anniversary of Abolition of Slavery

evaluation of the artistic and cultural life of the people have rescued Africa's past as one historian has said, *"from ignorance and error."*

Africa is the cradle of mankind. In the stone age its people were the first tool-makers and tool-users; and, over the millennia since then, in a continuum of human development, they established mastery over their environment. They domesticated grain, cultivated food crops, and reared cattle, sheep and goats. They became expert in mining, smelting and working with metals such as copper, iron and gold. They established cities, states and federations and learned to trade both within and outside of Africa.

From early times high civilisations developed along the Nile, of which Meroe, the Kingdom of Kush, and Axum were notable examples. During Europe's middle ages, there flourished in Africa important centres like Timbuktu, a university city famous for its vigorous and sophisticated intellectual life, its commerce and its splendid buildings. There were other celebrated examples of states, rich and powerful cities, and kingdoms which, with their well-organised governmental and social systems, contributed in various ways to the evolution of Africa's history and its culture. These included Songhai, also noted for its scholarship and commerce; Ashanti and Benin whose sculptors created religious art of great power and sensitivity, the Monomtapa and Rwozi confederations covering a large area south of the Zambezi, peopled by master-masons who built marvellous stone structures as can still be seen by the impressive ruins of great Zimbabwe; and Kilwa, whose trading contacts reached as far away as India and China. Since the second century A.D., Ethiopia had established itself as strong power. It became a bastion of Christianity, built majestic monuments and traded with Ceylon and Persia, Arabia, India and Byzsntium. These are only some examples.

The majesty and grandeur that was Egypt could not be denied, even by the most prejudiced of eurocentric historians. But to admit that Egyptian civilisation was *"African"* would not accord with their myth of the non-history of Africa; so they resorted to what has been called *"the practice of*

Address at 150ᵗʰ Anniversary of Abolition of Slavery

beheading the African continent. " Geography was turned upside down and Egypt was transformed into "South Europe." Most modern scholars of African history today stress the cultural unity of Africa. Despite all the diversity and differences apparent to the eye, there is, as Colin Turnbull noted, *"a unity, and a powerful one, that runs through all African societies, all African peoples, and all African cultures. "* There are two great themes underlying the development of Africa: these are unity and continuity of cultural growth.

As Amadou-Mahtar M'bow, the former Director General of UNESCO, has observed, *"it is now widely recognised that the various civilisations of the African continent, for all their different languages and cultures, represent to a greater or lesser degree the historical off-shoots of a set of peoples and societies, united by bonds centuries old. "* This "set of peoples" included the ancient Egyptians. Cheikh Anta Diop, the Sengalese scholar, has argued that the history of Africa cannot be correctly written until African historians connect it with the history of Egypt. He himself, with skilfully marshalled evidence and cogent, persuasive arguments, has made that connection. Egyptian civilisation was African.

An enormous amount of work has been done to confirm the fact of African history and reveal its complex, fascinating and powerful contribution to world civilisation. Yet, even today, the prejudice is still deep-rooted. In 1984, when Basil Davidson presented his BBC Television series on pre-colonial Africa, no less person than Connor Cruise O'Brien was so roused to anger that he denounced it with a vehemence that belied his reputation for scholarship, sophistication and open-mindedness. In a remarkably intemperate letter to the Observer newspaper, he accused Davidson of, among other crimes, flattering the Africans! Despite the evidence, O'Brien would not accept the fact that Africa had a history and had made an immense contribution to human growth and civilisation.

The struggle to recover the history of Africa and give it its rightful place in the context of world history is still a most difficult one, despite the brilliant work being done by many historians, anthropologists,

Address at 150th Anniversary of Abolition of Slavery

archaeologists and other scholars in assembling, interpreting and publishing the evidence. In a sharp criticism of people who passed off prejudice, ignorance, false reports, wilful error and ill-founded assumptions as history, Ibu Khaldun the celebrated 14th century Arab historian, in a striking phrase, described them as feeding *"in the pasture of stupidity."* Because the matter touches us closely, and because in any event we cannot allow our young people to become the victims of a false view of history, we in Guyana cannot tarry in the pasture of stupidity.

Therefore, our school curricula must ensure that we teach our children from their earliest days about their origins, the history of their ancestors and the nature of world civilisation. They must know that all peoples, including their own ancestors, made contributions to its growth and development; and that no one people has a monopoly of beauty, culture, intelligence or creativity.

And it seems to me, too, that the interrelationship between the history of Africa and Asia (particularly the Indian sub-continent) and that of Guyana should be a major preoccupation of our university and a subject for intense and continuing research, evaluation and teaching.

The history of the world is a story of the migration of peoples. People have constantly been on the move, sometimes under compulsions of one kind or another, sometimes voluntarily. Africa has always been central to this process of migration - both as a contributor and a receptor. There has been continual movement within the continent itself; but, from earliest historical times, there was also an African presence outside of the continent, in all parts of what was the then known world. Africans were to be found in the Graeco-Roman world, in Arabia, Persia, in India and in China. They were travellers, scholars, artisans, musicians, entertainers, soldiers and slaves. They held high political office; they commanded armies and governed states outside the continent of Africa. They served in Britain with the Roman Legions, and were to be found in many parts of continental Europe. Outside of the continent itself, Africans are today most widely dispersed in the western hemisphere. They are the descendants of

Address at 150ᵗʰ Anniversary of Abolition of Slavery

those millions of persons who were brought here by what has been described as the greatest mass deportation the world has ever known and incorporated into a brutal slave system in North America and in Latin America and the Caribbean.

There is little point today in denouncing the atrocities of the slave trade. These are well authenticated. Captain John Newton, himself the captain of a slave-ship, described it as a *"vile traffic...Abounding with enormities. "* (It is an interesting sidelight that he later became a clergyman and a great hymn-writer, and was the author of those two well-known Christian hymns: "Amazing Grace" and "How sweet the name of Jesus sounds"!) Slavery brought the African into the new world in a violent and traumatic manner. As Bernard Magubane said, *"it cut him off from all traditional human ties of kin and nation and even his own cosmology. "* They became exiles from the culture that sustained them, confirmed their humanity and preserved the integrity of both their social systems and their personality. To be exiled as the poet reminds us,

**" is to know your own tune
and not to sing.
The steps of your own dance
and not to dance
remain in darkness
knowing light."**

If the exile is long enough, cruel enough, confining enough, the song and the dance are forgotten and darkness becomes mistaken for light.

And so it tended to be with us of the African diaspora in Guyana. Cut off from our past and living in ignorance of our great heritage, our personality could not but be diminished, our vision restricted, and our spiritual and social development distorted by self-depreciation and insufficient confidence in our collective capacity to aspire and achieve. This was the damaging legacy of the long period of slavery which our ancestors endured in this country.

Address at 150th Anniversary of Abolition of Slavery

Although they were trapped in the system, the great majority of them refused to be slaves; for slavery is a state of mind, a passive acceptance of a status of inferiority and subjection as a permanent condition. Our forefathers never accepted the system; they refused to acquiesce tamely in their thraldom and resisted with all the vigour and ingenuity at their command. The revolts against the system of 1731, 1733, 1734, 1741, 1749, 1751, 1752, 1763, 1814, 1823, 1834, tell their own story. These are only the recorded incidents. There must have been many more, but they provide the most cogent evidence of the relentless nature of their resistance. They rose up in arms; they resorted to sabotage; they constrained productivity in many ingenious ways; they withdrew their labour from the system by fleeing the plantations. Today, we salute Cuffy and Accabre and Quamina and Damon and all the other heroes whose names we do not know, who kept aloft the torch of freedom.

But emancipation was merely a stage in the struggle of our people for real independence. The abolition of the slave system did not mean full freedom. The role envisaged for us was not one of full and equal opportunity to become involved in the economic, social and political life. According to an official report at the time, we were to constitute *"a labouring class in a civilised community,"* that is to say, we were to continue as an underclass in service of the European settlers. The writer shrewdly advised that whether or not we would be disposed to fulfil this function would depend entirely on the exercise of power over our minds. He identified education as the instrument for achieving this objective.

And how right he was! For education is the means of influencing people's way of thinking about themselves and others; and the whole purpose of colonial education, as can be inferred from successive official reports on education policy, was to impress on our consciousness a sense of inferiority and a belief that this status was fully in accordance with divine law and the natural orders of things. A prime objective of education according to colonial office directives was to teach us *"the domestic and social duties of the coloured race,"* and *"to combine manual labour ... With a proper*

Address at 150ᵗʰ Anniversary of Abolition of Slavery

cultivation of the mind" and to train us *"in the habits of docility, humility, obedience and usefulness."*

Here was a classic prescription for under-development, suppression of the creative impulse and a deepening of the sense of cultural loss and alienation. It was not an agenda for enabling us to liberate our spirit, develop our creative talents and take charge of our own lives. It was a programme for fragmentation of the human personality.

Ours has been a history of fragmentation, that has distorted our perspective. Not only politically and culturally, but psychologically we have suffered fragmentation. If we are going to improve the quality of our contribution to the development of our country, we must piece together the fragments and restore the broken images, so that we can re-integrate our personality. One way in which we can help this process is by re-establishing our association with Africa in ways both formal and informal. We cannot return physically *en masse*; but we can do so psychologically and intellectually. For this purpose, we must study the history of Africa, not in isolation but also as it relates to our own country and to the African diaspora. Many scholars have suggested, with some justification I believe, that an understanding of the history to the development of the world cannot be divorced from a study of the African diaspora.

My call for us to rediscover Africa and to restore our links does not derive from emotionalism or romanticism; nor yet from a desire to launch a mere scholarly or intellectual enterprise. It is more fundamental than that. Today, in the wake of decolonisation and the traumatic damage inflicted on the psyche of the peoples of Africa, they are now struggling against tremendous odds to restore their historical interconnectedness and restablish something of their ancient unity. We of the diaspora cannot be divorced from or indifferent to the process. For as Shepperson reminds us, *"People of African descent abroad played a major role in the emergence of the idea of African Unity, political and cultural, which has come to be known as Pan-Africanism."* Essentially, Pan-Africanism's central project has been the reclamation of Africa's past, the assertion of a distinct African

Address at 150ᵗʰ Anniversary of Abolition of Slavery

personality, the upholding of African dignity and pride in African dignity and pride in African culture as the building blocks of African unity.

For us in Guyana, these are not mere academic pursuits. We empathise with these ideals.

Our society is built upon the right of all of our citizens to have their humanity respected and to have equal opportunities that must in no way be abridged by considerations of ethnic origin, culture, religion or other irrelevant factors. We are therefore affronted as individual citizens and as a people, by the evil system of apartheid practised in Southern Africa. Such a system stands by itself. Its very existence is an insult and a threat to us in Guyana; for its underlying thesis, publicly and unapologetically proclaimed by the Pretoria regime, is that people who are not Caucasian - and "that are not Caucasian" includes the vast majority of people who constitute our nation - are less than human beings, incapable of development and therefore condemned to a status of permanent inferiority as the servants and beasts of burden of others.

Apartheid, then, is not a domestic South African matter; it is an assault on the humanity of all of us. We have a self-interest in helping to bring about its total destruction. We must therefore intensify our cooperation with that great continent, in all ways possible, in this decisive battle now being waged against the evil, barbarous forces of apartheid in South Africa.

But for economic reasons, too, we need to strengthen and multiply our ties with Africa. As members of the Third World and the Non-Aligned Movement, we are interested in, and have strongly supported, the principle of South/South cooperation to create and expand opportunities not only for the exchange of goods and services, but also for the sharing of experiences, expertise and technology. There is an enormous potential in such cooperation for increasing our development choices and for influencing changes in the system of managing the increasingly complex world economy with a view to securing more equitable arrangements and more beneficial results for ourselves.

Haslyn Parris

Address at 150th Anniversary of Abolition of Slavery

We have a multi-racial, plural society. Over the centuries the earliest immigrants to this country, the Amerindians, have been joined by people from Africa, Asia and Europe. The presence here of the overwhelming majority of us is explained by the workings of the systems of slavery and indentured labour, and by voluntary migration. But, whatever the origins of our forefathers, for all of us today, Guyana is home. We, the Guyanese people, have travelled a long, rough and dangerous road from slavery and indenture through the colonial period to independence. During that arduous journey there were, to be sure, misunderstandings, confrontations and conflicts. The slave-owner and the colonial authorities were not slow to foster and exploit divisions among us. They sedulously implanted the idea in our minds that we were different from one another, that we had, as one colonial administrator wrote, *"No common bond of union. "* Differences of ethnic origin, colour, cultural background, religious beliefs, were all manipulated to create barriers to social cohesion and common action.

But we did have much in common. And, in the end, those things we had in common proved to be a unifying force, more powerful than the superficial differences that existed in our society.

And what were these things which proved to be a unifying force, which exerted a pressure upon us to come together for common action in our own interest? They were an acknowledgment of our common humanity; and a recognition of our common experience of suffering and of struggle and our common aspirations for a just, harmonious and humane condition of life. We had undergone the cruelties of slavery and indenture. We had suffered systematic humiliation. We were relegated to a status of permanent inferiority from which it was not intended that we should escape. We were, in sum, all victims of the same system.

But we aspired together. We had a fierce yearning to have our humanity respected, to have access to equal opportunities to develop our individual talents and to strengthen our economic base. And we realised that such conditions would not emerge for us in the absence of political independence

Address at 150th Anniversary of Abolition of Slavery

for our country. And so, together, we launched the anti-colonial movement which won us the prize of independence.

In the performances of the Nigerian troupes we have had the rare and happy privilege of witnessing aspects of the rich and varied cultural life of Africa which is the product of long centuries of social development. We, in Guyana, can only benefit from deepening our relations with Africa in the field of culture. We have strong survivals and an enduring memory of the old African culture and traditions, particularly in the rural areas. They are all around to be seen if only we could master the difficult task of "learning to see". They manifest themselves in cultural forms like queh-queh songs, dances and ceremonies; the masquerade band; in our anancy stories and folklore; in artistic forms like our sculpture; in the food we eat like the foo-foo and the conkey. In our indigenous religious practices and beliefs; in words and expressions we use; in the games we played as children; in our village tradition of cooperative endeavour and mutual support.

Here is a rich field of research for our historians, sociologists and other professionals working in related fields. They must study these vestiges of the old African culture, evaluate them, trace them back to their sources in Africa and put them in their proper context. This is vitally necessary work for us; but we must be very clear in our minds why we would wish to pursue this task. It would not be to accentuate differences between our citizens of African descent and other members of our society; for such an objective would be undesirable, unacceptable and self-defeating. We must pursue this task so that, as a nation, we can benefit from a more powerful and rewarding contribution to the evolution and enrichment of our Guyanese national culture and the validation of our unique identify as a Guyanese nation. This would be of practical value to us as we seek to strengthen the bases of our multi-ethnic, multi-cultural, but non-racial and cohesive society.

It is understandable that, at this time of commemoration citizens of African descent should feel a sense of pride in the contribution they have made to the building of this nation. It was their physical labour that made this

Address at 150th Anniversary of Abolition of Slavery

coastland habitable and productive during the period of slavery and after. They brought many skills from Africa. They acquired those that were necessary to maintain machinery, equipment and to maintain the production process on the plantations. They were masons and builders, carpenters, mechanics, coopers and artisans of all kinds. They built the roads, the bridges, the kokers, the dams. They dug the drainage and irrigation canals. They built the river and sea defences. They constructed buildings. A massive amount of physical labour went into these activities. In the post-emancipation period, they continued to provide the artisan skills that were required in the economy; but they also became teachers, nurses, midwives, mechanics, policemen, stevedores, pan-boilers. They became sailors and captains on coastal and riverain vessels. They went into the forests to pioneer the forest industries. They braved the rivers and the rapids and the dangerous hinterland terrain to develop the quarries and the bauxite, the gold and diamond mining industries.

It is right that we should note prudence in, and that the nation should applaud, this mighty contribution. But let us also remember that all people who live in this country also made important contributions to the evolution of our nation. The Amerindians, the East Indians, the Portuguese, the Chinese, the Europeans were all, in their different ways and according to their different skills and aptitudes, involved in the development of our country. We developed this country together. That is why, today, all of us rightly lay claim to it as being our own. It belongs to all of us. None of us is a trespasser, none of us here on sufferance. All of us, then, have to work together to secure its future.

Our national culture must therefore be based upon the contributions from the heritage of all of our peoples. Our cultural situation is dynamic and receptive: it is always moving in the direction of synthesis. We are mature enough to understand that even as we respect ourselves, we must respect one another and the various strands of cultural heritage which we are weaving into the fabric of national culture. We are intelligent enough to understand that racism can have no place in our society. We must continue to stand resolutely against it and reject it in all of its forms and

Address at 150th Anniversary of Abolition of Slavery

manifestations. As the UNESCO declaration of international experts in the field of anthropology and genetics has noted: **"race is not so much a biological phenomenon as a social myth"** and **"in the present state of knowledge there is no justification for the belief that human groups differ in natural aptitudes either intellectual or emotional."** All the various groups in our society have contributed enormously in the past and must continue in the years ahead to contribute in exciting and stimulating ways to the development of all aspects of our national life.

Let us then make this anniversary not merely a time for commemoration, but a time for renewal and commitment: renewal of the spirit of enthusiasm, of discipline, of purpose; commitment to the ideal of national unity based on one permanent, indivisible loyalty, to this great land of ours. We have traversed a long and arduous road in the course of our history. We have reached this stage of our progress and development, to borrow the words of a Guyanese poet, Syble Douglas,

- *Across the chasm of hate*
- *Across the barrier of race*
- *Across the bigotry of class*
  to share in words,
  our hopes, our fears and our dreams
  of a better to-morrow

To that world of a better to-morrow, then, let us turn with our collective strength.

[Note: The granting of permission for me to use this Address as an appendix to this Essay, should not in any way be interpreted to imply that the author of the Address endorses, or has in any way commented on, the content of this book.   Indeed, he has never seen the manuscript.]

Appendix # 3
Tourism - A Counter-Intuitive Conjecture [1995]

Intuition is to be respected, but not always implicitly trusted. There are just too many cases in real life where our intuition leads us astray seriously. However, there are several instances where reason, or logic as it is frequently loosely called, deserves the same caveat - respect it, but don't trust it implicitly.

Consider the following example which comes from a branch of mathematical logic. The exposition is simplified for the non-mathematical reader.

Suppose you had five different books named A, B, C, D, and E, and a friend asked you to send him *"some of the books"*. You and your friend would have the understanding that he would receive more than one book but less than five. If he had said **"send me *all* the books"**, you would have understood that you should send the five books. This way of thinking entrenches the idea that *"some"* is less than *"all"*.

Now let us approach the same issue a little more pedantically. **The *size* of a set of things is *the number* of things in the set.** Thus, for instance, the size of the set of people in a room is the number of people in the room. We use this concept of size to give meaning to the statement that **"one set of things is *larger (or less)* than another set of things"**. Thus, for instance, if X represents the st of people in the bedroom, and Y represents the set of people in the kitchen, we say **"X is *less than* Y"** (or **"Y is *greater than* X"**) if the number of people in the bedroom is less than the number of people in the kitchen.

In the case of the five books, the set **"all the books"** has the number **5** associated with it. Thus the size of that set is **5**.

Now consider the set **"some of the books"**. Any one of the following combinations of books qualifies as being in the category **"some of the books"**. The different combinations are:

A&B; A&C; A&D; A&E; B&C; B&D; B&E; C&D; C&E; D&E;

A&B&C; A&B&D; A&B&E; A&C&D; A&C&E; B&C&D; B&C&E; A&D&E; C&D&E; D&E&B;

A&B&C&D; A&B&C&E; A&C&D&E; A&B&D&E; B&C&D&E.

If you sent your friend any one of the combinations he would say that you did send him **"*some* of the books"**.

There are 25 of those combinations, so the set **"*some* of the books"** has a size of **25**. But the set **"*all* of the books"** has a size of **5**. It follows, counter-intuitively, that **"*some*"** is greater than **"*all*"**. In this case, **"*some*"** is five times as large as **"*all*"**!

Whatever you make of this conundrum (be assured it is not trivial) its only purpose here is to put the reader on guard for what is to follow as an assault on the reader's intuition. It is uncontentiously asserted that Amerindians are human beings - sometimes downtrodden, often disadvantaged, and almost always not understood; but human beings nevertheless. As all human beings, they are interested in their own survival and in the progressive betterment of their material state. Indeed, our current view of "human rights" says that they have an inalienable right to pursue their own survival and prosperity. Among other things, this means that they ought to have the freedom and the right to earn and to deploy those earnings to improve their material state as they see fit.

The vision that comprises what they might see fit will obviously be determined by the norms to which they subscribe, and those norms are almost bound to conflict with the tenor of the existing legislation called the Amerindian Act (Chapter 29:01 of The Laws of Guyana).

But maybe we are moving too fast and getting ahead of ourselves. About whom are we speaking anyway? Who is an Amerindian? If you are of the view that the conundrum at the beginning of this essay is a bit of unnecessary silliness to which mathematical types are uniquely prone, consider the definition given in the law as an answer to the question: "Who is an Amerindian?" The Act asserts that "Amerindian" means:

"(a)   any Indian who is a citizen of Guyana and is of a tribe indigenous to Guyana or to neighbouring countries;

(b)   any descendant of an Amerindian within the meaning of paragraph (a) of this definition to whom, in the opinion of the Chief Officer, this Act should apply;"

And if you are not now clear then you can ask the "Chief Officer" who is *"the Chief Interior Development Officer, and includes any officer authorised in writing by the Minister to perform any of the functions of the Chief Officer for the purposes of this Act:"*

If, like me, you are dissatisfied with this piece of circular rubbish, you might try deriving a definition of your own that is not prone to the criticisms which you have sensed. Your intuition would then have led you into the same problem that the National Party of South Africa had when they felt compelled to promulgate the Population Registration Act that sought to label all South Africans by race, and devised an arbitrary and meaningless set of tests to decide Black from Coloured or Coloured from White.

The importance of finding a test for who is an Amerindian derives from one's intuitive conviction that some set of people, definable as Amerindian, needs the special treatment of "protection" of the Central Government from non-Amerindians; in a way that no other ethnic group currently does.

It probably doesn't occur to you that neither you nor the existing Law currently poses the same question in relation to any of the five other ethnic (or racial groupings) that allegedly comprise Guyana - African, East Indian, Portuguese, Chinese, European. The Amerindian Act is clearly based on the persistence of the intuitively satisfying assumption that the Amerindians in their hinterland communities need to be protected from exploitation by non-Amerindians in a special way that other ethnic groups do not need protection. It fits in with the developed world's popular views enshrined in the terminology "Indigenous People", and we appear to accept those views.

Such an understanding is the only explanation I have found for the open way in which Amerindian Communities have been given a place in the activity "tourism" by the rest of us. It is the only ethnic group to have been given such a place - a fact which gives the lie to society's alleged acceptance of the Amerindian as an equal in Guyanese society.

It is against this background that a significant aspect of tourism in Guyana has to do with tourists visiting Amerindian Communities, where, as one tourist operator's brochure puts it **"you will observe the Amerindians' humble way of living in traditional thatched roof houses."** Because of this aspect of involvement of Amerindians in tourism, it has been intuitively argued with the force of high morals that the Amerindian communities which participate in tourist activity should be prime beneficiaries of the income from those visits - including proceeds from the sale of their craft and artefacts. It is only fair and decent, we argue with righteous enlightenment.

However, we seem less predisposed to argue that there is something undesirable and unpalatable about inviting streams of strangers specifically to inspect the poverty of any particular ethnic group, and to invade the privacy of the lives that adjust to that poverty - even if the visitors pay so to do. What is more, it does not seem to occur to us that if the Amerindian views his life as humble, he may well be imbued with a desire to better it to live like those of us, including the foreign tourists, who agree that his life is humble and pay to see that humility. He who is beheld would like to become like the beholder.

What is it that makes us believe that when the Amerindian communities earn from the tourist-gawking activities, they will not use those earnings to replace their thatched roof houses by concrete bungalows and multi-storied buildings equipped with (modern?) devices such as television sets, Bose radios and stereo sets, refrigerators and deep freezes, personal computers, and upholstered furniture? Is it our expectation, and perhaps our hope, that some principle of "sustainable development" will preserve the pristine purity of their poverty, and therefore the persistent attraction of the afflictions of their communities to the tourist?

If that is neither our expectation nor our hope, then either we expect the Amerindians' earnings from tourism not to be large enough to finance the transition of their communities in the near future; or we simply are reneging on our assumption that Amerindians are human beings like the rest of us with similar capabilities for and visions of material betterment, Western style! The alternative scenario is that tourism based on visiting humble Amerindian communities will grow quickly, generate great income from which the communities will benefit substantially, and stop as suddenly as those communities come into the twentieth century losing their appeal of underdevelopment.

These conjectures may at first sight appear ridiculous, but they demand consideration. If earnings from this aspect of tourism do not have a significant impact on the income of Amerindian communities, it must be that someone else is getting the lion's share of those earnings, and major concerns about equity should arise. If the earnings are made to go to the communities, then the stage is set for them to have a short-lived business cycle. So if a certain kind of equity prevails, there is need to plan for the demise of the source of the initial success. The greater the initial success, the faster the material improvement and the shorter the life of the circumstances which gave rise to the income in the first place. This aspect of tourism therefore seems unlikely to be a long term growth industry unless there is an artificial preservation of the Amerindians' humble state.

The situation is not formally different from that faced with a so-called wasting asset like a mineral deposit. The faster the extraction, the greater the stream of the revenue, and the shorter the life of the mine. After the depletion of the deposit, what then? As the transition of the particular Amerindian community away from "humbleness" takes place, what then about its likely continued prosperity at the newly achieved level? Is the process an inherently self-defeating one, sustainable only by inhibiting transformation of the community?

Much of the previous paragraphs has highlighted problems in the context of tourism; but the issues go much, much deeper. The chapter pertaining to Guyana which appears in the United States Department of State's Country Reports on Human Rights Practices for 1994 states:

> *"The Amerindian Act regulates Amerindian life, and is legislation dating from colonial times designed to protect indigenous people from exploitation. The Act gives the Government the power to determine who is an Amerindian and what is an Amerindian community, to appoint Amerindian leaders, and to cancel or annul decisions made by Amerindian councils. It also prohibits the sale of alcohol to Amerindians and requires government permission before any Amerindian can accept formal employment, although these provisions generally are not enforced."*

having previously noted in relation to the Amerindian population mostly living in reservations and villages in remote parts of the interior that:

> *"Their standard of living is much lower than that of most Guyanese, and their ability to participate in decisions affecting their lands, cultures, traditions, and the allocation of natural resources is limited."*

The allegation is that the Select Committee of Parliament, authorised in December 1993, is intended to make revisions to the Amerindian Act, thereby making it more democratic and enhancing Amerindian self-determination. Intuitively, this mandate and its objective seem laudable and uncontentious. But are they? Is it possible by revision to correct something that is fundamentally flawed? Is it not a fundamental flaw to have a law referable to only one ethnic group? Is it not a fundamental flaw to have a law whose focus cannot escape the definitional problem of saying who is an Amerindian, when no other law requires definition of any other ethnic grouping? Are we not, led by our intuition, in danger of indeed destroying what we purport to be trying to preserve (Amerindians and their culture); and of denying rights by passing a law designed to restore those rights - in circumstances in which we allege those rights to be inalienable?

Again, the South African experience pops up disturbingly in my mind. This time it is in relation to the Tomlinson Commission for the Socio-Economic Development of the Bantu Areas. That government-created Commission, focusing on ethnic enclaves referred to as "bantustans", argued in an intuitively appealing way that a program of development for African areas should allow them to develop along their own lines, and provide industrialisation and other economic activities for Africans in their own geographical areas.

Neither the Tomlinson Commission Report, nor its watered down offshoot, the Bantu Authorities Act, highlighted the likely systemic result that three million whites would continue to own 87 percent of the land, while eight million Africans would own the remaining 13 percent. Is it that the reversed demographic characteristics of the Amerindian in Guyana intuitively might persuade us that a similar effect in Guyana would be equitable - a kind of democratically permissible tyranny of the majority over the minority who would be kept in their place?

Intuitively, there can be no denying that the weaknesses associated with the Amerindian Act need to be corrected; but it is possible that such correction cannot be achieved by revision of the Act. Maybe what is required is its abolition, based on its flawed origins! Maybe, the excesses and injustices which a law of this type is expected to avoid, if perpetrated on any ethnic or other group, would be equally reprehensible. If that is so, then it is not an **Amerindian** Act that is required, but perhaps an **Hinterland Communities** Act. The focus of such an Act would then be on the avoidance of the excesses and injustices, and not on any particular ethnic group, which in any event will defy definition.

I am reminded of an attempt made many decades ago by some eminent statisticians, in the field of multivariate analysis, to define a Coefficient of Racial Likeness (CRL). Intuitively it seemed possible, and at the time was probably morally desirable, to identify a set of parameters whose measurements when applied to individuals could determine the value of a single index that would with a pre-determined degree of confidence accurately categorise individuals by race. The attempt failed abysmally, and was eventually abandoned, when the Coefficient categorised an Inuit *(this is the name that Eskimos prefer to call themselves)* as something entirely different - or maybe it was vice versa.

Really, these points should not need to be stressed in a community like Guyana, where a girl named Chin may appear to be East Indian; a man named DeFreitas may appear to be African; a man named Persaud may appear to be Portuguese; and an Amerindian might be named Alphonso, Adams, Romascindo, or Allicock.

But back to tourism itself. Some time ago, long before it became popular to apply the prefix 'eco' to it, there were concerns expressed about the likely impact of tourism on the development process of so-called underdeveloped countries like Guyana. In Guyana, the issue, pre eco, got settled in large part because we had no easily accessible white sands and clear blue bodies of water. Our mud imposed on us the commonsense benefit that we should value the prawns off our continental shelf more than the tourists who might otherwise have come to swim and sun themselves. We were well advised to have decided to eat our prawns rather than bemoan the absence of tourists whom we should not eat.

Now that "eco" has arisen, and tourism is on the rise, so might the original concerns - except that prevailing international opinion, and current views on the path to economic progress have persuaded us to not discuss those concerns either openly or seriously. Here I am referring to concerns such as those about distortions of our cultural norms; politeness and hospitality versus subservience; psychological changes in our attitudes to work - the likely attraction of our young to become the analogue of sexually appealing beach bums and layabouts rather than manufacturing entrepreneurs; and the spread of sexually transmitted diseases imported by tourists.

Those cases seems to have been closed, the concerns to have been relegated to the realm of archaic and uninformed paranoia, their relevance to be of importance only to those who wish to stand in the way of progress. There is a conspiracy of silence about these possible undesirable systemic effects. Maybe if we play possum, these undesirable things will not arise - but I doubt that.

Supplier protection legislation is the term I use for that body of legislation currently ruled out by the current wave of thinking about things like market forces, free trade, the dismantling of trade barriers, and the protection of fledgling industries from unfettered international competition (including subsidies). Included in the idea of supplier protection legislation is the protection of hinterland communities, the suppliers of the goods and services for some branches of tourism, from the middle men and the consumers - the tour promoters and the tourists. In the prevailing situation where the Amerindians are having little say in the issues that arise through the promulgation of tourism (there is already an outcry about howler monkeys being a delicacy), what preparation are we making about the problems which tourism may pose for the development process in the hinterland communities? Do we believe that any serious problems may be posed? Do those communities believe that any serious problems may be posed?

The impression I have is that tourism (eco-tourism) has been labelled a "good thing", not so much because we have considered its likely systemic effects, but more so because it is an internationally popular idea. Our national intuitive response seems to be that it is a good thing so let's do it. The result is that we are vibrantly pursuing activities to encourage the influx of tourists without expending similar effort in considering and preparing for the main systemic effects ("good" and "bad") of our likely success.

We have been this way before, doing things without in-depth consideration of the likely systemic consequences of our actions; and without the cybernetic precaution of monitoring the results to see whether our expectations are indeed being met. Cybernetic approaches are not our strong point; and the maturity to deem our actions not *"wrong"* or *"right"* but *"considered experiments associated with probabilities of bettering our material state"*, is still to become a way of life. We resolutely refuse to accept and respond to the "Unthinkableness" of the world we inhabit, and misplace our trust in our intuition and in a deity whose record does not unassailably confirm that He is overwhelmingly concerned.

It is possible to pronounce with erudite conviction on matters about which one has no personal experience. Thus celibate virginal priests and nuns do so about sex, inspired and informed by their unimpeachable source, God through the Pope, whose alleged only experience in the matter was vicariously through the Holy Ghost. The jeopardy is that similarly, but with less supernatural assurance of correctness, coastlanders will pronounce on Amerindians and tourism into Hinterland Communities, relying on the guidance of their cherished prejudices and intuition.

END (1995)

Postscript (2003)

This essay began with a caveat about the reliability of one's intuition. Maybe, as a matter of style, the essay should have ended with an appropriate *da capo al fine* leading back to intuition. This postscript suggests the following problem *(mentioned in Lewis Carroll's Diary on December 21, 1893)* as appropriate:

> **A monkey is clinging to one end of a rope that goes over a pulley with a weight on the other end. The weight is equal to the monkey's weight. Initially, the monkey and the weight are at the same distance below the pulley. If the monkey climbs the rope, what happens to the weight?**

What does your intuition, or indeed any other device you choose to use, say is the answer?

END (2003)

Post Postscript (2005)

On August 11, 2005, the author wrote a short essay entitled "**The Act of the Amerindians**". It was written as a response to the Government tabling in the National Assembly (on Thursday August 4, 2005) an Amerindian bill. The essay is given below at the end of this Appendix, immediately after the Post Postscript (2010).

Post Postscript (2010)

1.   In the Stabroek News of Wednesday, March 10, 2010, the Pages 1 and 10 Article entitled "**Indigenous leaders call for hold on LCDS, REDD+ projects - until resolution of land issues**"; the

Thursday, March 11, 2010 Page 16 response by the Office of Climate Change (OCC); the anonymous Letter on Page 6 to the SN Editor of Friday 12 March, 2010 re Consultations in Amerindian communities; the Page 3 Article of SN of Saturday 13 March, 2010 re some Indigenous leaders being 'harassed' for voicing concerns; the Page 6 Letter to the Editor by Jocelyn Dow in SN of Wednesday, March 17, 2010; and in the Page 3 SN Article of Thursday , March 18, 2010, entitled 'Toshaos council needs $$ to continue LCDS, REDD+ consultations - Pearson'; all together confirm the relevance of the comments made in this essay which as written fifteen years ago, i.e. in 1995!

2.   As a recurrence of the urge to warn against reliance on intuition I offer the example of the MÖBIUS strip (named after one of its two discoverers, August Ferdinand MÖBIUS). In 1858, he discovered that a one-sided surface can be constructed by affixing the ends of a rectangular strip after first having given one of the ends a one-half twist. This construct has two counter-intuitive properties: It has only one side; and remains in one piece when split down the middle! Even now in 2010, more than 150 years later, its existence is still intuitively uncomfortable to accept.

END (2010)

Haslyn Parris

The Act of the Amerindians

It must be a peculiar human trait that causes us to be prone to ignore, or misinterpret, the significance of events that we know have occurred or of information that we have been given. For instance, Article 149 (1) (a) of our Constitution says "no law shall make any provision that is discriminatory either of itself or in its effect;" and Article 140 (2) states *"In this article the expression "discriminatory" means affording different treatment to different persons attributable wholly or mainly to their or their parents' or guardians' respective descriptions by race, place of origin, political opinion, colour, creed age, disability marital status, sex, gender, language, birth, social class, pregnancy, religion, conscience, belief or culture whereby persons of one such description are subjected to disabilities or restrictions to which other persons of the same or another such description are not made subject or are accorded privileges or advantages which are not afforded to other persons of the same or another such description."*

In the light of this information, shouldn't the event of the Government tabling an Amerindian Bill raise the question of whether such an act is in conflict with the Constitution? Might we look forward to the occasions on which we will be presented with bills relating to the other ethnic groups of Guyana - an African bill, an East Indian bill, a Chinese bill, a Portuguese bill, a European bill, a Mixed bill? And might the presentation of each such bill not be attended by the presence in the gallery of the National Assembly of a grouping of prominent citizens of the relevant ethnicity, as was the case on Thursday August 4, 2005?

But the conundrums do not end here. The various Amerindian Leaders, gathered under the umbrella of the Seventh General Assembly of the Amerindian Peoples' Association, have contended that the consultation processes with indigenous leaders were seriously flawed as they are consulted more in tokenism than in substance on the various matters in the bill.

Many Guyanese political Leaders have taken to describing our Constitution as one of the most advanced in the Caribbean, and inclusive governance based on *'meaningful consultation'* is one of the bases of this claim. A guide to the protocols and processes that should be involved in consultation is provided in Title 10 - the Interpretation section of the Constitution. There, it is stated that " *"consultation" or "meaningful consultation" means the person or entity responsible for seeking consultation shall - (a) Identify the persons or entities to be consulted and specify to them in writing the subject of the consultation and an intended date for the decision on the subject of consultation; (b) Ensure that each person or entity to be consulted is afforded a reasonable opportunity to express a considered opinion on the subject of the consultation; and (c)Cause to be prepared and archived a written record of the consultation and circulate the decision to entities consulted."*

If the processes mandated by the Constitution had been followed, then the complaint about tokenism of consultation could not have been honestly made; and there are many reasons to believe the complaint since even at the point of the laying of the bill in the National Assembly, copies of the formal bill being laid were not available for MP's, or for the Amerindian leaders in the gallery. Also, since the National Assembly immediately went into recess until October, with the bill not being discussed, nobody, and certainly not any of the Amerindian Leaders, knows an intended date of final decision-making on this bill. Many of the matters dealt with in the bill have been criticized since the 1976 revision of the original Amerindian Act.

The consideration of simply renaming the Act as the Indigenous Peoples Act will not resolve the substance of the issues raised above. Perhaps conceptually renaming and treating the legislation as a regimen of rules intended to be applicable to Hinterland Communities rather than to a specific ethnic group might suffice. But really, is the foundation that we are laying for the grand idea of treating all Guyanese individuals and groupings as equal in the eyes of the Law not impaired by this attempt to show concern for land rights, etc. related to Amerindians without a simultaneous companion concern being shown for issues such as 'children property' and 'ancestral lands' among other ethnic groups?

These matters had all been considered by the Constitution Reform Commission (CRC) and had led to a recommendation that was accepted by Parliament but that has subsequently been ignored by the Government. That recommendation is Recommendation 9.3.3 (4) of the CRC Report of 17 July, 1999. The recommendation states *"That an Indigenous Peoples' Commission be established to look into and make recommendations for specific issues including: land rights; improvements in legislation affecting Amerindians; the Amerindian Act; the scope and authority of the Council of Toushaus; empowerment with regards to local government and the Amerindian village council system; economic and education policy; and cultural protection and preservation."*

W. H. Parris *(August 11, 2005)*

Appendix # 4
THE TERM OF GOVERNMENT - *1995*
(or What's so special about 5?)

Gematria fascinates me. The substitution of numbers for letters in an alphabet, and the use of those substituted values to ferret out meanings from text written using that alphabet, is quite intriguing. Thus did the medieval cabbalists generate mystical insights into Genesis 28:12. They concluded that the Law revealed to Moses on Mount Sinai is man's way to heaven - based on the Hebrew word *sullam* meaning "ladder" and the word **Sinai** having the same numerical value.

A not dissimilar exercise, applied to the original Aramaic language in which the Book of Revelations was written, has the number **666**, the number of the Beast (Revelations 13:18) translate into **NERO**. But since the original allocation of numbers to the alphabet is arbitrary, as indeed is the procedure for combining the numbers assigned, Jesuit Father Bongus translated the same number into **"Martin Luther"**; while the German mathematician, Michael Stifel, derived the answer **Pope Leo X.**

Of more recent vintage has been the idea of "Perfect Number-Words" in English. Here the idea is that of assigning positive and negative integers to the letters in the English alphabet to derive the effect of making the English names of numerals correspond to their numerical values. Thus, $Z+E+R+O = 0$; $O+N+E = 1$; $T+W+O = 2$; $T+H+R+E+E = 3$; $F+O+U+R = 4$; $F+I+V+E = 5$; $S+I+X = 6$; $S+E+V+E+N = 7$; $E+I+G+H+T = 8$; $N+I+N+E = 9$; $T+E+N = 10$; $E+L+E+V+E+N = 11$; and $T+W+E+L+V+E = 12$; if the right positive and negative integers are uniquely assigned respectively to each of the letters E, F, G, H, I, L, N, R, S, T, U, V, W, X, Z. It does not matter what values are assigned to the remaining eleven letters.

What does all this have to do with the term of a Government? Well, I can only assume that some jiggery-pokery of a kind related to gematria must have been applied to derive the number "five" in Articles 70 (3), and 70 (4) of the Constitution of the Co-operative Republic of Guyana. I have been unable to ferret out any other acceptable reason or set of reasons that lead unwaveringly to the number "Five" in those Articles. Why not "Six", or "Four", or "Seven", or "Three"? Should a document as important as the Constitution, occupying the position of supremacy so clearly set out in Article 8, contain such an arbitrarily selected number? Does our Constitution enshrine the paramountcy of arbitrariness?

I think in this respect of the term of the Government it does, not out of malice but out of our being mired in our preferred adherence to two flawed systems - one fundamental and inescapable, the other traditional.

The fundamental inescapable flaw arises out of our preference for democracy and voting as a basis for decision-making. I have elsewhere (cf. BUNARO, Page 29) discussed this matter. It has to do with Condorcet's paradox and the generalisation derived by Kenneth J. Arrow, the 1972 winner of the Nobel Prize in Economics, called "The Impossibility Theorem"[48]. Essentially, that theorem states that any decision rule based on voting **must** make "unreasonable" decisions at least some of the time! Our constitution is based on the persistent application of such rules.

The traditional concept to which I refer was captured by Bertrand Russell in the opening statement of his Presidential Address to the Students' Union at the London School of Economics and Political Science, October 10, 1923 - more than seventy years ago, fifty seven years before the promulgation of our Constitution. That statement is: **"One of the peculiarities of the English-speaking world is its immense interest and belief in political parties. A very large percentage of English-speaking people really believe that the ills from which they suffer would be cured if a certain political party were in power. That is a reason for the swing of the pendulum. A man votes for one party and remains miserable; he concludes that it was the other party that was to bring the millennium. By the time he is disenchanted with all parties, he is an old man on the verge of death; his sons retain the belief of his youth, and the see-saw goes on."**

It is faith in the necessity of preserving the opportunity of the "see-saw" that generates the need for a 'term' of Government. And each time we revisit the question of who should govern, allowing those who are not now governing a chance to be chosen to so do, we fall back on a decision rule based on voting - the very arrangement that must make unreasonable decisions at least some of the time!

---

48 Vol1, entitled *Social Choice and Justice*, of the Collected Papers of Kenneth J. Arrow, published by the Belknap Press of Harvard University Press, deals in depth with this matter.

The comments made above do not apply uniquely to Guyana. We can therefore take comfort in the fact that we are no more silly nor sensible than a large part of the rest of the world. However, there are a few circumstances that should give us cause for concern.

The first has to do with the idea that what we are trying to achieve is the best combination of persons to govern us. In this attempt it appears not unreasonable for us to adopt and adapt other successful models. In particular, when we want to get the best cricket team for Guyana, we do not simply choose the club team that won the most prestigious tournament. Intuitively we know that doing that would leave out some good cricketers who do not belong to the club that won. We find a way to pick across clubs, and it would be unusual to find that all members of the Guyana cricket team come from the same club. Why should a similar result not be aimed at when we wish to choose from political parties to get a representative competent government? The current system forces "good" people to be excluded from being in the government formed, because they did not belong to the winning party in the competition called elections.

The second circumstance relates to the first. We could ignore the exclusions inherent in what we do if the situation were one in which there is a very large number of competent people who might participate in forming the Government, and talent skipped over is reproduced in the winning party by virtue of the superfluity of extant talent dispersed among the contesting parties. However, we must acknowledge that our small size and human resource base would make such an assumption patently false. The difficulties which the political parties have in constructing their lists for national and local government elections are too well known for this point to need to be belaboured.

The third and fourth circumstances have to do with some illogicalities that the current system encourages. It is par for the course for the contesting parties to argue that each is by itself more likely to be competent at governing than every other by themselves. None needs to argue that by itself it is likely to be more competent than any combination of the rest, or any combination including itself. Accordingly, the illogicality of arguing for a sub-optimal solution to the question of who should govern, by restricting the choices of voters to **within** parties, is enshrined even though what is allegedly being sought is the best combination to govern (which may be found **across** parties).

This illogicality then feeds into the considerations of causation. The previous party in power is deemed by the new party in power to have been the "cause" of any undesirable economic effect which occurs during the new party's term; and the new party is the "cause" of any desirable effect that occurs. All this takes place without reference to the gestation periods of policies or projects. Whatever "good" happens during my term is the result of my competence. Whatever "bad" happens is the result of the incompetence of my immediate predecessor. That many complex problems are associated with solutions that have gestation periods is simply ignored. But those gestation periods may well exceed the period left in the government's term, and in any event may exceed the number "five". It may even be that the incumbent party feels a compulsion to undo as much as possible of whatever its predecessor did, on the basis of its predecessor's alleged incompetence, insipience, or improbity!

This way of treating causation derives primarily from the strategy of building up and destroying party reputations, preparatory to the next elections that will occur at the end of the Government's term. In such circumstances, though collaboration with its opposition may be espoused by the party in government, the kudos which would normally attach to a collaborator's contribution to solution derivation cannot be openly accorded to the opposition. Tactically, the opposition's image of at best second best has to be fostered and preserved with an eye on the next election. The opposition must for the same competitive reasons behave in the same way as the Government, withholding praise and maximising destructive criticism.[49]

What should signal that there is need for a change of government? Surely it should not be just the passage of time. So there is not a fixed time period, describable as an integer number of years, preventative maintenance style, at the end of which there is a need to ask the question as to whether the government should be changed (like engine oil). It must be possible to argue that mal-performance of the system being governed is the real circumstance that is the indicator of the need for a change of government. Then, the relevant parameter will not be time, but some other measure or set of social and economic measures of public dissatisfaction with systemic performance. These parameters should be monitored continually, and the

---

49 I concur with Bertrand Russell's observation that: *"the instinctive appeal of every successful political movement is to envy, rivalry or hate, never to the need for cooperation."* *(Presidential Address to he Student's Union of LSE - Oct 10, 1923.)*

need for change should be determined by their levels, the directions of their change, and their rates of change. The circumstance of the parameters signalling the need to consider a change of Government could occur in any year, say year three, or in year nine, of the Government's term. The real problem is constructing and operating the mechanisms that would yield the measures suggested. That problem is not insuperable; and its solution is required for cybernetic management of the economy anyway.[50] It is interesting to note that if this approach were adopted, then good past performance would become a much weaker justification for a Government staying in or assuming power. The achievements of a previous decade would weigh little in the decision as to what best to do in today's circumstances.

When change is to be decided upon, even if we insist on using the sub-optimal decision-making device of voting, the results of the voting could be utilised to avoid courting the sub-optimality of choosing the government ministers from only one party, thereby getting the best team from across contesting political parties to undertake this most important task of governing the country. Even in the circumstance where one party wins a so-called "landslide victory" at the polls, there is no justification for relying on the assumption that the totality of wisdom and competence resides in that winning party's list.

Acceptance of this objective of "getting the best team to govern" has a number of consequences that themselves have implications for the term of the Government. The fundamental task of the Government is resolution of the social dilemmas that present a conflict between the general good and the costs to individuals or groups of individual interests. Existing theory indicates that cooperation within groups on such matters is intensely affected by how long individuals expect to remain part of the group. In a general sense, although the matter is far more complicated than this simple generality, the longer the period over which the members of the group perceive they will have to interact, the greater the level of cooperation in pursuit of the general good. Removal of the constraint of a fixed time period (particularly if that period is 'short') after which the group must fight for its political life as determined by the various interests in the society, and replacement of it by some measure of the society's on-going level of satisfaction as a trigger for change seems a useful direction to pursue.

---

50   This matter of the importance of public dissatisfaction to the management of the economy is discussed in detail in BUNARO, Pages 42 to 51 of Chapter 1.

In summary, the concept and the practice of applying a predetermined automatic term to Government appear to be associated with at least the following indefensible deficiencies:

(a)   The whole question of whether the Government should be changed is raised regardless of whether the incumbent Government is governing well in the eyes of the general public. (It ain't broke, and it ain't malfunctioning; but let's fix it anyway.).

(b)   An already sub-optimally chosen group is deprived of the opportunity of growing into a really collaborative force for the general good by the Damoclean device of a time constraint associated with the determination of the life of the group.

c)   Except in the case of a national emergency, when commonsense says "Keep the current Government while we ride out the crisis", but particularly in the case when stability and progress prevail, commonsense will not prevail and the system insists on introducing the divisiveness of electoral propaganda aimed at possibly replacing the incumbent group, always at great financial cost.

(d)   An invariant time period for judging the efficacy of policies and projects is imposed, despite common knowledge that not all policies and projects have the same gestation period for generating results deemed desirable.

Surely, the abandonment of the arbitrary choice of the length of the term of Government, and its replacement by a system that would avoid these deficiencies and eschew the need to rely on rhetoric and misrepresentation of information, is a worthwhile objective in pursuit of effective government. END (1995)

Postscript (2003)

The first two paragraphs of this essay might give the impression that all this cabbalist stuff is nonsensical and long gone. That's not my view! As late as May, 2003 news broke that Madonna spent over US$5mn for a London town house that will become a new centre for the study of Kabbalah. Under the Leadership of Philip Berg, Kabbalism in America has greatly expanded; and celebrities including Madonna and Monica Lewinsky appear to have joined the cause. The pursuit of personal improvement and spiritual happiness for people of all faiths, and no faiths, using the once arcane wisdom of Kabbalah seems to be well underway.

END (2003)

Post Postscript (2010)

It is perhaps instructive to note that a not unrelated problem has been raised in 2009 & 2010 about a third term for the current President of Guyana.

END (2010)

Appendix #5
Who shall Govern Us? [1996]

Most of this essay was first written some eleven years ago. What has surprised me is that its concepts appear to me to be as relevant and as true today in 2007 as they seemed in 1996. I have concluded that either the concepts are perfectly irrelevant, and therefore need no revision despite the passage of time; or the part of the real world to which I have applied them - specifically Guyana and more generally CARICOM - has entered a state of stasis on the dimension of governance; or both. Readers are seriously invited to make the choice.

I have grown weary and wary of the spate of imported buzz words and buzz phrases that currently infest our everyday discourses - *Transparency, Level playing field, Empowerment, The Private Sector being the Engine of Growth, Democracy,* for example. The weariness is a kind of linguistic jadedness that derives from the very high frequency of utilisation of these buzz terms, giving them a kind of near iniquitousness across topics. The wariness arises from our treatment of the terms as though they convey self-evident truths, completely ignoring their inherent complexities and the agendas of their authors. In the same way that in matters of economic development we bemoan persistent balance of trade and balance of payments difficulties, we ought to be concerned about the balance of ideas and balance of concepts problems. Both suffer from the negative impact of high net inappropriate imports.

Sheer political and economic power, and persistent repetition, have endowed *"Structural Adjustment"* with the respectability of appropriateness for dealing in the long run with problems of economic malaise. An appropriate indigenous "adjustment" programme needs to be devised to deal with the problems of conceptual malaise. Indeed, the problems of economic and of conceptual malaise are intimately related; but *"the powers that be"* cannot be proselytizers of the belief in that relationship.

The essence and exercise of "Independence" is to dream one's own dreams. When someone else determines your dreams, you may not even be able to dream of being "Independent." There ought to be no "ought" about what a man, a woman, a child, or a nation dreams. To impose such a constraint, or to allow it to be imposed, or to foster its imposition, is to destroy the well-spring of progress - proliferating variety. Men become what they persistently think, and their thoughts create their future states. To control what a man thinks is the final act of irreversible enslavement.

The prevailing reality appears to be that there exists a Pied Piper virus that destroys the fundamental meaning of "Independence," where that meaning has to do with a nation making up its own mind about the kind of society it wishes to generate and sustain. Since he who pays the Piper calls the tune, the ability of the impecunious to cause a tune to be played that accords with their emotional and physical circumstances is near non-existent. **All** the world dominated by the Piper **must** dance to his music or not dance at all. As in Hamelin (there is tremendous pressure to make all the less developed world Hamelin) the children and the rats feel a compulsion to follow the Piper to God knows where - certainly not to where they individually or consensually have rationally determined they wish to go.

It is against this background that my mind rebels against the persistent loose usage of some terms, and there is one particular term on which this essay wishes to focus. By way of introductory preparation let us divert by looking superficially at the non-usefulness of one of the other terms - *"Transparency."* That look will provide an example of the need to examine carefully the analytical value of each of these terms we have adopted.

Current thinking appears to want to insist that "Transparency" is a fundamental requirement of good governance. That this **cannot** be true derives directly from the fact that governing cannot but take place in a milieu of non-benign competition among nations, corporate entities, individuals, and individual groupings with non-coincident interests. That is a characteristic of the real world. In the context of that reality, sometimes it is "best" to ensure that your competitors know what you're going to do. At other times it is immaterial whether they know since their knowing what you're going to do cannot lead to any action injurious to you or in any way inhibitory of your success. At yet other times it is overwhelmingly important that the competition not know what you're intending, lest they effectively counter your action and prevent you from achieving your objective. Accordingly, that *"transparency should characterise your behaviour"* is True, Immaterial, or False, depending on the nature of the competitive activity in which you are involved - regardless of whether you are an individual, a corporate entity, a Political Party, or a national Government making decisions for the State. Thus for it to be true that "Transparency" is a fundamental requirement of any specific aspect of good governance requires "Transparency" to be given a special meaning and for the competitive context related to that aspect to have special characteristics. These special requirements imply the non-usefulness of the term as a **general** test for correctness of action.

If *"Transparency"* is interpreted to mean *"making public what the Government has done, after it has done it,"* the issues become quite different and requirements of final disclosure by the Government become justifiable.

Now let us go to the term on which I really wish to focus - **"Democracy."** I have elsewhere initiated a general discussion of some of the complexities associated with Democracy and Decision Making [cf. *Chapter 1 of BUNARO* (Section B. Democracy, Consensus, National Interest, and Decision Making)]. This essay directs its focus more narrowly on Guyana (and hopefully by extension on other Caricom territories) and on the interpretation of voting as a basis for deciding 'who should govern us'.

Most of us are given to understand, and subscribe to the correctness of the view, that the way in which democratic societies make decisions about whom they should be governed by, is by voting in "free and fair elections" held for the purpose of choosing between two or more contestants. The difficulties of giving effect to that general principle have been recognised for the longest while (certainly since the eighteenth century when the philosophers Jean-Charles de Borda, the Marquis de Condorcet and others wrote and otherwise commented on the problem). The essential task is one of ascertaining individual opinions on choices, and then aggregating the individual opinions that have been ascertained into a declared overall societal choice or consensus. Usually, the relatively straightforward but not entirely simple part is that of ascertaining what each individual voter has chosen. The difficult part is going from those individual choices to a unique result of what the voters, taken as a whole, have impliedly said!

Before we look at the specifics of the Guyana situation, it is instructive to get a feel for the problem by examining the following example based on a model constructed by William F. Lucas[51].

---

51   [0]*l*.The Appendix to this essay gives an example of this problem drawn from real life. It refers to the attempt by one of our statutory bodies to determine who should fill an important post in a Ministry. The names have been changed but the numbers are exact.

Assume that there is a club of 55 persons who are attempting to determine by voting who should be their President. There are five candidates - Alfred; Bert; Charles; Dennis; and Eddie. Assume also, that to effect that choice the question put to a vote requires not only an indication of whom each voter has as first choice to be President, but also requires an indication of the relative rankings of the candidates. Thus each voter indicates their first choice, their second choice, their third choice, their fourth choice, and their fifth choice. The results of the voting - free, fair, and by secret ballot - were:

	1st Choice	*2nd Choice*	*3rd Choice*	*4th Choice*	*5th Choice*
18 Voters	Alfred	Dennis	Eddie	Charles	Bert
12 Voters	Bert	Eddie	Dennis	Charles	Alfred
10 Voters	Charles	Bert	Eddie	Dennis	Alfred
9 Voters	Dennis	Charles	Eddie	Bert	Alfred
4 Voters	Eddie	Bert	Dennis	Charles	Alfred
2 Voters	Eddie	Charles	Dennis	Bert	Alfred

What have the voters, taken as a whole, said about who should be President of the club?

An answer could be derived by using the rule that the person securing the most first preferences should win. This "plurality" method would declare **Alfred to be President.**

Another method could be that of saying that of the two persons securing the most first preferences, the more popular should be chosen. The choice would then be between Alfred and Bert. There are 18 voters who prefer Alfred to Bert, but 37 who prefer Bert to Alfred. On this basis, **Bert should be declared President.**

A third method of arriving at the club's consensus is also appealing. In this method we repeatedly throw out the person with the least first preferences, and re-look at what the first place preferences then become. Thus, we would eliminate Eddie as having the least first preferences, and derive the result that in the absence of Eddie, Alfred would still have 18 first preferences, Bert would now have 16, Charles would have 12, and Dennis would still have 9. We would then eliminate Dennis as now having the least first preferences, and derive a new ranking which says that if we are not going to have either Eddie or Dennis as President, the voting results indicate that Alfred would have 18 first preferences, Bert would have 16, and Charles would have 21. We would then eliminate Bert as having the least first preferences at this stage, and derive the answer that **Charles should be President** by virtue of his having the most first preferences (37 compared with Alfred's 18) in the absence of those progressively eliminated by this method.

A fourth method, based on awarding points for the ranks earned by each candidate (5 for a first place, 4 for a second place, 3 for a third place, 2 for a fourth place, and 1 for fifth) yields the points allocation based on the voting results of:
Alfred - 127; Bert - 156; Charles - 162 ; Dennis - 191; Eddie - 189.

This so-called Borda count method indicates that **Dennis should be declared President.**

A fifth method is to pick as President the person who when compared with any other person in pairwise comparisons is the most popular. Eddie beats every other candidate in these pairwise comparisons. In comparison with Alfred, Eddie is preferred 19 more times ; with Bert, Eddie is preferred 11 more times; with Charles, Eddie is preferred 17 more times; and with Dennis, Eddie is preferred 1 more time - so **Eddie should be chosen as President.**[52]

Each of these five methods has a claim to rationality, and therefore its conclusion has a claim to validity. Each of the methods purports to be interpreting what the voters, taken as a whole, have said. **Yet each method supports a different person for the position of President!** Which one should be chosen?

In summary, the demonstrated fact[53] is that there exists no foolproof way of always deriving group preferences from individual choices where that derivation meets some minimal conditions for acceptability with respect to "fairness", "non-dictatorialness", and "consistency".

Every voting system has flaws and allows undesirable consequences, but depending on the circumstances some are more appropriate (better?) than others.

---

52   ^{0}2. *In the jargon of these matters, Eddie is called the Condorcet winner.*
53   ^{0} 3. *The mathematical economist Kenneth J Arrow proved what is known as the Impossibility Theorem on this matter and was awarded the Nobel Prize in 1972 for this and related work on social choice.*

The following paragraphs and tables demonstrate some of these problems in the specific case of General Elections in Guyana. For the sake of definiteness the statistical data used refers to the 5 October, 1992 General Elections. Those results are set out in Table 1 below.

Table 1. 1992 General Elections - Percentages and Votes

	PPP	PNC	WPA	TUF	DLM	
REGION	(PERCENTAGES)					VOTES
1	31.85	**51.18**	2.03	12.70	1.12	**4,726**
2	**63.01**	29.80	0.80	0.74	1.22	**18,338**
3	**72.59**	25.12	0.90	0.31	0.74	**42,803**
4	41.74	**54.27**	2.97	0.47	0.22	**121,685**
5	**61.59**	37.01	0.53	0.28	0.16	**24,380**
6	**75.75**	22.35	0.49	0.24	0.68	**62,525**
7	26.45	**68.33**	2.47	1.67	0.34	**6,409**
8	29.44	**44.19**	24.39	0.45	0.59	**2,021**
9	32.97	**37.01**	4.36	25.45	0.00	**5,274**
10	4.88	**89.04**	3.45	0.42	1.35	**14,858**
TOT Votes	162,053	128,125	6,068	3,183	1,557	303,019
PR %	**53.48**	42.28	2.00	1.05	0.51	100
SUM %	440.27	**458.30**	42.39	42.73	6.42	

(The Table deals with only the top five contesting parties based on PR%)

INTERPRETATION #1

The Table highlights the fact that under the current system of PR[54] the winning Party is deemed to be the **PPP with 53.48%** of the overall vote.

INTERPRETATION #2

If, however, the results of the voting were treated in a manner analogous to that in which we often treat examination scores - that is we behave as if

54 [0] 4. *It should be noted that there are very many types of PR systems. The one we use is a list PR system (i.e. one in which voters vote for a list of candidates), and seats are allocated according to the Hare quota and the Largest Remainders after application of the quota.*

the contestants had taken ten (10) examinations and scored percentages as indicated in the table - then the last row of the Table which shows the totals of their percentage scores on each of the ten "examinations" would declare the **"best" overall performer** to be the **PNC with 458.30 percentage points**!

INTERPRETATION #3

The conceptual basis of the second interpretation relates naturally to another method we often use to determine the overall results of competitions - it is the one most prevalent in dealing with athletic competitions, but is also used in other cases.   It is the method based on rank performances in the various events, e.g numbers of Gold, Silver, and Bronze medals won. Table 2 below translates the results of Table 1 above into ranks, i.e. 1st, 2nd, 3rd, 4th, and 5th with respective ranks of 1, 2, 3, 4, 5.

Table 2. **1992 General Elections - Rank Performances and Votes**

	PPP	PNC	WPA	TUF	DLM	
REGION	(RANKINGS)					**VOTES**
1	2	1	4	3	5	**4,726**
2	1	2	4	5	3	**18,338**
3	1	2	3	5	4	**42,803**
4	2	1	5	4	3	**121,685**
5	1	2	3	4	5	**24,380**
6	1	2	4	5	3	**62,525**
7	2	1	3	4	5	**6,409**
8	2	1	3	5	4	**2,021**
9	2	1	4	3	5	**5,274**
10	2	1	3	5	4	**14,858**
BORDA COUNT	44	46	24	17	19	
	PPP	PNC	WPA	TUF	DLM	POINTS
RANK 1	4	6	0	0	0	**5**
RANK 2	6	4	0	0	0	**4**
RANK 3	0	0	5	2	3	**3**
RANK 4	0	0	4	3	3	**2**
RANK 5	0	0	1	5	4	**1**

The Table records that the PNC had 6 first places and 4 second places, while the PPP had 4 first places and 6 second places. On this basis the Borda Count[55] declares the PNC performance to have been the best overall performance. Interestingly, the third best performer by this method is clearly the WPA, and the TUF is relegated to fifth!

If the practice of considering only the top 3 contenders in the race is used, then the 53 General Election seats in Parliament might be allocated in proportion to their Borda Counts and would yield 40.4% of the seats for the PNC; 38.6% for the PPP; and 21.0% for the WPA - yielding PNC- 22 seats; PPP- 20 seats; and WPA- 11 seats.

In terms of the currently popular practice of deeming the General Elections to be a statement of the mandate given to the winning Political Party by the electorate, it is interesting to note that the six(6) Regions which deem the PNC to be their first choice contain 154,973 of the total votes cast of 303,019; i.e. 51%; while the four(4) Regions that deem the PPP to be their first choice contain 148,046 voters, i.e. 49% of the votes cast. If one interprets these numbers on the basis of what the society is saying as a matter of consensus, the result clearly conflicts with the answers derived by the straight application of Guyana's PR formula![56]

The three interpretations given above clearly do not cover the totality of possible variations in interpreting the society's view based on the results of individual votes. They do however raise some interesting questions about what the society has indeed said about whom it should be governed by. Statistically (as opposed to what the Constitution decrees) it is a moot point as to who has been given what mandate (cf. the Lucas example above). Precisely what mandate has been given to whom becomes a moot point if **all** the information inherent in the voting results is taken into consideration

---

55 ⁰ *5. Based on 5 points for first place, 4 points for second place, 3 points for third place, 2 points for fourth place, and 1 point for fifth place.*

56 ⁰*6. The explanation of this apparent contradiction lies in understanding the effect and distribution of the Power Indices (discussed later in this essay) of the 10 Electoral Districts. The Electoral Districts in which the PNC and the PPP respectively won, with their Power Indices given in square brackets, are as follows:*
PNC wins:
District 4[408]; District 10[48]; District 1[16]; District 7[16]; District 9[16]; District 8[0].
PPP wins:
District 3[104]; District 6[104]; District 5[72]; District 2[48]

- just as in the case of the 55 person club discussed earlier[57]. Even if one cannot resist the urge to choose one statistical interpretation in preference to any other on the basis of one's own political bias, it remains useful to note that the problems and ambiguities inherent in voting systems and the interpretation of their results are realities of democracy. With such realities in mind, the temptation to believe one's own, or anybody else's, rhetoric about the mandate which the society has given any particular political party can be resisted. Such resistance is necessary if the concept of representativeness in decision making is to be given pride of place in the matter of who governs us.

This issue of representativeness in decision making leads to at least two questions that will now be pursued. The first has to do with the implications of the voting system about the power to influence decisions; and the second has to do with mechanisms that we choose to use in attempting to ensure that voter preferences inform the composition of the group assigned the responsibility for governmental decision making.

A convenient point of departure for dealing with the first aspect of the power to influence decisions, is a re-look at the concept of one person, one vote. The current presumption, taken as a self-evident truth, is that there is equity in the equality of each person having one vote to exercise. On the basis of this equality it is presumed that each person has an equal say **and therefore the same degree of influence** in determining which Party is mandated to form the Government.

The assumed synonymity of "equal say" and "same degree of influence" is worthy of our attention. Is it indeed true that the equality of influence which *"one person, one vote"* allegedly gives to individuals translates into equality of influence for groups of individuals? More specifically, does equality of influence on an individual basis translate into equality of influence among the ten Regions into which Guyana is divided for electoral

57   [0] 7. *Though there may be ambiguity about who has been given what mandate, that a mandate has been given (in the sense that a consensus has been expressed) is supported by an interesting statistical measure. This measure, Kendall's Coefficient of Concordance, is a test of how close the consensus is among those judging - in this case the 10 Regions. For the statistically inclined it may be noted that Kendall's Coefficient of Concordance calculates as 0.778 - associated with a Chi-Square of 31.12 with 4 Degrees of Freedom. The 1% Probability level for Chi-Square with 4 degrees of freedom is 13.28. Put simply, the voters were pretty much at one on the matter of how overall they ranked the contesting Parties!*

and other purposes? Or do some Regions exert greater influence than others in the determination of which Party shall govern us? And if I reside in one of the Regions that exerts lesser influence, am I as an individual not exerting less influence than someone who resides in a more powerful Region?

To facilitate the investigation we need to introduce the concept of a **"Power Index"**. The following example does so.

Assume that in an election a candidate is aware that there are four charismatic individuals (Tom, Harry, Dick, and Joan) each of whom can influence groups of voters to vote for or against the candidate. Of a total of 58 voters, Tom controls 18, Harry controls 20, Dick 12, and Joan 8.

There are seven (7) possible combinations or coalitions of voter types which include Tom, viz.: Tom/Harry; Tom/Dick; Tom/Joan; Tom/Harry/Dick; Tom/Harry/Joan; Tom/Dick/Joan; and Tom/Harry/Dick/Joan. If we define a **"winning coalition"** as one that provides more than 29 votes (one-half of 58) for the candidate, then there are six (6) winning coalitions that include Tom, viz.: Tom/Harry (38); Tom/Dick (30); Tom/Harry/Dick (50); Tom/Harry/Joan (46); Tom/Dick/Joan (38); and Tom/Harry/Dick/ Joan (58). Of these six (6) winning coalitions, four (4) of them would not remain winning coalitions if Tom withdrew his 18 vote support for the candidate. These are: Tom/Harry; Tom/Dick; Tom/Harry /Joan; and Tom/ Dick/Joan, where support would drop to 20; 12; 28; and 20 respectively. We define Tom's **"Power Index"** to be **4**, meaning that there are four (4) coalitions of all the coalitions to which Tom might belong, for which Tom's support is required for the coalition to be a winning one. **Tom's support is of pivotal influence in only these 4.**

To ensure a clear understanding of this "Power Index" concept, the reader should verify that Harry's Power Index is also four (4); that Dick's is four (4); and that Joan's is zero (0). It should be noted that Tom, Harry, and Dick all have the same Power Index, even though they control different numbers of voters. One conclusion that could be drawn is that the candidate need not bother to court Joan's support since there is no coalition for which what she does will change it from a winning coalition into a losing one! Another is that the candidate would be ill-advised to consider Harry more important than Dick because Harry controls 67% more votes than Dick! Tom, Dick, and Harry merit equally strong lobbying by the candidate because they are of equal influence, as measured by the equality of their Power Indices.

Let us now perform the thought experiment of treating each Region as a homogeneous unit[58], and asking the following hypothetical systemic question for each Region:

> *If all voters in a Region voted the same way*[59], *for how many coalitions*[60] *with one or more other Regions would a specified Region's view make the difference between a Party getting more than or less than 50% of the total votes cast?*

We can define that number of coalitions as the **"Power Index"** of the specified Region. Conceptually, such a Power Index does give a systemic measure of how influential a particular Region potentially is in determining which Party wins a simple majority in the election.

To facilitate the examination let us revert to the actual 1992 statistics of the ten Electoral Districts and the voters distributed across those Districts. The following Table provides that information, where for convenience (and with no impact on the argument or its conclusions) the numbers of voters are taken as the numbers of valid votes cast, as opposed to the numbers registered to vote. The ten Regions are ranked by Power Index.

---

58   [0] *8. This is not as unreasonable an assumption as it may at first blush appear, since the Regions have been allegedly demarcated to achieve homogeneity on geographical, economic, and social dimensions. It is therefore not inappropriate to consider a Regional consensual community of interest.*

59   [0] *9. We therefore allow differences across Regions, but not within Regions. Each Region's consensus is treated as a unanimously held view within the Region, thereby treating the Region as if it contributed a bloc of votes favouring the consensual opinion.*

60   [0]*10. There are 511 coalitions to consider for each of the ten Regions.*

POWER INDICES AND RANKING
OF
ELECTORAL DISTRICTS

Electoral District	Valid Votes	Seats On Basis of PR	Power Index	Ratios Of Power Indices	PERCENTAGE COMPARISON OF POWER INDICES
4	121,685	21	408	25.50	49.0%
3	42,803	8	104	6.50	12.5%
6	62,525	11	104	6.50	12.5%
5	24,380	4	72	4.50	8.7%
10	14,858	3	48	3.00	5.8%
2	18,338	3	48	3.00	5.8%
7	6,409	1	16	1.00	1.9%
9	5,274	1	16	1.00	1.9%
1	4,726	1	16	1.00	1.9%
8	2,021	0	0	0.00	0.0%
TOTALS	303,019	53			100.0%

The Table indicates that Region 4 is the most influential Region, being 25.5 times as influential as each of Regions 7, 9, and 1, and wielding nearly half the influence of all the Regions put together. By this measure, poor Region 8 wields no influence at all! Indeed, generally, the Hinterland Regions wield little influence by comparison with their coastal counterparts[61] - **so much for this being the decade of the Indigenous People!** [62] *(The Table makes it obvious, but it is nevertheless useful to point out, that the Power Index is not simply determined as being proportional to the number of*

61 ⁰ *11. This imbalance can be corrected by allocating seats to Regions in such a manner that the Power Index of each Region is a constant multiple of the number of voters in the Region - a tricky bit of arithmetic not likely to be undertaken by the coastal seat of Government as a basis for Constitutional reform.*

62 ⁰ *12. I am reminded of the comment in the United States Department of State's Country Reports on Human Rights Practices for 1994, which states about Amerindians:* **"Their standard of living is much lower than that of most Guyanese, and their ability to participate in decisions affecting their lands, cultures, traditions, and the allocation of natural resources is limited."** *The extant voting system is a component of this lack of "empowerment".*

voters in the Region as the second and fourth columns clearly indicate. For example, Region 7 is no more influential than Region 1, and Region 4 is nearly four times as influential as Region 6.)

Obviously, all Regions are not created equal, and some Regions are more equal than others, as indeed are their voting inhabitants, in the matter of influencing who wins the Elections.

Let us now turn to the issues of governmental decision making. Everyone knows that Parliament (or more strictly the National Assembly) is not the main forum in which Governmental decision making takes place.

Given its infrequency of convening, and the selectiveness that attends the issues which it considers, it is clear that Parliament was never intended to, and cannot, be that main forum. The main forum is the Ministerial structure, including the Cabinet. Nevertheless, let us make the erroneous assumption that Parliament **is** the main forum on which we should focus to ensure as close as possible a reflection of expressed voter preferences. The following Table 4 is a good device for highlighting what we in fact do.

PARTY BREAKDOWN OF MEMBERS OF
THE NATIONAL ASSEMBLY
(As at October 10, 1996)

Table 4

	PPP/C	PNC	WPA	TUF	Totals
From the General Elections	28	23	1	1	53
	53%	43%	2%	2%	100%
From the NCLDO	1		1		2
From the Regions	7	3			10
Total Elected	36	26	2	1	65
	55%	40%	3%	2%	100%
Non-Elected Ministers (Non-Voting)	6*				6
Total Elected & Non-Elected	42	26	2	1	71
Speaker (Non-Voting)	1				1
Totals	43	26	2	1	72
	60%	36%	3%	1%	100%

As of October 11, 1996 this number was increased by 2 to 8.

If decision-making **is** influenced by the voices that can be raised in any debate in the Assembly, and we wish the balance of voices available to participate to represent the relative Party percentages as determined by the results of the General and Regional Elections, that objective is totally thwarted by the device of adding Non-Elected Ministers to the Assembly, exacerbating the skewness already introduced by horse-trading the results of the Regional Elections. The more non-elected Ministers we introduce the worse the problem becomes (cf. the first and last % rows of the Table)!

In any event, the argument being put is that if there is to be an attempt to have the composition and the deliberations of the group to be assigned the responsibility for governmental decision making reflect the expressed voter preferences, the mechanisms to ensure achievement of that objective must focus not only on the composition of Parliament, but even more on the composition of the Ministerial structure and the Cabinet. A Ministerial structure and Cabinet comprising only members of the Party deemed *(most likely ambiguously in terms of what the societal consensus is)* to have won the Election cannot possibly reflect voter preferences on this matter.

Declaration of the winning Party arising from the Election is at best a statement primarily about the societal consensus on the vision which that Party has for the society and the methods of making that vision a reality. What the society taken as a whole has said about who has won has already been shown to be very likely to be ambiguous. The variations of views of the voters need to be reflected in the composition of the Ministerial structure and the Cabinet. If those variations are not so reflected, then the major governmental decision-making forum will not be reflective of the electorate's view and the "democratic" process will have been thwarted.

Attempts at collaboration by the method of the winning Party consulting on a case-by-case basis with the other Parties represented in Parliament **must** turn out to be inadequate, unsatisfying to all concerned, and not reflective of the electorate's preferences.

There are several reasons for this, not the least of which are:
> (a) That such attempts cannot escape being sporadic, given the overall necessary fast pace of responsible government decision making;
> (b) That such attempts represent discussion among participants whose access to information in the government system is severely unequal; and

(c) That final responsibility for the decisions eventually made is not shared equally among the participants in the discussions leading to those decisions.

These types of inhibitions can be overcome if, and only if, the decision making forums routinely contain members whose views represent those of the other Parties in Parliament. Then, and only then, will deliberations routinely benefit from the vantage points of all the Parties which the electorate chose to place in Parliament.

This is **not** an argument for a national consensus Government! It is simply a statement of a statistical fact, rather than a plea for political horse trading. The winning Party must be made to operate under the **obligation** to include representatives of the other Parties represented in Parliament in Ministerial and Cabinet positions that comprise the forums for routine government decision making. While the Party deemed to have won the Election is required to form a Government, that requirement should be met **in keeping with the views that the electorate has expressed about the non-winning contestants** - and that is not capable of being handled with finality in Parliament while the Ministerial structure and the Cabinet comprise only members of the winning Party.

Also, as I have argued elsewhere (cf. The Essay *"The Term of Government"*) in the context of our shortage of human resources it is highly unlikely that the best Ministerial team to govern can be found from among only members of the "winning" Party. Thus both prudence (or the absence of arrogance), and the "democratic" dictates of translating voter preference into our governing mechanisms and decision making, argue for a system in which the "winning" Party accepts the responsibility to govern, and also honours the requirement to structure its governing team (Ministers and Cabinet) to reflect voter preferences and to pursue the "best" composition of administrative and analytical talent.

Admittedly, this approach will make the job of the President more complex, demanding as it will the ability to take account continually of the variations in vantage points represented among his Ministers and in his Cabinet, and to manage a possibly rambunctious team of strong individuals some of whom do not owe him political loyalty. But whoever said that the job of President of the country was supposed to be easy? And certainly this next step along the road of "democracy" should not be eschewed purely on the basis of possible difficulty!

Members of the society can then support the Government without necessarily changing their Party loyalties, and debates in Parliament will be far better informed. Who governs us will be then more reflective of the electorate's perspectives, and the chances for creative problem solving will have been enhanced by the bringing to bear of more diversified views. In any event, the continual formal process of *"creative problem solving"* **requires** a proliferation of vantage points for each problem faced.

I recollect the comment by Sydney J. Harris that *"The chief test of civilisation is the amount of "difference" it can tolerate and absorb, the one characteristic of all primitive societies is a horror of diversity."* [63] I juxtapose this idea with my perception that the task of the President is to stimulate nationally a harmonising process out of which should come a synergy of individual talents. This synergy could generate a wave of creative problem solving in relation to the most resistant problems of development. What better place to begin, in a civilised society, than with the Cabinet! Of course, if you embrace as correct the following statement attributed to Walter Lippman: *"A democratic society might be defined... as one in which the majority is always prepared to put down a revolutionary minority,"* then all the above would have been of little more than passing academic interest. But you should be uncomfortable if, on the other hand, you subscribe to the view of James Russell Lowell that *"Democracy is that form of society, no matter what its political classification, in which every man has a chance and knows that he has it."*

END

---

63 [0] *13. Mark you, by this measure it is tempting to conclude that many a developed country, and perhaps the world taken as a whole, is slipping into a technologically advanced "primitive" and "less civilised" state. After Hems-Burton, Castro might be inclined to agree; as indeed, for similar reasons, might the top Administration of the UN!*

APPENDIX (Commentary on an Actual Case)

The Problem

The six (6) members of a Statutory Body set out to choose the best candidate from among four (4) applicants (A, B, C, & D). Their decision was to be based on the results of the six members, a group that included the Chairman of the Statutory Body, having each ranked the candidates. Those individual rankings produced the following composite results:

3 persons preferred	A to B to C to D
1 person preferred	D to B to A to C
1 person preferred	D to A to B to C
1 person preferred	D to A to C to B

The task was to interpret these results as a consensual decision - i.e. to answer the question **"What is the consensus on who is the best candidate?"** It was the classic case of deriving a group decision from, and consistent with, individually expressed opinions.

The Solution

(1)   In cases such as this, it is not unusual to use the decision rule: **"Pick the best candidate as the one with the most first choices."** In this case, however, this rule does not prove to have enough discriminatory power to derive a unique answer. There are two candidates (A & D) each with 3 first choices. It is not consistent with the information contained in the rankings, and therefore statistically incorrect, to conclude that these two candidates have been equally favoured by the group. Declaring the result a "tie" is based on making this statistical error. It is the insufficiency of the rule rather than the inherent equality of the candidates that should be highlighted.

(2)   Particularly in cases such as this, another decision rule can be utilised. This is the device known formally as the **"Borda Count."** This rule takes account of all the rankings. It assigns points in the following manner: 5 points for first place; 4 for second place; 3 for third place; 2 for second place; and 1 for fourth place; and calculates a score - the candidate's Borda Count - for each candidate ranked. Application of this rule produces the following result:

CANDIDATE	BORDA COUNT			RANK
A	$3 \times 5 + 2 \times 4 + 1 \times 3$	$= 15 + 8 + 3$	$= 26$	1
B	$4 \times 4 + 1 \times 3 + 1 \times 1$	$= 16 + 3 + 1$	$= 20$	2
C	$4 \times 3 + 2 \times 1$	$= 12 + 2$	$= 14$	4
D	$3 \times 5 + 3 \times 1$	$= 15 + 3$	$= 18$	3

A should be chosen; and the illusion that A and D are equally preferred is certainly destroyed by use of the Borda Count.

(3)   Two more comments may be useful in throwing light on the statistical peculiarities of the problem. The first comes about by considering **"Pairwise Comparisons."** This is the technique of counting the number of more times a candidate is chosen in preference to a competitor.

> A is preferred 4 more times than B
> A is preferred 6 more times than C
> B is preferred 4 more times than C
> D is preferred 0 more times than A
> D is preferred 0 more times than B
> D is preferred 0 more times than C

The consensual view could not possibly be that D is the consensually preferred candidate. The equality of preference between D and A is illusory.

The second comment deals with this illusion of the A/D equality of preference based on simply the number of first choices being equal. If D is equally preferred to A in a consensual manner, and they are both equally superior to the other candidates, then if A were removed from the competition D should be the clear winner. This amendment (i.e. the removal of A) if made to the actual rankings would show that D continues to have 3 first preferences while B would then also have 3 - hardly statistical evidence of D's dominance over **all** the remaining competition. On the other hand, if D is removed from the competition, A would have 5 first preferences, and B would have 1, indicating the clear dominance of A over all the remaining competition.

(4)   As a final comment on the matter, I draw attention to the fact that in the circumstance in which the Chairman was a member of the 6 persons doing the original ranking, then the device of using the Chairman's vote as a **"tie-breaker"** is statistically equivalent to introducing a seventh person into the ranking exercise where that person's view is identical with that of the Chairman (*The Chairman's ranking was A-2; B-4; C-3; D-1)* . Predictably, this would give D 4 first places to A's 3! This is statistically indefensible as a method for deriving a group decision from the individually expressed opinions!

As indicated in the footnote referring to this Appendix, this is an actual case! I am not surprised that the Chairman's declaration that D should be given the job led to formal objections by the other Commission members, and to accusations of ethnic bias in the public's attempt to understand the decision.

END

Appendix # 6
Whither goest we?[1996]

(Some worrying Conjectures by an Afro-Guyanese Quinquagenerian)

> *We're poor little lambs who've lost our way,*
> *Baa! Baa! Baa!*
> *We're little black sheep who've gone astray,*
> *Baa-aa-aa!*
> *Gentlemen rankers out on the spree,*
> *Damned from here to Eternity,*
> *God ha' mercy on such as we,*
> *Baa! Ya! Baa!*
>
> *Rudyard Kipling*

This essay takes its title from that of a book on which I am working, and represents a kind of summary of some of the main ideas with which that book will deal. The ideas, however, should not be made to wait for their introduction to this collection of heretical works because they are associated with the urgency of survival; and because also I subscribe to the truth and relevance of the quotation from Oliver Wendell Holmes used in the introduction to this volume, i.e. that *"Many ideas grow better when transplanted into another mind than the one where they sprang up."* It is for these reasons that I now provide these 'shorts' or 'trailer' to the 'coming attraction' of the book, in the tradition of the cinema (the theatre as we called it then) when I was a little boy interested in 'serials' like Fu Manchu.

The urgency to which I have alluded in the paragraph above has to do with the impact of ideas on our actions. There has always been a problem of correlating our actions with our rhetoric. This is partly because we have never properly applied the cybernetic approach to dealing with our development problems. Ours has not been the systemic approach of setting targets, of assiduously monitoring actual performances, of checking how what is actually resulting as we try to implement our cherished strategies compares with the targets we have set, and of then continually adjusting our strategies and actions in response to the variances observed between actuals and targets.

Instead, we have tended to adopt philosophical stances that have informed 'what we should do' and have elevated those stances, at least by implication, to the level of unalterable truths, supposedly invariant over time and changes of circumstances. This problem was difficult enough when our rhetoric comprised our own homemade slogans (Feed, Clothe, House; Making the small man a real man; etc.). Recently, however, we appear to have succumbed to feeding frenzy on imports, using imported slogans. The nuances of these slogans often escape us by virtue of their foreign origins; and we become more prone to treating them as revealed truths, revealed by knowledgeable foreign experts or institutions whom we revere, partly by virtue of our predisposition to xenophilia.

In this context I am reminded of the following quotation from John Maynard Keynes that I consider apt:

> *"The ideas of economists and philosophers, both when they are right and when they are wrong, are more powerful than is commonly understood. Indeed the world is ruled by little else. Practical men, who believe themselves to be quite exempt from any intellectual influences, are usually the slaves of some defunct economist. Madmen in authority, who hear voices in the air, are distilling their frenzy from some academic scribbler of a few years back. I am sure that the power of vested interests is vastly exaggerated compared with the gradual encroachment of ideas."*

I have succumbed to the temptation to coin a word. It is a word that must convey the idea of *'arrogance'*; juxtapose that idea with the descriptions *'false'* and *'foolish'*; capture the notion of *'fragrance'* in the sense that what smells good to some smells awfully bad and repulsive to others (English Blue Stilton cheese?); include the Guyanese usage of the synonym for phallus, i.e. *'cock'*, to mean *'trickery'*; and conjure up the notion of power associated with the Pharaohs of Egypt.

My word is '**PHAROGANCE**'. It is a noun. Its pronunciation is what you phonetically please, as determined by the aspect of the meaning you wish to accent.

The world in which we live, looked at from Guyana's vantage point, appears to be characterised mainly by five Pharogances. These are among the major legacies which many years of virulent, continuous, and continuing colonial domination and praxis have left imprinted on our picture of the world. These pharogances have the status of stereotypical truths. The fundamental set may be stated as follows:

PHAROGANCE # 1

Generally, white people are superior to non-white people, the visual cue being darkness of skin colour.

PHAROGANCE # 2

Though from time to time some group of non-white people may be considered 'honorary white' (e.g. Japanese), the invariant rule is that gradation of skin colour is highly correlated with 'worth' so that black people are at the bottom of the ranking. Melanin is the first measure of human value. As Louis Armstrong sang: *my only sin was the colour of my skin.*

PHAROGANCE # 3

God exists. He is, and has a preference for, white. He resides in the Northern Hemisphere. His emissaries, armed jointly with His infallible prescriptions for remedying the ills of the South, and individually with prophylactic kits to protect them from some of those ills, visit the South primarily during the periods of seasonally inclement weather in the North for the purpose of delivering those prescriptions to the leaders of the South. Rejection of the prescriptions leads to ostracism of the whole country from the comity of sane nations.

PHAROGANCE # 4

Poverty is a disease to which black people, especially the black people of the South, are particularly prone because of their indolence and ignorance of the scientific and other truths known to the whites of the North. The disease would be progressively eradicated if they were to become mentally 'like white', and behave, at least in matters of business, like the Asian groups that have learnt this trick.

PHAROGANCE # 5

A necessary condition for Guyana's overall social well-being is its material well-being as measured by the yardsticks of the materially well off countries of the North, and as propounded by the International Financial Institutions which they control. This serves as justification for accepting as desirable and attainable the objective of closing the material well-being gap between Guyana and rich countries.

These five pharogances appear to circumscribe our thinking, define our goals, and inform our actions in terms of what we try in our efforts to achieve those goals.

It is against this background that this essay seeks to draw attention to three of the points made more carefully and comprehensively in the book mentioned above:

(i)   That we have lost our way in the development safari - no independently determined Promised Land is envisioned, nor is there any compass to tell us where we are going;

(ii)   That in Guyana there exists at least one ethnic group whose need for real emancipation we appear unwilling to recognise and secure;

(iii)   That we're teetering on the edge of chaos because rhetoric, cant and apostrophe, rather than indigenous analysis, underpin our misunderstanding of cooperation.

There are many advantages associated with growing up in the countryside. Not the least of these is early familiarity with the principle that growth and well-being are not synonymous. Every laden fruit tree with blight or hairy worm, every fast growing "maaga" or mangy dog, every fowl with"pip", teaches the lesson. Also, wherever we have grown up, we have been surrounded by examples of differences in growth rates not signalling malady. Children in the same family growing at different rates, pups in the same litter not all growing at the same rate, the short slow-growing boy who suddenly shoots up into a tall adolescent, the chubby girl who loses her baby fat and becomes svelte - all are familiar examples of differential growth rates that signal nothing about ill health, even though there is the colloquialism *"Yu growin so fas yu grow out yu sense"*. One does not have to wait for a formal course in Development Economics, nor need to become a Head of State, to recognise that growth is almost certainly **neither a necessary nor a sufficient condition** for well-being.

Yet, despite all the experience of our childhood and our adulthood, we appear to have agreed to construct, and worship sacrificially at, the altar of 'growth'. For the longest while it has been suspected that economic growth, as measured by the standard economists' measures such as GDP or GNP, is neither a necessary nor a sufficient condition for the well-being of the people in an economy. Its non-sufficiency is coming to be better understood and accepted as the realities of the co-existence of 'growing poverty' and 'growing economy' force this rustic commonsense principle into the hallowed halls of economic development theosophy.

But there are still many cognoscenti who will insist on the necessity of growth, almost as a self-evident truth!

For instance, the World Bank's report of May 1996, entitled "Poverty Reduction and Human Resource Development in the Caribbean" states in a footnote on Page 2 that *"For the purposes of this report, poverty is broadly defined as the inability to attain a minimum standard of living and an acceptable quality of life."* The Executive Summary of that report begins the section labelled **"Causes of poverty"** with the following two paragraphs:

> *"Several complex, interrelated factors have contributed to poverty in the Caribbean. These include low economic growth, macroeconomic instability, deficiencies in the labor market resulting in limited job growth, low productivity and low wages in the informal sector, and a decline in the quality of social services. Accordingly, countries that have sustained high economic growth rates over time and invested heavily in the social sectors have achieved relatively low levels of poverty (for example, Antigua and Barbuda, the Bahamas, Barbados, and St. Kitts and Nevis).*

> *Economic growth is fundamental to poverty reduction. Growth reduces poverty through rising employment, increased labour productivity and higher real wages. Countries in the Caribbean that have sustained positive growth rates and invested heavily in human development such as Antigua and Barbuda, the Bahamas, Barbados, and St. Kitts and Nevis have relatively low levels of poverty. Poverty has increased in countries that have had low or negative growth rates for protracted periods such as Guyana, Haiti, Jamaica, Suriname and Trinidad and Tobago. The low growth is attributed in part to external shocks, such as adverse changes in a country's terms of trade, changes in global demand for a country's exports, changes in the global interest rate on a country's external debt, increases in external borrowing and expansionary monetary and fiscal policies. Although it is not possible to quantify its direct impact on poverty, low growth has resulted in overall declines in per capita gross domestic product (GDP), in real wages, and in social sector expenditures. These combined forces undoubtedly caused poverty to increase some during the 1980s."*

The Heads of Governments of the Caribbean are expected to use this report as an important input to their decision-making on the matters of pursuing the economic well-being of their countries. I personally hope that each Head is familiar with Rudyard Kipling's "Just So Stories"[64] (e.g. How the Camel Got His Hump; How the Whale Got Its Throat; How the Rhinoceros Got His Skin; How the Tiger Got His Stripes) - those stories that are convincing conjectures based on a peculiar use of evidence, and which have the characteristic of reasoning backwards from the fact. Such familiarity **may** give them cause for pause before they accept, as they probably will, the explanations and associated advice of the report.

This essay's conjecture that 'Growth' is neither necessary nor sufficient for well-being does not make growth either unimportant or trivial. What does follow is that 'Growth' should not be given center stage in considerations of the pursuit of economic well-being.

The matter has had light shed on it from a variety of sources. For example, nearly two decades ago, specifically in September 1978, there was published by the Overseas Development Council (ODC) in Monograph # 11, an article by Jams P. Grant entitled *"Disparity reduction rates in social indicators - a proposal for measuring and targeting progress in meeting basic needs."* In the section dealing with "The Measurement of Physical Well Being", both the economy-specific nature of the problem, and the absence of correlation across countries between some macroeconomic measures and measures of physical well-being are starkly highlighted. Where correlation is absent, both necessity and sufficiency are also absent, and causation is an alien.

Grant pointed out that:

> *"The limitations of using per capita income figures alone to measure progress in overcoming the worst consequences of absolute poverty can be illustrated more specifically by noting the experience of several developing countries - as well as of Washington, D.C. In the early 1970's, Costa Rica's life expectancy was roughly comparable to that of Washington, D.C. - although Costa Rica's annual per capita income was approximately $700, while Washington's was well over $5,000. Both Hong Kong, with a per capita income of $1,480, and Jamaica, with a per capita income of $930, have longer life expectancies (72 and 70 years, respectively) and lower infant mortality rates (19 and 26 per thousand births, respectively) than Washington, D.C., which has*

---

64   *They are, time apart, a not distant relative of Sparrow's "Lying Excuses".*

a life expectancy of 66 years and an infant mortality rate of 29 per thousand."

As a response to "the limitations of using per capita income figures alone to measure progress in overcoming the worst consequences of absolute poverty", the article opts for the use of a composite index - the Physical Quality of Life Index (PQLI) - which consolidates three indicators (infant mortality, life expectancy at age one, and literacy) into a single index on a scale of 0 to 100. As ingenious as that PQLI turns out to be in terms of its construction, measures of this kind do not get to the heart of the social dimension problem. For a start, one is still trapped in the web of looking for a universally acceptable measure of quality of life, applicable across countries; and of having to deal with the fact that the currently accepted macroeconomic variables traditionally used to discuss economic performance in a planning context do not correlate neatly with such quality of life measures.

In my view, Grant's monograph (Pages 41 & 42) gives evidence of these aspects in the following words:

> *"....Pakistan and Niger may have very similar per capita GNP figures, but Niger clearly lags in terms of physical well-being. While Sri Lanka's PQLI level is remarkably high, it needs special attention to improvement of its GNP base to ensure maintenance and improvement of its PQLI level in the future; it has urgent need both for increased effective investment growth and for assistance on concessional terms. Conversely, Pakistan (at the same income level as Sri Lanka) and Iran (at a much higher level of per capita income) need to apply special attention to their relatively poor PQLI performances; Pakistan requires substantial concessional assistance to do so. Niger requires substantially increased efforts (and assistance) to advance both growth and physical well-being; Iran and Jamaica, with their relatively high GNP levels and growth rates, do not need concessional assistance for increasing output, but could benefit from selected need-oriented assistance of the types provided by the United Nations Children's Fund and the Inter-American Foundation to accelerate progress among disadvantaged groups."*

This kind of evidence indicates that not only is 'growth' an insufficient parameter on which to focus, but also that there is an intensely economy-specific aspect to identifying economic well-being.

In this matter of measuring economic well-being, it is useful to mention the efforts of the Institute for Research on Poverty of the University of Wisconsin in the USA. The Institute was established in 1966, pursuant to the provisions of the Economic Opportunity Act of 1964, by a grant from the Office of Economic Opportunity. The Institute accepted that its primary objective was *"to foster basic, multidisciplinary research into the nature and causes of poverty and means to combat it."* Bob Haveman, when he was director of the Institute, expressed the view that a large proportion of research by Institute staff could be considered as dealing with the question *"How should economic welfare be measured for policy purposes?"* In the year in which Guyana achieved political independence, leading academics in arguably the 'richest' nation in the world were admitting difficulties in measuring economic well being in their own country.

After a decade of endeavour, there was the published admission by researchers of the Institute that *"issues of appropriately measuring the economic status of families and of defining the poor remain to be settled"*, despite the long history of attempts at the measurement of poverty - at least since 1890 when Charles Booth discussed the development of a poverty line. Work continues, but the problem currently retains elements of intractability.[65]

I suppose that in a very rich economy the issue of poverty **is** an important one; but in a nation like Guyana, both intuition and political rhetoric make it not just important. It becomes **pivotal!** After all, was the political justification for pursuing Independence not the Promised Land of very improved economic well-being for all citizens of the new nation? Where, then, do we as Guyanese stand on this matter?

The position appears to be as follows:
(i)   We have no settled, indigenously determined, consensual view as to how our economic well-being is to be measured. Accordingly, there is no computable definition of the Promised Land, and

---

65   As late as the year 2010, this matter has not been resolved, and I am reminded of the comment by Piet Hein that *'A problem worthy of attack Proves its worth by fighting back.'*

therefore no way of estimating unambiguously whether we are getting closer to or farther away from it.

(ii)   The surrogate measure that we appear to have been persuaded to accept, i.e. economic growth, is easily proven to be neither a necessary nor a sufficient condition for economic well-being. The insufficiency is tending to be recognised by force of the reality, persistence, and pervasiveness of 'poverty', but many still harbour the belief of growth's necessity!

(iii)   In the light of (i) and (ii) above, and in the context of the five Pharogances listed earlier, we cannot but dissipate our energies like hens in their own barnyard, chased round and round and often caught by the roosters of the International Institutions whose development credos we feel constrained to accept and to attempt to apply.

Among the more recent "barnyard" phenomena is the one referred to as "The Private Sector being the engine of growth". The whole concept of 'the engine of growth' is such a mightily inappropriate way of viewing the economy that it would be ludicrous were it not supported by the soi-disant cognoscenti and their followers, just as was the case in the story of the King's new clothes where the King turned out to be naked. To pick any complex adaptive system[66], with its myriad interconnections and interactions among its component parts, to devise some fairly blurry categorisation of those component parts, and then to rank as most important some one group of those artificially classified parts in accounting for the behaviour of the system is to misunderstand considerably the behavioural characteristics of complex adaptive systems. The economy is a complex adaptive system. The 'main cause' notion associated with the term 'engine' is, in this context an inadequate concept. To argue, therefore, about which of the two artificially and vaguely defined sectors, public and private, is the 'engine' is to indulge in an exercise in futility, surpassed only by arguments about whether the private sector is yet capable of undertaking the role of 'engine'. In any event, when such argumentation leads through a focus on 'privatisation' to it being deemed important to decide whether

---

66 This term *'complex adaptive system (cas)'* is used in the sense explained in the book *'Hidden Order - How Adaptation Builds Complexity'* written by John Henry Holland, and published in 1995 by Addison-Wesley. The ideas are not unrelated to those examined in Chapter 1 *of BUNARO (published in 1993)* where the economy is characterised as *'unthinkable.'*

the Government should own 3% of the shares of the Pegasus Hotel, all the bells of disbelief and irrelevance should peal.

We **have** lost our way in the development safari, and have no compass to get onto the right track. Our current compromise is to talk about building the social dimension into plans to generate rapid GDP growth - Development with a human face, we say. This approach is one of trying to have the fundamental and most important subjugated to the incidental. The fundamental purpose or objective of managing the economy is to provide economic well-being. In this endeavour, such growth as arises should be incidental to and driven in its nature and extent by the cybernetically ordered pursuit of well-being. The significance of 'cybernetically' in the previous sentence lies in the idea that our future actions should be determined by the differences between the results of our previous actions and the targets we had set out to achieve. The targets must be determined and put in command as the points of our compass. Management must be made subordinate to objectives and targets; and objectives and targets must be determined by **us** in pursuit of **our** notion of well-being.

This matter of specifying **our** Guyanese notion of well-being lies at the very heart of the idea of being an independent country. Unfortunately, if we were to come up with such a specification of well-being, we would feel a compulsion to 'justify it to the rest of the world, particularly the developed world, for their approval. We have the monumental difficulty of dealing with the reality that we see ourselves as if we are part of the rest of the world that is viewing us.

Perhaps the best insight that I can give into the idea I am trying to bring forth is to quote the words of W.E.B. DuBois from the first chapter of "The Souls of Black Folk", first published in 1903[67]: *"It is a peculiar sensation, this double-consciousness, this sense of always looking at one's self through the eye of others, of measuring one's soul by the tape of a world that looks on in amused contempt and pity."*

Everyone, nations and individuals, has problems, and one of life's most pervasive activities is problem-solving, sometimes in very "creative" ways.

---

67   *Professor Saunders Redding wrote in the Introduction to the paperback edition of this classic: "**The Souls of Black Folk** may be seen as fixing that moment in history when the American Negro began to reject the idea of the world's belonging to white people only, and to think of himself, in concert, as a potential force in the organization of society."*

But the countries deemed 'developing', and their inhabitants, have been slotted into a very special category. It is the category of not only **having** problems, but also of **being** the problem.

In relation to the American Negro, DuBois captured the essence of this same idea in the following words that preceded the statement quoted above:

> *"Between me and the other world there is ever an unasked question: unasked by some through feelings of delicacy, by others through the difficulty of rightly framing it. All, nevertheless, flutter around it. They approach me in a half-hesitant sort of way, eye me curiously or compassionately, and then, instead of saying directly, How does it feel to be a problem? They say, I know an excellent colored man in my town; or, I fought at Mechanics ville; or, Do not these Southern outrages make your blood boil? At these I smile, or am interested, or reduce the boiling to a simmer, as the occasion may require. To the real question, How does it feel to be a problem? I answer seldom a word.*
> *And yet, being a problem is a strange experience - peculiar even for one who has never been anything else, save perhaps in babyhood......"*

As an official dealing with International Financial Institutions on behalf of Guyana as a developing country, I could have said the same thing with relevant amendments to the references to "an excellent colored man in my town", to "Mechanicsville", and to "Southern outrages."

Independence has made little impact on us perceiving ourselves and our economy to **be** a problem. We consistently discuss it from this vantage point among ourselves and with the International Institutions. Yet, we cannot break away from this vantage point without a new sense of self; and as a nation we cannot derive a new sense of self if we do not recognise and deal with the fact that a major ethnic group in our nation has had its history woefully misrepresented or obliterated, its rites of passage forced into defuction, more so than any of the other ethnic groups. I refer here to the Afro Guyanese.

For instance, it is popular and correct these days to note the rapid advance and impact of technology on all aspects of life. Driving these advances are matters of mathematics and science. In both areas, a relatively formally well educated Guyanese can point, even if vaguely, to some contribution that historically the Chinese, or the East Indians, or he Portuguese, or the Europeans, or the Amerindians (the Mayans?) have made to the knowledge in these two areas. Those same Guyanese would be hard put to state, if they rely only on the basis of their formal Guyanese education, any contribution that Africans have made to the world of science (not necromancy) or mathematics. So the average Afro-Guyanese youngster is left by the formal education system to form the opinion that at no time in history did his ancestors contribute to this important body of knowledge; and none of the mooted revisions of the education system appear to be concerned with this aspect!

Similar comments can be of other areas of knowledge and culture, e.g. great world literature, as served up by Guyana's formal education system; and if we focus on females, the same examples will suffice - so the prognosis for the psyche of the Afro Guyanese female is doubly bad, and she will pass all this on to her children, male and female.

Real emancipation cannot occur without the deliberate obliteration of the phenomenon described by DuBois as *'double-consciousness'* , or the correction of the tales comprising the non-history of a significant proportion of our population's ancestors. A fundamental restructuring of our formal education system seems required if these aspects are to be dealt with effectively. In particular, African History needs to be taught at all levels of the formal education system in a manner that would reveal the truth about the contributions of Africa and Africans to world civilisation, including the development of writing, science, medicine, mathematics, architecture, engineering, religion, and the fine arts. But of course no such teaching can take place without knowledgeable teachers and severely changed curricula. I have no reason to believe that such a fundamental restructuring is underway; that if it were mooted it would receive the support of the International Institutions that help finance education projects; and that such a change would attract full support from the general Guyanese public who will probably consider it as the entrenching of racism in favour of Afro Guyanese.

I therefore conclude that in Guyana there exists at least one ethnic group whose need for real emancipation we appear unwilling to recognise and secure; and that for the foreseeable future that group will continue to be perceived and perceive itself as deriving from a race of nobodies, with no worthwhile history in which it could have justifiable pride. The five pharogances, and our entrenched double-consciousness, leave us all (but particularly Afro Guyanese) open to what I call the "Robert Whitmore" jeopardy, after the following poem by the American poet Frank Marshall Davis:

> *"Having attained success in business*
> *possessing three cars*
> *one wife and two mistresses*
> *a home and furniture*
> *talked of by the town*
> *and thrice ruler of the local Elks*
> *Robert Whitmore*
> *died of apoplexy*
> *when a stranger from Georgia*
> *mistook him*
> *for a former Macon waiter."*

The third point this essay seeks to highlight is perhaps best introduced by recounting a story, allegedly true. One place where the story is told is in the book "Jamaica: A Junior History" by Dr Beryl Allen, first published in 1989, and revised in 1993, by Carib Publishing Limited of Jamaica. A paraphrase of the part of the story to which I refer goes as follows:

> *When Columbus and the Spaniards first arrived in Jamaica (5 May, 1494), the then native population, the Arawaks, assumed the Spaniards were Gods. Columbus planted the Spanish flag there, and the Arawaks did not understand what the planting of the flag meant to Columbus. The Arawaks, who allegedly were kind and peaceful, gave Columbus and his entourage gifts of food, otherwise welcomed them, familiarised them with the island, and worked for them. These acts of hospitality, friendship and collaboration, given the Spaniards' interest in gold, facilitated the enslavement of the Arawaks who were driven to work much harder than they were accustomed, or needed to before Columbus' arrival. Understandably, the Arawaks objected to the cruel treatment which included beatings, and this Arawak resistance led to the Spaniards destroying their crops, hunting them with dogs, and brutally killing those who retaliated. It is estimated that 65 years after Columbus' arrival, the entire population of Arawaks in Jamaica had died. This pattern was replicated in Cuba, in Barbados, and in other*

territories where Arawaks had established a tranquil lifestyle with which supposedly they were content.

If we treat this story as a cautionary tale, it will highlight several principles that we are well advised to understand and observe. First, that in all collaborative exercises, one is well advised to apprise one's self of the agendas of those with whom one is collaborating, and of whose agents would-be collaborators are. Second, that we should beware of the analogue of the Arawak "Gods" presumption, arrived at on the bases of strangeness and real or apparent technological superiority. Third, that we should neither distrust our capacity to conduct analyses and to set objectives indigenously, nor uncritically replace those analyses and objectives with imported concepts - our own interests and objectives should be indigenously determined and remain centrally in command, even as we seek to improve them with imports.

One does not have to be paranoid to accept the validity of these cautions. Even as we embrace the rhetoric of the efficacy and relevance of the concept of 'Market Forces', we should recognise its relationship with principle that 'Competition' is a fundamental concomitant of living in a society, and therefore the need to decide when and how to collaborate with others is ever present. The reality of this world, perhaps unpalatable, is that cooperating with others, or exploiting them for personal gain, are the two main ways members of society can interact. Which you choose to do depends on a complex variety of moral, judgmental, and personal objective circumstances. Individuals in groups continually choose between acting selfishly or cooperating for the common good, even when the major hurdle of deciding consensually "what is the common good to be pursued" has been surmounted.

Blinkering out these considerations will leave us ill prepared to deal with a number of jeopardies; not the least of which is that problems of ethnic polarisation and divisiveness can become exacerbated by the disparities between ethnic groups in terms of access to political power, and the distribution of wealth. The fact is that, looked at from an amoral vantage point, crime (e.g. robbery) is simply a device for redistributing wealth from the alleged haves to the have-nots; and crime efficiently executed can pay for the perpetrators! History (including Guyanese history) is replete with examples of business empires that have had their genesis in efficiently executed criminal activity of one kind or another. The passage of time and the accumulation of wealth do tend to rewrite history, but they cannot change the facts. Unpreparedness for dealing with these jeopardies derives from a misunderstanding of the nature of cooperation.

It is against this background that I end this essay with an uncomfortable, apparently xenophobic, question related to the Columbus story. Is there an analogue with the way we treat representatives of international institutions, of foreign governments, and of various other entities who send representatives here? Often, these representatives arrive here, all at sixes and sevens, are deluged with Guyanese hospitality, and subsequently evolve into persons telling us how we ought to live, what we ought to think, and being free to be destructively critical of those whom we choose as leaders - an activity which we are not encouraged to pursue in relation to theirs! Patterns are in the eye of the beholder, and what this essay has sought to say emanates from the eye of an Afro Guyanese quinquagenarian who is committed to living in Guyana, has never met an Arawak, but does recall how a number of Guyanese women avidly pursued rankers of the Black Watch.

Refrain of Despair
How long shall Sambo's problems las'?
For as long as there's life in Sambo's arse.
Anonymous

END

Appendix # 7
Some further Comments on Guyana's Electoral System [1998]

This essay, together with the one to which it refers, i.e PEC, comprised Submission No 11 to the Constitution Reform Commission. The submission was not discussed at any of the meetings of the Commission, despite my prodding as Secretary of that Commission. I concluded that it was simply too heretical, and maybe "too egg-headish". That conclusion was my justification for including it and its companion "PEC" in the collection of "Heretical Musings".

November 13, 1998

A. *INTRODUCTION*
These comments are further to those already made in the two monographs: *"Some of my favourite heresies;"* and *"Some more of my favourite heresies,"* with particular reference to the essays dealing with constitutional reform, the ethnic problem, and who shall govern us. They are also further to the conjecture written separately and entitled PEC (this essay is published as an Appendix to Part II of this book), in conjunction with which they should be read.

The objective of these comments is to suggest **computable criteria** that should be used to judge the acceptability of the electoral system, and to apply them to derive and justify a recommended system for Guyana. The idea is that the recommended system is itself to be the subject of continual review against the yardstick of these computable criteria, thereby allowing stepwise systemic change over time as we review how the system actually performs.

The comments are thus intended to help provide a firm quantitative basis for reform through the process of continual electoral engineering.

This approach is preferred to that of simply looking at how other countries have conducted their affairs, and then attempting to emulate what they have allegedly achieved by adopting and adapting the electoral systems which we feel made such alleged achievements possible. In identifying the criteria to be used, however, the traditional practices, definitions, and formulae in the area of analyses of electoral systems are adhered to; and pride of place is given to the concept of *"representativeness,"* in the sense captured by the following quotation from the opening paragraph of the Introduction to Arend Lijphart's publication: *"Electoral Systems and Party Systems A Study of twenty-seven Democracies, 1945 - 1990."*

> "EXCEPT in very small communities, democracy necessarily means *representative* democracy in which elected officials make decisions on behalf of the people. How are these representatives elected? This indispensable task in representative democracies is performed by the electoral system - the set of methods for translating the citizens' votes into representatives' seats. Thus the electoral system is the most fundamental element of representative democracy."

One source of support for this approach is the following quotation from Paragraph 17 of the Handbook *"Human Rights and Elections (Professional Training Series No.2)":*

> "United Nations human rights standards relating to elections are broad in nature and thus may be achieved through a wide variety of political systems. United Nations electoral assistance does not seek to impose any given political model. Rather, it is based upon a realization that there is no single political system or electoral methodology which is appropriate for all peoples and States. While comparative examples provide useful guidance for the construction of democratic institutions that both respond to domestic concerns and conform to international human rights norms, the best formulation for each jurisdiction will ultimately be that shaped by the particular needs, aspirations and historical realities of the people involved, taken within the framework of international standards."

B. *SOME CONCEPTS and DEFINITIONS*

There are several inter-related dimensions involved in the general idea of ***"representativeness."*** The ones on which this comment will focus are:

    (a) Representation of Regions in the National Assembly.

    (b) The Influence of Regions on the overall Party composition of the National Assembly - Regional Power Indices.

    (c) Disproportionality -the deviation of parties' seat shares in the assembly from their vote shares garnered in the elections.

(d) The effective number of political parties. *(This important aspect is defined and discussed in some detail in later sections of this paper.)*

Each dimension has been chosen, not only for its conceptual relevance to the general idea of representativeness, but also for its capacity to be associated with a computable index. In these indices inhere the advantage of guidance to choose between alternative configurations of electoral systems.

To facilitate the presentation, the following definitions and explanations are offered of terms that will need to be used. Where relevant, the symbol used to refer to the variable is given in brackets.

> ***Electoral Formula:*** This term is used to refer to the mechanism employed to ascertain individual voter choices and to the algorithm applied to convert those individual voter choices into seats gained by each contesting party in the national assembly.

> ***District Magnitude*** (M): The number of representatives elected per electoral district.

> ***Assembly Size:*** The total number of seats to be allocated to all parties represented in the national assembly.

> ***Threshold*** *of Representation* (T): The threshold of representation is the minimum percentage of voter support that a party needs under the most favourable circumstances to earn a seat in the national assembly. If a party passes this threshold it becomes possible for it to win a seat. In the LR-Hare system, the *"threshold of representation"* is given by the formula: 100%/Mp (where p is the number of contesting parties).

> ***Power Index*** (PI): For each Region, this is the answer to the following hypothetical question:
> ***If all voters in a Region voted the same way, for how many coalitions with one or more other Regions, or by itself, would a specified Region's view make the difference between a Party getting more than or less than 50% of the total seats in the assembly?***

The importance of this measure derives from the concerns perhaps best expressed by Paragraphs 68& 69 of the Handbook "Human Rights and

Elections (Professional Training Series No.2), which state as follows with respect to the concept "One person, one vote":

> "68. Universal suffrage is, of course, only one element of fairness. Another is the concept of equal suffrage. This is the idea traditionally expressed as "one person, one vote". Constituency delimitation, registration or polling procedures designed to dilute or discount the votes of particular individuals, groups or geographic areas are unacceptable in the light of the international norm of equality of suffrage. In short, each vote must carry equal weight in order to satisfy the element of fairness.
>
> 69. The 1962 Draft General Principles expressly provide that each vote shall have the same weight and that electoral districts shall be established on an equitable basis, to ensure that the results accurately and completely reflect the will of all the voters."

In addition, Principle XI(b) of the 1962 Draft General Principles deals with the need to ensure: *"the balanced representation of the different elements of the population of a country."*

C. EVALUATION OF THE CURRENT SYSTEM

Appendix (I) of this paper gives a summary description of the current system, and presents the results of the 1992 elections. Since the 1992 elections represent the most recent uncontested results, those results are used as the basis of this evaluation. The liberty is taken of excluding from consideration those contesting political parties that have garnered less than 0.5% of the valid vote in the General Elections. The magnitude of this threshold accords with the practice of analysts who have traditionally looked at similar matters. In the case of the 1992 Guyana elections, it reduces the focus to five (5) of the eleven (11) contesting parties, viz.: the PPP/Civic (53.48%), PNC (42.28%), WPA (2.00%), TUF (1.05%), and the DLM (0.51%), thereby considering 99.32% of the 303,019 valid votes (this total of 303,019 excludes the 171 non-resident votes cast). The evaluation is done with a focus on the four dimensions of representativeness detailed as sections B (a), (b), (c) and (d) of this paper.

(a) Representation of Regions in the National Assembly

The two-tier system which Guyana uses (i.e. ten electoral districts for Regional Elections, with a national district superimposed on the lower-level districts for General Elections) is a form of "complex districting." It ensures that each Region contributes at least one (1) representative to the National Assembly; and that overall, through the choice of two (2) additional representatives from the NCLDO, there are at least twelve (12) representatives originating from the Regions in the National Assembly. Thus, given the Assembly size of 65 members, the Regions are guaranteed, in their own right, a minimum of approximately 18.5% of the seats in the Assembly, although these are expressed in terms of Party affiliation.

This representation should, however, be seen more as representation from the local government (RDC's and the NCLDO) sector rather than from the Regions. Indeed, since only one (1) representative comes from each RDC, the fact that the seats in an RDC are themselves apportioned among parties on a PR basis does not translate into anything significantly different from the single RDC representative in the national assembly having been chosen on a first-past-the-post basis among political parties. None of the inherent advantages of PR systems should therefore be attributed to that part of the existing electoral formula that chooses representatives of the Regions for seats in the national assembly.

There are therefore two questions:
- Whether 18.5% is an appropriate level of representation from the RDC / NCLDO sector; and
- Whether the electoral formula for deriving the representatives at that level of representation is itself adequate (given the preference for a PR formula)[68].

We postpone the attempt to answer these two questions until some other considerations are dealt with; but note at this stage of the argumentation that the answers to the two questions are not independent.

(b) The Influence of Regions on the overall Party composition of the National Assembly. (Regional Power Indices)

We begin by looking at the General Elections, using the 1992 experience to calculate the Power Index of each of the ten (10) Regions. The following **Table 1** shows the results of the calculations.

---

68   The issue of whether we should stay with a PR system, and indeed with LR-Hare is dealt with separately in Appendix II

Table 1.
Power Indices and Ranking of Regions (1992 General Elections)

REGION	Valid Votes	SEATS on PR BASIS	PI	PI / SEATS
4	121,685	21	408	19
3	42,803	8	104	13
6	62,525	11	104	9
5	24,380	4	72	18
10	14,858	3	48	16
2	18,338	3	48	16
7	6,409	1	16	16
9	5,274	1	16	16
1	4,726	1	16	16
8	2,021	0	0	NA
TOTALS	303,019	53		

NA=Not Applicable

For ease of reference we repeat the definition of **"Power Index"** given above in section B.

Power Index (PI)
For each Region, this is the answer to the following hypothetical question:
If all voters in a Region voted the same way, for how many coalitions with one or more other Regions, or by itself, would a specified Region's view make the difference between a Party getting more than or less than 50% of the total seats in the assembly?

For each of the ten Regions there are 511 possible coalitions to be considered.

The most startling and obvious observation is that Region 8 has a PI of zero!

What this means is that in the hypothetical situation where Regions vote as blocs, voters of Region 8, even when acting in concert, make no difference to the matter of any party getting more or less than 50% of the total votes cast, and therefore of the total seats in the assembly associated with the general elections. This, we assert, is an untenable situation in the context of "representativeness."

The situation occurs because of the small voter size of Region 8 which is less that the Hare quota of 5,717 (i.3. 303,019 / 53), leading also to an inability to give meaning to the ratio "Power Index units per seat." We assert that "representativeness" should require that in the General Elections, the electoral formula should endow all Regions with a positive PI.

Also, we suggest that the number of PI units per seat represented by the voter strength of each Region should be roughly equal if Regions are to be considered about equally influential in determining the composition of the national assembly. The rightmost column of Table 1 shows Region 6 as a bit of an anomaly in this respect. We return to this issue in the section dealing with recommendations.

(c) Disproportionality
Of all the dimensions related to "representativeness" this is the one which often attracts most concern. It is simply not tenable to have a system in which there inheres the characteristic that the percentage of seats which a party is awarded in the national assembly differs substantially from the percentage of votes which that party garners in the elections. Indeed, perhaps the strongest argument in favour of the LR-Hare electoral formula is the fact that it is the most proportional formula, thereby not automatically favouring larger parties, and giving smaller parties a "fair" chance to earn seats.

The measure of disproportionality which perhaps best serves our need for a reliable index of disproportionality is Michael Gallagher's least-squares index (LSq). It is defined as follows:
Let

v_i = Percentage of votes garnered by the ith Party
s_i = Percentage of seats in the assembly awarded to the ith Party

Then
$$LSq = \sqrt{(\tfrac{1}{2}\Sigma(v_i - s_i)^2)}$$

LSq = 0 when the percentage of votes garnered equals the percentage of seats awarded to each contesting party; and is larger the larger the disparity between the two. As indicated above at the beginning of this section, parties that have secured less than 0.5% of the votes are excluded from the calculation.

The following Table 2 shows the results of the 1992 elections, and calculates LSq for:
(i)   A - the General Elections (based on the 53 seats so allocated);
(ii)   B -the General and Regional Elections taken together, using the voter shares of the General Elections as the basis of comparison; and
(iii)   C -the seats in the Assembly when non-elected Ministers (who are non-voting members of the Assembly but can contribute to debates) are included, using the voter shares of the General Elections.

Table 2 PARTY BREAKDOWN OF MEMBERS OF THE NATIONAL ASSEMBLY
(As at October 11, 1996)

	PPP/C	PNC	WPA	TUF	DLM	TOT
% Votes earned in General Elections	53.48	42.28	2.00	1.05	0.51	99.32
Seats Allocated on Basis of General Elections	28	23	1	1	0	53
%	53	43	2	2	0	100
Seats Allocated from Regions	7	3	0	0	0	10
Seats Allocated from NCLDO	1	0	1	0	0	2
Total Elected Seats in National Assembly	36	26	2	1	0	65
%	55	40	3	2	0	100
Non-Elected Ministers	8	0	0	0	0	8
Total Seats (Elected & Non- Elected)	44	26	2	1	0	73
Speaker	1					1
TOTAL Seat Representation	45	26	2	1	0	74
%	61	35	3	1	0	100

LSq (A) =1.149 ; LSq (B) =2.290 ; LSq (C) =6.763

Clearly, the part of the electoral formula that adds in representatives of the RDCs & the NCLDO approximately doubles the disproportionality of the composition of the assembly!

This is the result of the Regional seats being the subject of political horse-trading, thereby generating a "manufactured" majority which abandons the proportionality inherent in PR.

The device of adding non-elected Ministers, who can speak in debates even though they cannot vote, increases the influence of disproportionality by nearly a factor of six (6)![69]

These undesirable and indefensible results with respect to disproportionality derive from the mechanics of application of the electoral formula, completely destroying the proportionality which choice of the LR-Hare PR system sought to impose, and which it did capture in the General Elections phase.

It should follow that a different way has to be found to include the influence of the Regions.

(d). The Effective Number of Political Parties.
A short discussion on the concept of "effective number of parties" is necessary for clarity and intuitive understanding. The following are relevant quotations from the Lijphart publication mentioned in section A. Introduction, above.

Page 67 - The Effective Number of Parties
> *"The most important difference among democratic systems is that between two-party and multi-party systems. In parliamentary types of government, two-party systems make one-party majority cabinets possible, whereas such cabinets are not impossible but much less likely in multi-party systems. In presidential forms of government, two-party systems may have two quite different but equally significant results: either the president will enjoy majority support from the legislature or he or she will be faced by a hostile legislative majority. In addition to the distinction between two-party and multi-*

---

69 Little attention should be paid to the fact that I have chosen to treat the "Speaker" as not neutral. Neutral treatment will not make any significant difference to the impact of disproportionality.

party systems, a further distinction must be made between moderate and extreme multi-party systems -with commensurate consequences for cabinet formation in parliamentary systems and legislative support for presidents in presidential systems. The variable that underlies both of the distinctions is the number of parties.

The practical problem in measuring the number of parties is how to count parties of unequal size, and, in particular, how to count very small parties. The assumption in the comparative politics literature has long been that some kind of weighting is necessary. For instance, the British party system has long been described as a two-party system even though, throughout the twentieth century, there have always been more, and usually quite a few more, than two parties in the House of Commons - which means that third parties have simply been discounted."

Thus we cannot claim to be concerned about the representation of smaller parties, about disproportionality, and about "power sharing" in decision-making without considering some measure of the "effective number of parties" generated by our electoral system.

Such a measure called "the effective number of parties," and designated by the symbol "N" has been defined by Markku Laaksco and Rein Taagepera in their publication ' "Effective" Number of Parties: A Measure with Application to West Europe', in Pages 3 - 27 of Comparative Political Studies, 12 (1979).

Using the same definitions given in section C above for v_i an s_i,

$N_{v} = 1/\Sigma v_i^2$ measures the Effective Number of **Elective** Parties; and

$N_{v} = 1/\Sigma s_i^2$ measures the Effective Number of **Parliamentary** Parties.

The distinction between the two indices is that the effective number of parties can be based on either their vote shares or on their seat shares. Because electoral systems tend to favour the larger and to discriminate against the smaller parties, the effective number of parliamentary parties should be expected to be lower than the effective number of elective parties.

An intuitive feel for these indices may be achieved by noting that in a two-party system comprising two equally strong parties, i.e. $v=1/2$ (or $s=1/2$), $N = 2$; whereas if one party is considerably stronger than the other, e.g. respective vote (or seat) shares are 70% and 30%, $N = 1.72$, in accordance with our intuitive judgement that we are moving away from a pure two-party system in the direction of a one-party system. Similarly, if we had three equally strong parties, i.e. $v=1/3$ (or $s=1/3$) for each, N would be 3; and if one were weaker than the other two, N would be somewhere between 2 and 3.

If we consider the three cases based on the 1992 elections, i.e.:

(i)   A - the General Elections (based on the 53 seats so allocated);

(ii)   B -the General and Regional Elections taken together (the 65 seats); and

(iii)   C -the seats in the Assembly when non-elected Ministers (who are non-voting members of the Assembly but can contribute to debates) are included (the 73 MPs with the Speaker);

The following **Table 3** gives the results of the calculations for N(Elective) - i.e. N the effective number of elective parties, and N(Parliamentary) - i.e. N_s the effective number of parliamentary parties:

Table 3

	LSq	N(Elective)	N(Parliamentary)
A	1.149	2.149	2.136
B	2.290	2.149	2.137
C	6.763	2.149	2.024

For convenience we have repeated the Disproportionality indices for cases A, B, and C.

There are a few points worthy of note:

(i)   Disproportionality increases as we go from A to C, and the current system produces a progressively stronger movement towards a pure two-party system in Parliament, **further away from the electorate's wishes for movement in the opposite direction.**

(ii) It is the device of including non-elected ministers in the assembly that increases both disproportionality and the movement **towards** a two-party system.

(iii) The horse-trading in B predictably **increases disproportionality**, and moves the parliament slightly in the direction away from a two-party system as compared with A.

It is instructive to end this section by drawing attention to the following set of observations given in the reference by Lijphart, arising from analyses of the experiences of 27 democracies between 1945 and 1990. The quotation is from Page 144.

> *"Suffice it to say that the conventional assumption that two-party systems make for more effective and stable democracy than multi-party systems is not valid. As I have shown elsewhere, for instance, majoritarian parliamentary systems do not have a better record with regard to either macro-economic management (the stimulation of economic growth and the control of inflation and unemployment) or the maintenance of public order and peace than multi-party parliamentary systems.[70]*

> *What two-party systems do excel in, as G. Bingham Powell has demonstrated, is clear government accountability: the voters know that the governing party is responsible for past government performance, and they can decisively return this party to power or replace it with the other major part[71] But greater accountability does not directly translate into greater responsiveness to citizen interests. There is no evidence that coalition cabinets in multi-party systems are less responsive than one-party majority cabinets; on the contrary, coalition cabinets are usually closer to the centre of the political spectrum - and hence closer in their policy outlook to the average citizen - than one-party cabinets representing either*

70   Arend Lipjhart, 'Constitutional Choices for New Democracies', *Journal of Democracy*, 2 (1991), 72-84.
71   G. Bingham Powell, Jr., 'Constitutional Design and Citizen Electoral Control', *Journal of Theoretical Politics*, 1 (1989), 107-30.

the left or the right.[72] *But it is entirely legitimate, of course, to regard government accountability as a value in and of itself -just as proportionality is an ultimate value for many PR supporters.*

In the final analysis, therefore, the choice between PR (especially one of the more proportional forms of PR) and multipartism on the one hand and plurality and two-party systems on the other depends on personal normative preferences; does one value minority representation and the principle of proportionality more highly than the two-party principle and government accountability, or the other way around? This is not merely a matter of personal taste but also, and probably more so, of cultural background;........"

D. *A SET OF RECOMMENDED CHANGES*

1. Presumptions

P1. Electoral engineering is to become an on-going feature of the processes of our society.

This presumption generates the following corollary assumptions:

(i) there will be established a permanent review body with responsibilities for continual study, review, and reform of the electoral system;

(ii) at no stage will there be a one-shot attempt to devise a perfect system good for all time; and

(iii) the review and reform process will be a cybernetic one characterised by identification of relevant parameters and by the definition and application of target indices.

P1. The process of change will be an iterative, systematic one in which we will identify features for stepwise change and review, rather than an unsystematic one of attempting to tamper with all features at the same time.

P2. We accept the proposition that tampering with the electoral formula for translating votes into seats cannot resolve the

---

72 See S.E. Finer (ed.), *Adversary Politics and Electoral Reform* (London: Anthony Wigram, 1975); and id., 'Adversary Politics and the Eighties', *Electoral Studies*, 1 (1982), 221-30.

problem of ethnic polarisation; and accordingly a special recommendation is required to deal with the problem of voting along ethnic lines. *(PEC attempts to deal with this aspect of the problem)*.

2. Assumptions

A1. The key concern about the electoral system is *"representativeness."*

A2. The relevant quantifiable parameters that will be used for "representativeness" are:

(i) **Representation of Regions in the National Assembly** *(as measured by the number of seats associated with each Region)*;

(ii) **Regional Power Indices** *(the influence of Regions on the overall party composition of the National Assembly)*;

(iii) **An Index of Disproportionality** *(this will be Gallagher's LSq)*; and

(iv) **The Effective number of Political Parties** *(this will be measured by Laakso's and Taagepera's N_v and Ns)*.

A3. Given the well known difficulties of identifying at least 65 persons to comprise the list of each contesting party for the general elections, we assume that the Assembly Size will, at least initially be kept at 65, even though pursuit of proportionality under LR-Hare does benefit from increases in Assembly Size.

3. Criteria and Target Levels for the Quantifiable Parameters.

A2.(i)

The theoretical advantages of LR-Hare are by definition unobtainable if the number of seats associated with a Region is 0 or 1. This is the problem that has occurred with Region 8. Accordingly, the minimum number of seats associated with each Region should be greater than 1. **This recommendation uses a minimum of 3 within the total Assembly Size of 65.** When there are 10 contesting parties, this minimum of 3 is associated with a *"threshold of representation"* of 3.33%, a not unreasonable lower threshold.

A2.(ii)
No Region should have a Power Index (PI) of zero. Also, to ensure approximate equality of influence the number of PI units per seat should be approximately equal, even though variation in the number of seats associated with each Region will produce varying PIs, with PIs being numerically higher the higher the number of seats associated with the Region, in accord with voter population size. There are therefore two measures of equitable influence: PI units per seat; and higher PIs for Regions with larger voter populations (in the sense that a smaller Region should not have a larger PI than a larger Region).

A2.(iii)
The **LSq index** for the 1992 General Elections was **1.149**. This is to be treated as an **upper limit** to be observed by any system to which we propose to move, if the new system is to be deemed to be less disproportional than the 1992 system.

A2.(iv)
In order to satisfy concerns for representation in the Assembly of smaller parties, the **N(Parliamentary)** measure should treat the 1992 General Elections value of **2.136** as a **lower limit**. Taken together with the upper limit on disproportionality, this approach should satisfy the desire to ensure that smaller parties are not systemically shut out from representation in the Assembly, or put another way, the system is geared to move in the direction of multi-party representation insofar as voters' behaviour at General Elections so supports. Political pluralism is to be considered an essential element in providing a real choice to electors.

4. Some General Comments.

(i) The proportionality benefits of LS-Hare are best obtained by treating each of the ten Regions separately, applying the electoral formula to the results of General Elections to allocate the number of Assembly seats to parties for each Region, with the total allocation being 65. Regional Elections would still be used on a PR (LR-Hare) basis to determine the composition of RDCs. We would thus have abandoned the device of treating the nation as a single higher district contributing 53 seats to the Assembly, with the Regions as lower districts contributing one seat each to the National Assembly, and with two more from the NCLDO. The question of representation from the Regions as posed in Section C (a) above, would therefore have been put to rest, **provided that contesting parties choose Regional persons for inclusion on their lists.**

(ii)   The device of non-elected members of the Assembly (technocrat non-elected, non-voting Ministers) is recommended for abandonment. No person who has not faced the electorate can be a member of the Assembly.

In both of the abovementioned areas, we have already demonstrated (cf. Section C) the undesirable effects on disproportionality and on the Effective Number of Parliamentary Parties; and on that basis find preservation of the current practices indefensible.

5. The Proposed New System

The following **Table 4** defines the proposed system, and gives the levels of the various indices described in section 3 above. These are to be compared with the levels obtained from the 1992 elections. The basis of Table 4 is what the proposed system would have produced had it been applied to the 1992 voter behaviour.

Table 4

Proposed Configuration of Assembly Seats				1992 Valid Votes	1992 Voter Preferences				FINAL SEAT ALLOCATION				
Reg	Seats	PI	PI/Seats		PNC	PPP/C	WPA	TUF	Reg	PNC	PPP/C	WPA	TUF
1	3	46	15	4,726	51.18%	31.85%	2.03%	12.70%	1	2	1	0	0
2	3	46	15	18,338	29.80%	63.01%	0.80%	0.74%	2	1	2	0	0
3	12	156	13	42,803	25.12%	72.59%	0.90%	0.31%	3	3	9	0	0
4	17	258	15	121,685	54.27%	41.74%	2.97%	0.47%	4	9	7	1	0
5	5	86	17	24,380	37.01%	61.59%	0.53%	0.28%	5	2	3	0	0
6	13	196	15	62,525	22.35%	75.75%	0.49%	0.24%	6	3	10	0	0
7	3	46	15	6,409	68.33%	26.45%	2.47%	1.67%	7	2	1	0	0
8	3	46	15	2,021	44.19%	29.44%	24.39%	0.45%	8	1	1	1	0
9	3	46	15	5,274	37.01%	32.97%	4.36%	25.45%	9	1	1	0	1
10	3	46	15	14,858	89.04%	4.88%	3.45%	0.42%	10	3	0	0	0
TOT	65			303,019	42.28%	53.48%	2.00%	1.05%	Totals	27	35	2	2
									%Tot Seats	41.54%	53.85%	3.08%	1.54%
									%Tot Votes	42.28%	53.48%	2.00%	1.05%

Gallagher's Least Square Index of Disproportionality (LSq) 1,082

N(Elec) 2,149   N(Parl) 2,157

6. Summary of Recommendations

In summary, the recommendations are as follows:

    i.   Maintain, at least initially, the National Assembly size of 65.

    ii.   Discontinue the practice of having non-elected members in the Assembly.

    iii.   Treat the country simply as being divided into the existing 10 Electoral Districts, with no two-tier arrangement of a national district superimposed on the lower-level districts.

    iv.   No district shall contribute less than three (3) seats to the composition of the 65 member National Assembly. Thus each Region contributes a minimum of 4.5% of the seats.

    v.   Distribute the 65 seats among Electoral Districts / Regions as indicated in the second column of Table 4.

    vi.   Apply the LR-Hare system to each of the 10 Electoral Districts to determine the contribution from each District to party representation in the National Assembly.

    vii. Apply the LR-Hare system in Regional Elections to determine the compositions of the RDCs; but do not send representatives from the RDCs or the NCLDO to the National Assembly.

    viii. For each coming election, determine the seat allocations by District referred to in (v) above by ensuring that the immediately prior election's voter preferences, when applied as in Table 4 satisfy the characteristics and limits set for PI/ seats; LSq; and N(Parliamentary).

    ix.   Give effect to the presumptions listed above as P1, P2, P3.

    x.   While the party winning the largest percentage of the valid vote cast in the general elections shall have the responsibility to assume the Presidency and form the Government, the composition of the Cabinet must reflect the overall proportional support which the contesting parties were awarded in the general elections.

xi. Apply PEC as the basis for the application of LR-Hare as recommended in (v), (vi), and (vii), to attempt to minimise ethnic polarisation, and to empower voters.

The justifications for these recommendations are as stated in the foregoing sections, particularly in terms of the target values of the computable parameters: Seats allocated to Regions; PI/Seats; LSq; and N(Parliamentary). The justification for PEC is given in the paper on PEC.

END
W. H. Parris (Nov 13, 1998)

Appendix # 8
The Upsidedowness of Power Sharing [2002]

PART I

At the time of first writing (in February, 2002), the flow of argument and counterargument on the matter of Power Sharing in Guyana appeared to have dried up. Maybe, what had happened was that all the arguments for and against had been put, no new arguments were on the horizon, and there was a "time out" while the protagonists recovered their energy[73]. This is not the same as saying that there had been a resolution of the matter. Indeed, it appears that we had arrived at a stalemate, and neither of the main political parties could in the then existing circumstances do anything rational to cause the matter to arrive at a definitive closure.

In my own mind, I do not find this situation surprising. Indeed, I believe this result to have been predictable - the only uncertainty being when the state of stalemate would occur. The predictability to which I refer derives from at least the following circumstances:

1. Kurt Gödel's consistency theorem;
2. The use of argument rather than exploration in a situation where what is required is a paradigm shift; and
3. The perceptions about the PNC and the PPP.

It is perhaps easiest to begin with the third circumstance (the perceptions about the PNC and the PPP); and to do so with an illustrative conundrum. That conundrum goes as follows:

> *A traveller arrived at the intersection of two roads and was unsure which one to take to get to his destination, the town of Rook. At the intersection stood two men, one of whom always answered questions correctly, and the other who always answered questions incorrectly. The traveller was uncertain which man was the one who always answered correctly. What question might the traveller ask that would guarantee that he gets the correct direction to Rook?*

---

73 This situation has changed given the recent events in the tied Trinidad election, and crime etc. in Guyana.

The answer to this puzzle is: *The traveller should pick either of the two men and ask "What would that other man say is the correct road for me to take to get to Rook?" The traveller should then take the other road.* A little thought would demonstrate that this is what the traveller should do.

The current perceptions about the PNC and the PPP, fostered by both and believed by their respective die-hard supporters, is that one of them always answers questions correctly and the other always answers incorrectly. If you therefore wish to know whether there should be Power Sharing, do as the traveller did, by asking the question of either Leader: *"What would the Leader of the other Party say about whether we should have Power Sharing - Yes or No?"* ; and then accept the opposite of the answer you are given as being the correct answer. Of course, there are few die-hard supporters of either Party who would wish to entrust their country's fate to this device of irrefutable logic. It is too elegant, too slick, to be trusted; but I assure you that the answer would be correct in the same sense that the traveller's methodology is correct.

Now let us turn to Kurt Gödel. In 1931 Gödel published a relatively short but complex paper that revolutionised mathematics. Its German title may be translated into English as: *"On Formally Undecidable Propositions of PrincipiaMathematica and Related Systems"*. The *PrincipiaMathematica* mentioned in the title of the paper is the monumental three-volume treatise by Alfred North Whitehead and Bertrand Russell on mathematical logic and the foundations of mathematics. Gödel's paper has since been described as "a milestone in the history of logic and mathematics", even though at the time of its first publication, it attracted little attention, and few mathematicians understood its significance. Put very simply, Gödel furnished a proof that the internal consistency of a system cannot be proven without going outside the system whose internal consistency you wish to prove. One upshot of his theorem is that **Arithmetic** cannot be shown to be internally consistent not that this bothers us common mortals who persistently use it without demur or trepidation in our day-to-day lives.

The current approach to arguments about Power Sharing is not unrelated to this work by Gödel. One of the strongest assertions is that "winner-take-all" is unacceptable. Yet, the argumentation presented is an attempt to demonstrate that the "winner" of the argument would be deemed to have proven that "winner-take-all" is not acceptable as a principle! How justifiable is it to use a 'win/lose' mechanism (argument) to decide whether 'win/lose' systems are inappropriate for decision-making? Really, we should go outside the paradigm of "win/lose" to demonstrate the inadequacy/adequacy of the paradigm itself. What is required is not 'argument' but 'exploration'. Exploration could lead to a paradigm shift; while Argument cannot, given its selective use of contradiction to attack or defend a particular position with a view to labeling the position 'right' or 'wrong'. That dichotomous aspect of 'argument' allows no middle ground, no shift of perspective.

There is a sense in which the opportunity for such a paradigm shift has been presented to us, through the exploratory work done in the Constitution Reform Commission's deliberations. The opportunity resides in the **new Article 13** of the revised Constitution which says, under the marginal note "Objective of political system":

> "The *principal objective of the State is to establish an inclusionary democracy by providing increasing opportunities for the participation of citizens, and their organisations in the management and decision-making processes of the State, with particular emphasis on those areas of decision-making that directly affect their well-being."*

If the Constitution is the overriding regime, then **we are not legally allowed** to choose to not seize the opportunity presented! Pragmatism, born of the obvious and fundamental dissatisfaction with current circumstances and the incapacities of present arrangements in decision-making, has driven us to consider 'Power Sharing'. That same pragmatism should be allowed to push us in the direction of a paradigm shift. It should also alert us to the fact that paradigm shifts often require transitional or interim arrangements that can provide a breathing space in our conduct of the tasks of managing the society.

The main implication of the new Article 13 is a new paradigm of Government. It may be stated as follows:

The responsibility of Government is to:

(A) Stimulate the generation of creative solutions by the community to the community's perceived problems;

(B) Manage effectively and supportively the implementation of these solutions; and

    (C)   Account to the community for its stewardship in conducting the activities of (A) and (B).

This paradigm has as an integral component, the concept of "meaningful consultation", a term that is described in a new provision (alteration of article 232) of the Interpretation section of the Constitution.

It is thus apparent that "Decision-making" power is intended to remain with the electorate, and the result of National and Regional Elections in no way divests the electorate of that Power. It is not to be handed over to a Government, nor to any Political Party or coalition of Political Parties. There is therefore no Power that the elected Government has to share. It must simply undertake, and be held accountable for, the responsibilities described above, within a framework of relevant consultation protocols that have to be devised to accord with the meaning and intention of "meaningful consultation".

To speak therefore of "Power Sharing" is to adhere to the old upside down paradigm under which the Government of the day has unfettered decision-making power, and claims that the vote has given it that mandate, valid until the next election. This driving licence model under which the licence *(the mandate from the vote)* gives the designated driver *(the Government)* the right to drive the vehicle *(make all the important decisions about the society)* without the interference of *(meaningful consultation with)* back seat drivers *(the various interest groups in the society)* is the old paradigm. Under the new Constitution (Article 13) this is simply not so. The "passengers in the vehicle" are required to have a continual say in "where the vehicle is going", with "continual" not being restricted to a maximum of "once every five years".

To speak of "Power Sharing" is also to ignore the inappropriateness of Parliament as a decision-making body, since a government majority in Parliament, under a regime of the "Party Whip" and "no crossing of the floor", guarantees that whatever the government proposes **must** pass into law unless the government chooses to change its mind. Unlike exploratory discussion in a Select Committee, debate in Parliament is not capable of conducting "exploration" of any topic. It is only capable of laying bare some arguments in support of or against a particular decision, scoring debating points for recording in Hansard, with no or little hope of causing the decision to be changed, regardless of the debating points scores, once the government is resolute.

Exploration of solutions must therefore take place intensively **before** we reach the stage of a decision presentation to Parliament for ratification masquerading as debate. It must take place under a regime of consultation protocols, where the relevant subsets of the community can explore the solution landscape in a creative manner; and on the basis of that exploration arrive at what the government should be mandated to try to implement as a solution. Under the new paradigm, the already existing constitutional option for interest groups to propose legislation to be put before Parliament must be activated. This will push Parliament in the direction of veering away at least sometimes from the dichotomy of Government and Opposition - a dichotomy necessary for 'argument' but destructive of 'exploration'.

Sharing of Ministries has nothing to do with the new paradigm of decision-making. At most it has to do with the sharing of responsibility, accountability, and Ministerial perks and prestige; but not the sharing of decision-making power, which is mandated by the current Constitution to reside firmly and inalienably in the relevant communities that comprise the society whose affairs are to be managed. Thus the Panday type rush to a structural 'Power Sharing' solution to the current Trinidad impasse is an ill-advised proposal that seeks to use **'amended structure'** rather than **'amended process'** as a solution device to the problem of deriving national consensus on key management issues. It is based on the old driving licence paradigm. It is based on the presumption that if the drivers concur, with whatever political horse trading underpins that concurrence, all would be well among the occupants of the vehicle being driven. We should not make the same mistake!

The real difficulty is twofold. First, the communities of electors have **not** been apprised of the actual Constitutional changes, particularly those that underpin the paradigm shifts such as that with respect to decision-making a la Article 13 (and indeed Articles 14, 15, 16,17, and 149C). Secondly, consultation protocols do not exist, and are certainly not endemic to our culture of governance. For the new paradigm to be made to work, relevant consultation protocols need to be constructed, and the populace needs to be instructed in their use in the decision-making process. It is only then that all the upside down talk of *"Power Sharing"* will truly cease, and be replaced by considerations of *"accountability and participation"*.

However, the process transition I argue for cannot be wrought overnight. What is required is **the resolution to change the process of decision-making**, and **the buying of time to construct and deploy the new process** one does not have the option of saying: *"Stop the world, I want to get off and repair it"* . The latter requirement implies the need to derive consensus on the **interim arrangements** to be put in place during the shift from the old paradigm to the new; and the deployment of a project type, task oriented, time-bound approach to a structured evolution.

PART II

To avoid cluttering up this presentation, but also to provide intuitive elucidations of some of the propositions stated as almost self-evident truths in Part I, this section comprises some separated out end notes that readers may find useful and interesting. As a logical construct, Part I can stand on its own; but its believability will probably be enhanced by these comments.

A. Quotations from the Amended Constitution

Article 14 of the Amended Constitution (Goal of economic development)
>   The goal of economic development includes the objective of creating, promoting and encouraging an economic system capable of achieving and maintaining sustainable competitive advantage in the context of a global competitive environment, by fostering entrepreneurship, individual and group initiative and creativity, and strategic alliances with domestic and global business partners in the private sector.

Article 15 of the Amended Constitution (Further goal of economic development)
>   The goal of economic development includes the objective of laying the material basis for the greatest possible satisfaction of the people's growing material, cultural and intellectual requirements, as well as the dynamically stable development of their personality, creativity, entrepreneurial skills, and cooperation relations in a plural society. The State shall intervene to mitigate any deleterious effects of competition on individuals or groups of individuals.

Article 16 of the Amended Constitution (State to foster forms of development)
>   The State shall foster the development of such relevant forms of cooperation and of business entities as are seen to be supportive of the goals of economic development as stated in articles 14 and 15.

Article 17 of the Amended Constitution (Private enterprise)
>   Privately owned economic enterprises are recognised, and shall be facilitated in accord with their conformity with the aims and objectives stated or implied in articles 13, 14, 15, and 16.

[These, together with Article 13, were passed by the National Assembly on 21ˢᵗ June, 2001 -Act No. 6 of 2001]

Article 149C (Right to participate in decision-making processes of the State)

 This article is part of Bill No. 18 of 2000, which was passed unanimously by the National Assembly, but **not** assented to by the President. The Bill deals with all the fundamental rights, and came a cropper when a phalanx of religious groups objected to the inclusion of "sexual orientation" as a matter on the basis of which the State could not discriminate against an individual. At the time of writing, the Bill is "dead" and all the new Fundamental and Human rights contained therein have not therefore been placed in the law. Specifically, this stymies the application of Article 149C which elevates participation by a trade union, for instance, to a fundamental right. The article states:

> **'No person shall be hindered in the enjoyment of participating through co-operatives, trade unions, civic or socio-economic organizations of a national character, in the management and decision-making processes of the State.'**

Alteration of Article 232 of the Constitution (Re "Consultation" or"Meaningful Consultation")

 Article 232 of the Constitution is hereby altered -
 (a) by the insertion immediately after the definition of "local Democratic organ" of the following definition: ' "consultation" or "meaningful consultation" means the person or entity responsible for seeking consultation shall-
 (A) identify the persons or entities to be consulted and specify to them in writing the subject of the consultation and an intended date for the decision on the subject of consultation;
 (B) ensure that each person or entity to be consulted is afforded a reasonable opportunity to express a considered opinion on the subject of the consultation; and
 (C) cause to be prepared and archived a written record of the consultation and circulate the decision to each of the persons or entities consulted;..............'

[This was passed by the National Assembly on 15ᵗʰ Dec, 2000 - Act No. 17 of 2000]

B. Some other inherent Logical Difficulties with the Power Sharing Concept

A basic reason given for the pursuit of the 'Power Sharing' concept is that Guyana is a plural society in which *'ethnic voting'* is a standard characteristic of elections. It is posited that the results of these elections, which are a mechanism for determining the popular view of *"Which Party should Govern us"* , are, in the context of ethnic voting, not determined by considerations of the policies of contesting Parties in relation to the main issues of management of the society, but almost entirely by entrenched ethnic preferences. The elections therefore cannot but result in the *"winning"* Party being the one which enjoys the support of the ethnic majority. In a multi-ethnic society, this circumstance spells disaster, since the Party that enjoys the majority ethnic support will always win; and, in a *'winner take all system'* all ethnic minorities will harbour the intense dissatisfaction of perpetual formal exclusion from the corridors of serious decision-making -with consequent effects on the distribution of material wealth and well-being.

As intuitively appealing as the presentation given above may appear, it **must** however be flawed since there are serious inadequacies in the underlying concept that *'there is ethnic voting'* - a concept that is treated axiomatically, i.e. as though it has the status of a self-evident truth. There are at least three sets of reasons for not accepting, or at least challenging, the truth of this axiom. They may be stated as follows:

(i)   There is an inherent conceptual imprecision of definition associated with the term *"ethnicity"* . Nowhere is this imprecision more evident than in the existing legislation called the Amerindian Act (Chapter 29:01 of the Laws of Guyana) which attempts unsuccessfully to define *"Who is an Amerindian"*. A not dissimilar difficulty will exist if we try to define the categories East Indian, African, Chinese, etc. If such definitions are not achievable, then the unambiguous grouping of the electorate into these categories becomes impossible. Accordingly, even if the vote were not secret, no clear meaning could be given to the answer to the question of which ethnic group voted how.

(ii)   No one seriously claims that **all** East Indians vote for the PPP and **all** Africans vote for the PNC. **'All'** in our belief system is replaced by **'Most'** or by the idea of **'Very likely to'**. There is thus a serious probabilistic element associated with the concept of *'ethnic voting'*. There is, however, no settled view of what the probabilities might be, other than that they are large.

(iii)   (i) and (ii) above lead to the statistical impossibility, in a system of secret balloting, of looking at the results of an election and determining whether and to what extent there has been ethnic voting; or whether ethnic voting in one election was stronger or weaker than in any other. *(This dimension has been discussed in my essay 'Red balls, Blue Balls, & Ethnic voting patterns' republished in this book.)*

It follows that no serious non-anecdotal analysis can be based on the concept of *'ethnic voting'*; although perceptual analyses can always be done. However, conclusions born entirely of perception derive from untestable hypotheses, and should not be the main basis of serious decision-making for a society - no more so than any other popular belief or perception. **My point is that the concept of *'ethnic voting'* belongs to the category of *'untestable perception'*.** Accordingly, it cannot merit the pivotal position it has been accorded in analyses of the desirability of Power Sharing.

However, I am aware that, as with all perceptions and beliefs *(cf. Ishmael's lecture to Queequeg about Yojo and his Ramadan in Herman Melville's Moby-Dick)*, this perception of ethnic voting is not pervious to logic. One has come across this type of problem in religion with respect to the existence of God.   The fact that we are in the realm of untestable perception does **not** mean that belief in God is any of: undesirable, crazy, or erroneous.   It does mean that we should be very careful about how we apply the concept of God to our day-to-day affairs!

In the final analysis, the existence of the perception that non-East Indian groups, and especially African based groups, are disadvantaged in decision-making does require that a system be devised to deal with the results of that belief.   As I have suggested in Part I, decision-making based on consultation protocols is the way to go; rather than Power Sharing deriving from perceptions of ethnic voting that lead to the need for a dynamically stable balance of power among inevitably vaguely defined ethnic groups.

C. "Argument" versus "Exploration"

In the text of Part I, I have drawn a distinction between 'argument' and 'exploration'.   Some further explanation may be useful.

The art of argument is the art of causing the destruction of the arguments of those who are not in agreement with one-self and of stopping one's arguments from being open to like attacks.   It is a process designed to place one's position in the category "True", and all other positions in the category "False"; or equivalently in the categories "Best" and "Less than Best". Accordingly, in the process of argument, if one discovered a presentation that would strongly support the position of one's opponent, that discovery would not be offered to one's opponent; and if one discovered a presentation that would obliterate support of one's position, one would not offer that presentation to one's opponent.

There is in argument an underlying 'True / False' or 'Best / Less than Best' type dichotomy assumed.   The result of the process is that the cleverer debater will prevail - and this may have nothing to do with 'Truth' or 'Best'.

There is no possibility of considering that both proponent and opponent may be 'wrong', or that both may be 'right' depending on the contextual circumstances. There is no middle ground, and no possibility of a paradigm shift. However, the world is based on "fuzzy" sets, where there are shades of grey rather than simply black and white, degrees of membership rather than the clear distinction between belonging to the set and not belonging to the set. It is this perception that led Albert Einstein in 1921 to state: *"So far as laws of mathematics refer to reality, they are not certain. And so far as they are certain, they do not refer to reality."*

In the process of 'exploration', as opposed to the process of 'argument', there is no position to resolutely defend, and creative pursuit of solution rather than resolute justification of a preferred solution is the order of the day. All ideas are allowed to contend, even the most initially ridiculous or outlandish sounding ones, during the process of exploration; and the usefulness of the idea is not a function of the alleged cleverness of its presenter. Inclusive democracy demands use of the process of exploration, rather than of argumentation, because in exploration there inhere the foundations of creativity without which paradigm shifts are often impossible.

The current preoccupation with the dichotomies like *'right/wrong'* or *'true/ false'* which underpin argument, probably derives from Christianity. After all, the author of the statement : *'He that is not with me is against me'* was neither Burnham or the PNC driven by the malevolence of dictatorship, nor Jagan or the PPP motivated by dialectical materialism, but no less historically prestigious a personage than Christ (St. Matthew 12, 30). Indeed, Christ went even further and insisted that: *"Anyone who says something against the Son of Man can be forgiven; but whoever says something against the Holy Spirit will not be forgiven - now or ever."* This draconian treatment of those who are arrogant enough to attack the fundamentals of any belief comprises the foundation of heresy, which must never be tolerated. The current American stance on Afghanistan, and indeed on many other matters, follows this model faithfully. This strong attachment to the dichotomy of 'argument' needs to be eschewed if inclusive democracy is to become the new paradigm; and if the complexities of globalisation are to be successfully confronted. Inclusive democracy is the very antithesis of heresy, and the foundation of creativity. Without the proliferation of variety of ideas, an Inquisition type atmosphere will be entrenched, and a Dark Age will be assured -prerequisites for the avoidance of paradigm shifts and consequent progress.

D. The Necessity for an "Opposition".

There are those who feel wedded to the concept of a need for an *"Opposition"* in our Parliamentary democracy. In part, this insistence on the desirability of an Opposition derives from the equal attachment to the value of *"argument"* as opposed to *"exploration"*. The perception appears to be the same as that used by the courts of the Inquisition. There it was perceived as being unfair to condemn a heretic without affording them the defence by someone whose purpose was to challenge the prosecutors (typically the same concept as used in our courts of law with the lawyers for the defence[74]). Thus there arose and was implemented the concept of a *"devil's advocate"*. Equally clever antagonists (the prosecutor and the devil's advocate) in the contest called *"trial"* was the device accepted as the best mechanism to ferret out *"truth"*; even when life depended on it, and in the context of *"argument"* not being recognised as an inappropriate device for determining *"truth"* (cf. Copernicus and Galileo[75]) In our current embrace of this same principle, we have held on to the "Opposition"

---

74   A position to which we adhere despite the possibility that a Jury is a group of twelve people who determine which client has the better lawyer.

75   In 1632 Galileo was deemed by the Inquisition, after his second trial, to be *'vehemently suspected of heresy'*, was sentenced to spend the rest of his days under house arrest, and forbidden to talk about the movements of the planets. He died in his bed in 1642; and was finally cleared of heresy by Pope John Paul II through a Vatican commission in 1992! It took 350 years after his death for the "truth" to be **officially** recognised.

as Parliament's "devil's advocate"; and think of the Opposition" as the alternative government.

But our perception of the role of an Opposition is at variance with the device we deploy to generate the composition of Parliament. There exists no nontrivial electoral system that will faithfully reflect the variety of support for contesting political parties, and also guarantee the avoidance of overwhelming support for one party, or the avoidance of near equal support for the winning party and the rest. Accordingly, **inherent** in our electoral system to determine the composition of Parliament, are the possibilities of no opposition *(the winning party wins all the seats in a landslide victory)* or an opposition as strong as the Government *(the seats gained by the winning party being equal or nearly equal to the seats gained by at least one of the other contestants)*. Also, there is the possibility of the winning party having less seats than the other contestants combine[76]. Under what I have called the old paradigm, whenever one of these circumstances occurs, we will deem ourselves to have arrived at a crisis of governance; but the crisis derives not from the results of the voting system, but from our definition of the role of the Opposition in decision making - a direct result of the old paradigm of decision making. **Accordingly, our adherence to the old paradigm of decision making is systemically at variance with our concept of the preferred role of *"Opposition"*, for any given non-trivial electoral system.** A focus on the 'winner take all' aspect of the old paradigm obfuscates this systemic core contradiction.

The conundrum is completely avoided if: (a) we change the paradigm of decision making in accordance with Article 13; (b) we change the role of the Opposition to that of participant in exploration rather than devil's advocate in argument; and (c) we give primacy to meaningful consultation under a suitable regime of consultation protocols.

E. The Rationality of the PNC and the PPP.

In the first paragraph of Part I, I made the statement that *"neither of the main political parties can in the existing circumstances do anything rational to cause the matter to arrive at a definitive closure."*

The basis for this assertion is that I consider the two main Parties both 'rational' in the sense that no person playing a game whose rules they

---

76   The simplistic solution of making the number of seats in the National Assembly an odd number does not avoid these difficulties.

know, will choose to play in a sub-optimal manner. The current 'game' being played is determined by what I have described as the old paradigm of the driving licence model. Two things flow from this model: first, there is no rational consistency in an attitude that accepts the paradigm to play the voting game, but then immediately rejects its results by embarking on Power Sharing; and second, ability to win the game is no guarantee of competence at making the decisions to manage the economy. But adherence to the old paradigm does not allow a focus on this second concern that ability to win an election is not a sufficient condition for capability to govern well. It is ruled out by the paradigm itself.

It is therefore against this background that I submit that neither Party would be behaving rationally under the old paradigm if it were to accept a Power Sharing model. If, however, the paradigm were shifted to the one implied by Articles 13 through 17 of the amended constitution, sharing of Ministries would have a different meaning and consequence, and could then become classified as rational behaviour in accordance with the new paradigm. **In the end, the issue becomes one of whether the amended constitution will be allowed to prevail.**

But that is a matter of adherence to the Rule of the Supreme Law, and of considerations of the internal consistency of the Constitution itself. The enormity of this dimension of the issue of the Constitution's internal consistency is clearly highlighted by the observation that Government, speaking as spokes-entity for the State, is, under the old paradigm, treated as both omnipotent and omniscient. It is a clever reincarnation of Christ with the difference that the new incarnation has the power to avoid or significantly delay its own crucifixion, while it can order the peremptory crucifixion of others. Thus, for instance, one can sue the State; but having won, one cannot levy on State property to give material effect to the judgement. State Property is protected from forced sale and is thus insulated from the excesses of any Government against an individual, who is in turn not assured of material redress under the version of the Rule of Law which embraces the principles of the State Liability Act. The timing of your receipt of any monetary award is entirely in the hands of the Minister of Finance; and that official can choose to be as tardy as he/she pleases. You cannot, for example, cause the sale of Parliament Building to get any sum of money that the Courts say you are owed by the State!

It is in this context of the old paradigm that Article 13 of the Constitution specifies the direction of the paradigm shift; **but it does not specify the**

speed of the shift. The net result is that the momentum of change in the process of governance is left unspecified and in the decision making responsibility of the body politic.

F. Consultation and Consultation Protocols

Part I asserts that "consultation" and "consultation protocols" are pivotal to the implementation of the new Article 13 of our Constitution. The only government source of which I am aware that formally has pursued this matter is the Australian Capital Territory Government, Canberra, in which the Chief Minister's Department has published (Dec 1997) a *"Consultation Protocol A guide to consultation processes for the ACT Government"*. The document is available on the ACT Government Homepage, the Internet address of which is: **http://www.act.gov.au**

I do not know, or care, whether the Constitution under which the ACT Government operates has any article that is similar to our Article 13; but the following excerpts, quotations from the Consultation Protocol, are interesting:

"What is Consultation?

Consultation is a central principle in sound planning and decision making. It allows Government to make informed decisions about issues which affect its citizens. The consultation process aims at allowing maximum opportunity for citizens to be informed and to make their concerns heard and be taken into account, before a final decision is made by Government. It involves the use of methods ranging from information sharing to participatory decision making, to ensure Government is aware of the views of citizens affected by a potential decision or policy change.

Consultation provides an opportunity to identify major differences, as well as areas of agreement, which can be taken into account by Government in its decision making process. Appropriate consultation needs to commence early in any decision making process. The choice of appropriate consultation method should be based on input from relevant key stakeholders, who will have an understanding of how best to access and involve the citizens most affected by or interested in, a potential decision or policy change..."

"Why Consult?

.................There are a number of objectives that Government achieves by consulting before making or acting on a decision. These include:

- demonstrating the transparency and accountability of Government processes;
- learning about the needs of its citizens by canvassing a range of alternative views and ensuring greater representation in decision making processes;
- building a cooperative and responsive relationship between Government and its citizens to deal with potential problems. Exploring a range of solutions by all stakeholders and learning more about each other's roles and constraints;
- providing an opportunity for people to exercise their rights as citizens in ensuring Government makes considered and informed decisions when developing local programs and services;
- enabling individuals and groups to participate as citizens in taking responsibility as members of the community and maximising ownership of issues and decisions;
- providing expertise to Government to assist in the provision of programs and services for specific population or special needs groups, such as older people;
- ensuring cost effective and appropriate programs or services are developed through a consultation process which clearly identifies the community needs;
- developing comprehensive understanding of the objectives of Government services through enabling different interest groups to hear each other's points of view;
- enabling Government to understand the full range of impacts of proposed action."

I am of the view that the requirement of demonstrating *"transparency and accountability of Government processes"*; and *"providing an opportunity for people to exercise their rights as citizens in ensuring Government makes considered and informed decisions when developing local programs and services"*; and *"enabling individuals and groups to participate as citizens in taking responsibility as members of the community and maximising ownership of issues and decisions"* are all within the objectives intended by our Article 13.

Further, consultation appears to me to be the best way to avoid two difficulties that exist and will persist under the old paradigm:

–   the desire for a Party to lay claim to ideas when their implementation is 'successful', even though ideas can have no unique owners (this is allied to the compulsion to rewrite history); and

–   the compulsion for a Party to pretend that within it resides the requisite wisdom to give 'best' answers to **all** problems – a compulsion which if not yielded to forces that Party to not be able to claim the kudos for whatever successful solution is put forward.

The preparation of Consultation Protocols for Guyana appears to be one of the most pressing tasks to be undertaken, if satisfaction of the demands of Article 13 is to be achieved. That is, however, a formidable task since it includes, for instance, solutions to the problem of how to deal with resolutely recalcitrant stakeholders (e.g. a Government; or the minibus group?) who may choose to torpedo the process of exploration by resorting to 'strong-arm' tactics, or 'ignar' proclamations. In this respect we may be well advised to promulgate legislation to the effect that the right to be consulted is allied with the responsibility to participate in consultation without resort to such tactics / proclamations during the period determined for consultation! But in the end, the core problem is that of spreading the memes that consultation and compromise are preferable to confrontation or imposition by some supposed authority; and that requires a paradigm shift!

W. H. Parris Friday, August 23, 2002

POSTSCRIPT (4 Feb, 2003)

I am convinced that there has been a serious misinterpretation of Desmond Hoyte's statement about Power Sharing -"adjusted governance is an idea whose time has come"- in his Leader's Address to the 13th Biennial Congress (August 16-18, 2002)*. The popular view seems to be that Hoyte was signalling that he had been converted and was then finally 'on board' with a specific model of Power Sharing, having been initially opposed. I believe this view is almost certainly inaccurate, based on the following observations:

1   Hoyte's awareness of the positions taken over the decades of the prolonged political pas de deux between Forbes Burnham, as founder leader of the PNC, and Cheddi Jagan in a not dissimilar position in relation to the PPP, with respect to the concept of a National Front Government;

2   Hoyte's awareness of the positions officially presented by various interest groups - specifically those of the PNC in the memorandum which he substantially authored and signed as the submission to the Constitutional Reform Commission, and those of the GTUC in their memorandum, which contained the signed views of Joseph Pollydore and Lincoln Lewis to the same Commission. *[These have been published verbatim in my Annotated version of the Report of the Constitution Reform Commission]*; and

3   Hoyte's support for the PNC's Central Executive decisions in 1999 and subsequently, to commission an internal study to generate a Power Sharing model in implementable detail as opposed to a general conceptual framework

My conclusion: Hoyte was almost certainly referring to the evolution of the meme of Power Sharing in the pursuit of 'inclusive governance'; and declaring that in his view a not inappropriate mutant in governance was emerging and would probably survive - an idea whose time had come. **He was being both political participant and perceptive historian.**

* The quotation from the actual speech: *'Second, an adjusted system of governance for our country - whether we call it "power-sharing", "shared governance", 'inclusive governance" or any other name - appears to be an idea whose time has come. It could hardly be claimed that our present arrangements are working in the best interests of the country and its citizens. The imperfections obtrude everywhere and are a serious obstacle to national cohesion and development. In the circumstances, the imperative of constitutional adjustment appears to be unavoidable. We cannot stand on the seashore and bid the waves recede. I suggest,* *therefore, that we as a Party give careful and anxious consideration to the insistent voices that are calling for constitutional and political reform. We should not shy away from examining possible modalities for a transformed system of governance that meets the needs of our peculiar situation; nor should we be diffident, as a Party, about putting forward proposals as part of any national debate on this subject.'*

END

Appendix # 9
Ethnic Voting - a Myth [2004]

I know most men, including those at ease with problems of the greatest complexity, can seldom accept even the simplest and most obvious truth if it be such as would oblige them to admit the falsity of conclusions which they have delighted in explaining to colleagues, which they have proudly taught to others, and which they have woven, thread by thread, into the fabric of their lives.
Leo Tolstoy

The mind is slow to unlearn what it learnt early.
Seneca

In previous essays (e.g. the ethnicity suite, the suite on Education, and the suite on Electoral Systems in *Heretical Musings, 1993 to 2003)* I have suggested and sought to demonstrate that current theories of ethnic voting in Guyana have neither explanatory nor predictive power about voting behaviour in Guyana. Indeed, it has struck me that the assertions about ethnic voting in Guyana, with their companion allegation that each election is simply an ethnic census of the electorate, may well qualify for inclusion in the category of the great malignant myths of my lifetime.

Perhaps of these the myth most relevant to me personally, and to persons of my perceived ethnicity, is the one that asserts that Africa had no history until the Europeans discovered it, and consequently that the peoples of Africa had made no significant contribution to human growth and civilization. Proselytizers like Hegel (in the mid 1820s with his lectures on the Philosophy of History) and more recently Trevor-Roper (in the 1960s)[77] thus relegated my ancestors to the status of a race of inferior nobodies, and set the stage for me and persons of my ethnic origin to be assigned no more than an inferior role in the saga of the development of the world, and therefore of Guyana - we who have among our ethnic forebears the likes of Aleksandr Pushkin, the three Dumases (General, Pere, and Fils), and Chevalier de St. Georges; and who had inculcated in our architecture, our hairstyles,

---

77   Trevor-Roper's capacity for fallibility was interestingly demonstrated when the 60 or so diaries that he certified as Hitler's in 1983 were subsequently challenged as forgeries.

our fabric designs, and our urban plans, concepts of fractal geometry long before the developed West hit upon Fractals and chaos theory[78]!

Another of those myths is the set of dream theories of Sigmund Freud and Carl Jung. Those theories comprised a powerful meme with a high survival characteristic, even though they were simply subjective speculation without empirical support. My understanding is that Freud's *Interpretation of Dreams* was published in 1899 (1900 appears on the title page by mistake); that Freud's work was most fashionable in the United States in the 1920s and 1930s; that Freud was a heavy user of cocaine in the period during which he made up his dream theory; and that by the end of the 1970s the American academic establishment had relegated Freudianism to the category of interesting misplaced conjectures, totally unsupported by the scientific method. The late 1980s and early 1990s saw many books declaring Freud to be an unscientific eccentric, and even a quack. Nevertheless, Freudianism is respectably ensconced in the English language - note the use of *'Freudian slip'* to mean *'an unintentional error regarded as revealing subconscious feelings.'*

This last observation perhaps makes it inappropriate to compare the theories of ethnic voting in Guyana with now discredited Freudianism, since Freudianism's 40 year reign in American academia has ended, while the meme of ethnic voting in Guyana is alive, well, and fecund! The theory espouses a certain Newtonian determinism, based on an algorithm linking voting behaviour to ethnicity. It is a chimera cherished by the cognoscenti in their analyses and predictions about the outcome of free and fair elections in Guyana. This view is bolstered by the existence of a correlation between ethnicity and voting preferences; but the fuzziness of ethnicity apart, correlation does not unwaveringly either imply causation or offer explanation.

Further, while Freudianism had a Freud and a Jung associated with it, Ethnic Voting in Guyana has no person's name popularly associated with it[79]. Like many ideas, it is capable of assuming and maintaining an aura of fundamental, self-evident, truth through frequent repetition, and thus needs no parentage. Indeed, the idea is not unlike that

---

78   See 'African Fractals: modern computing and indigenous design' by Ron Eglash - Rutgers University Press (1999)

79   Although there **are** allegations about who subscribed to the theories through the introduction of the tactic of Apan Jhaat.

associated with the demise of the dinosaurs being attributable to their failure to adapt to new conditions. The success of that meme has caused the term *'dinosaur'* to become entrenched in English to mean *'a large unwieldy system of organisation, especially one not adapting to new conditions' [cf. The Concise Oxford Dictionary, Ninth Edition].* Similarly, belief in the theory of ethnic voting in Guyana persists, certainly bolstered by anecdotal evidence, and perhaps by an Occam's razor type of preference - a preference that flies in the face of the reality that sometimes problems are made easier to solve by adding complications.

Against this background of observations, I am convinced that a better myth with which Ethnic Voting in Guyana might be compared is that of cannibalism. Here I am referring to the idea that there exist or have existed 'primitive' societies in which the routine practice of eating fellow humans has been followed - as opposed to known rare cases of aberrant behaviour by individuals under stress.

Not only is the derivation of the word *'cannibal'* associated with the Caribbean through Spanish mispronunciation of the word *'Caribs'* as *'Canibs'*[80]. It is also associated with our dear friend Colombus who, though he never saw anyone being eaten, helped spread the man-eating myth about our part of the world, (although there is good reason to think that he himself did not believe it). Thereby he contributed to our musical heritage by helping to lay the foundation upon which Sparrow composed his masterpiece of double entendre called *'Congo Man'.*

A good appreciation of the myth of anthropophagy perhaps can best be gained through a reading of the book by W. Arens entitled *'The Man-Eating Myth'.* Early in that book he cautions that *'scholars in all fields occasionally have functioned as little more than erudite purveyors of attractive pedestrian myths'*; and he adverts to Michael de Montaigne's advice that *'we are to judge by the eye of reason, and not from common report'.* Arens also suggests that *'in examining a problem it is just as important to demonstrate how a particular idea, whether true or false, becomes part of conventional wisdom'* to avoid the jeopardy of

---

80 An interesting parallel is the derivation of the English word 'bugger' and the French word 'bougre', both of which derive from the word 'Bulgarian' through the meme that a Bulgarian medieval sect , the Bogomils, practiced sodomy.

uncritically lending *'support to collective representations and thinly disguised prejudices........'*

I have arrived at the view that Ethnic Voting in Guyana is a 'pedestrian myth' of dubious attractiveness (like that of Santa Claus), but of malignant effect. A myth is a kind of meme infected with falsity. As with all untruths, it can be categorised as *'Benign', 'Neutral',* or *'Malignant'* depending on the time and circumstances related to the categorisation attempt. For instance, the myth that Adolf Hitler had refused to shake the hand of Jesse Owens at the 1936 Berlin Olympics presents such a difficulty. Purveyors of the Ethnic Voting myth have relied, perhaps understandably, on little more than repetitious anecdotes in the context of secret balloting and allegations of rampant vote rigging prior to 1992. Before summarizing the arguments I have already given in the essays of Heretical Musings, let me examine somewhat the origins of the idea.

The most coherent account that I have been able to find on this matter has been the book 'From Pain to Peace, Guyana 1953 -1964' by Hamilton Green, a former Prime Minister of Guyana with a wealth of hands-on experience in Guyana's political affairs.

For many Guyanese, their sensitization to the idea of racial voting (note that I have begun to use 'racial' interchangeably with 'ethnic') is associated with the term *'Apan Jhaat'* which is translated to mean *'vote for your own race'*. Nobody wants to claim ownership, or accept responsibility for the introduction, of the idea of Apan Jhaat; but that the idea was introduced during elections of 1957, and reinforced during those of 1961 appears indisputable.[81]

The Waddington Commission had resulted in the introduction of Universal Adult Suffrage into Guyana in 1953 - once a person was over twenty-one years of age they were entitled to vote; and for the first time in the history of Guyana a large number of persons (men and women) could exercise the right to vote in national elections[82], without having to satisfy criteria of the value of property owned or the level of wages earned. Yet, as a tactic for winning elections based on the

---

81   Green asserts (Page 58) that this appeal to race was *'fuelled by elements within the PPP for obvious reasons (The demographic reality showed that East Indians were the largest single ethnic group in the Colony)'.*

82   In village elections, emancipated slaves had long ago enshrined the practice of women's participation in decision making in the villages' affairs.

demographic reality of East Indians being the ethnic majority, and on perceived prejudices, advice to indulge in ethnic voting could not have made sense nor have had any relevance prior to the split in 1955 of the then PPP into the Burnhamite PPP and the Jaganite PPP. But, as Green points out (page 49), there was the circumstance that '*....some of the most influential Indo-Guyanese in the PPP as well as some of the principal activists of the party elected to support Forbes Burnham, while a number of Afro-Guyanese leaders clung to Cheddi Jagan.*'

What this suggests to me is that some person or group of persons, in pursuit of political power through elections, perceived that despite the racial heterogeneity of the two PPP factions, the different ethnicity of the two leaders, and of individual contesting candidates, should be caused to be focused on by the new wider electorate. It appears that the effectiveness of this tactic was tested in the elections of 1957. According to Green, it worked in favour of the Jaganite PPP when Balram Singh Rai defeated Sydney King who contested as an independent candidate, and against whom the Burnhamite PPP chose not to put up a candidate, thereby tacitly supporting King's candidacy in the constituency of Central Demerara. Maybe that same group of persons interpreted events in the same manner as Mr Green, since in 1961 the tactic was repeated. By that time (actually in October 1957), the Burhamite PPP had changed its name to the PNC. The interesting question is whether, with 89.4% of the electorate voting in 1961, the result of 42.6% of those voting supporting the PPP; 41% of those voting supporting the PNC; and 16.2% of those voting supporting the UF is clear statistical evidence of the operation and efficacy of *Apan Jhaat*.

I have never seen any statistical analysis of this hypothesis; but the view, strongly supported by anecdotal evidence, and facilitated by our innumeracy, has become firmly entrenched that ethnic voting is an overwhelmingly important characteristic of voting in Guyana. Story telling should not be the basis for establishing acceptability of hypotheses, even if it is a not unuseful intuitive basis for generating them. As Montaigne advises in his essay 'Of Cannibals': '*we are to judge by the eye of reason, and not from common report.*' But when an idea is powerful enough, it generates its own evidence.

Thus, we appear to be hostages of an idea that could have emerged as a relevant tactic in the pursuit of political power no earlier than 1953 (Universal Adult Suffrage is a necessary condition), became relevant in

1955 (two main political factions led by persons of different ethnicity is also a necessary condition), and was deemed to have been effective since 1957. This, so far, approximately 50 year reign of the idea that voting is primarily ethnically determined, very likely formed part of the stimulus to electoral rigging by contestants who subscribed to the idea and considered themselves to be demographically disadvantaged; *and counter-rigging by their opponents*[83]. And it currently apparently also partially informs the pursuit of executive power sharing by some members of the PNCR.

It is against this background that I worry about a 'persistent myth' being the basis for pursuit of the idea of inclusive governance. The 'myth' of ethnic voting has all the hallmarks of the cannibalism myth. Not only is it persistent, and supported by eminent opinion-formers, but also it has the characteristic that one ethnic group claims that the other votes ethnically while their own ethnic group does not so do, or does so to a much lesser degree. Evidence to the contrary does not lead to rejection of the 'myth'. Instead it leads to explanations of what is seen as a conundrum in the context of the assumed 'truth' of the myth.

For instance (note its date), the survey entitled:

HOPES AND ASPIRATIONS:
"Political Attitudes and Party Choices in
contemporary Guyana"
An Opinion Survey
sponsored by
"THE INITIATIVE"
a group of Guyanese civil society
and conducted by

ST. AUGUSTINE RESEARCH ASSOCIATES (SARA)
August-September 2000

contains the following text:

"How important to respondents was race or religion when exercising their franchise? One would assume that in a country

---

83   The only counter one can have to rigging, where the system in which one exists is being controlled by the putative rigger, is counter rigging.

such as Guyana, where the ethnic factor was evident in past voting behaviour, and where it is said that elections are ethnic referenda or censuses, voters would find such considerations important. Most of our respondents, - 67 per cent – however claim that race was not important at all, and one is left to decide whether they were giving an answer that they felt was politically or ideologically correct, or whether they were genuinely not conscious of what they did when they voted – i.e. they actually felt they were making the right choice based on the issues or non-ascriptive criteria, and that the race of the candidate was not the dominant factor which influenced their choice. Only 9 per cent acknowledged that race was a very important consideration, with another 7 per cent saying that it was of "some importance".

Even more Guyanese – 77 per cent – felt that the religious persuasion of the candidate was unimportant. Only eleven per cent felt it was "very important," while 8 per cent deemed it to be of "some importance."

The responses varied by the ethnicity of the respondents. More Afro-Guyanese felt that both race and religion were important in the voting choices which they made, a finding that may surprise some who believe that *apanjhat* is an exclusively Indian phenomenon and that Afro-Guyanese do not vote race, which is clearly not the case."

An equally enlightening insight into the widespread nature of the idea of ethnic voting, and of the use (abuse?) of statistics to support it, is provided by the Final Report of the Needs Assessment Mission for the Organisation of General Elections in Guyana, done by consultants for the European Union Delegation of the European Commission to the Co-operative Republic of Guyana and to the Republic of Suriname. That report is dated 31 March, 2000. Its methodology (cf Section 2 of Page 8) states that: *'A survey of as wide a range of viewpoints as possible within Guyanese society was conducted , to give a full view of the electoral process and its context;'*

Section 3.4 beginning on Page 11 of the 90 page report, and entitled *'Wider perceptions relating to the electoral process'* begins with the following two paragraphs:

"The first section of the survey gave a good insight in the perception by Guyanese society of elections in general and especially the 1997 elections. The history of elections in Guyana since 1953 is still very much in the minds of many politicians, especially those who have been personally involved throughout. Between 1957 and 1964, two boundary redistributions and then a change in the electoral system were put in place by the colonial authorities in an attempt to disadvantage the PPP. From 1968 to 1985, elections were systemically rigged by the Burnham government.

The 1992 and 1997 elections have demonstrated the depth to which ethnic voting is entrenched, and the interviews, both inside and outside the political parties, showed nothing to suggest that this pattern is changing. They are backed up by the numbers from the elections and the demographics. 1990 figures show IndoGuyanese to be 48% of the population, predominantly rural; AfroGuyanese to be 33% of he population, predominantly urban. The 1992 elections show a 53% vote for the PPP and 42% for the PNC: the declared 1997 results show 55% for the PPP and 40% for the PNC.'

I deem it sufficient to make only three comments.

First, I assume that the caption of the Section is accurate, i.e. that what is recounted in both paragraphs of the section is not necessarily fact confirmed by the consultants, but simply an accurate recounting of what they discovered the popular perceptions to be. *However, the wording of the second paragraph leads me to be not sure.*

Second, with respect to the first paragraph, since Burnham died in August,1985 before the election of that year, the government perceived to have rigged that election could not have been the Burnham government, unless we define the government to have been invariant under changes of leadership consequent upon his death (the hand of Burnham from beyond the mausoleum).

Third, with respect to the second paragraph, I have been unable to demonstrate to myself, or to have anyone demonstrate to me, how the statistics quoted lead unwaveringly to the conclusions about the existence, depth, and persistence of the characteristic of ethnic voting. Also, I have been unable to determine by any statistical calculations whether ethnic voting in 1997 was more (or less) pronounced than in 1992.

The virulence with which the idea of the existence, persistence, and relevance of ethnic voting in Guyana has pervaded the corridors of power is demonstrated by the following quotation from the World Bank's Guyana Development Policy Review The Challenges of Governance and Growth (dated June 23, 2003). On Page19, that Report asserts that a necessary condition for the private sector to lead the process of economic growth and poverty reduction is that:

> "…. the ethnic political divide is bridged and a bipartisan political commitment to good economic governance emerges".

The endnote associated with this statement asserts:

> 'A recent inter-agency technical team of the UN Executive Committee for Peace and Security visited Guyana in December 2002. Their mission reported that: "the economic decline, insecurity, and fear described above are affecting the very fabric of Guyanese society. There is growing conviction among many Afro-Guyanese of an Indo-Guyanese political plot to keep them permanently disempowered; conversely, many Indo-Guyanese perceive Afro-Guyanese political organizations as deliberately fostering criminality in order to create conditions for the overthrow of the elected Government."'

'Apan Jhaat' now has a place as an instruction that has generated a reality to be considered in the hallowed international halls of economic development conjecture on a diarchal Guyana. 1992 is deemed to be the watershed year in which Guyana moved from the autarchy of Burnham's PNC to the diarchy of Jagan's PPP/C and Hoyte's PNCR (28 years of autarchy to, so far, 12 years of diarchy).

It appears that the phenomenon of ethnic voting has been presumed as one that obviously exists as a result of Guyana being a 'community of several races'. As the 1951 Report of the Waddington Commission stated more than half a century ago:

*"race is a patent difference and it is a powerful slogan
ready to the hand of unscrupulous men who can use it as
a stepping stone to political power."*

Clearly, such unscrupulous persons exist and have existed, and have tried
to press Apan Jhaat into service to achieve the ends of political power.
It does not follow automatically, however, that the exhortation has been
and is being followed. Recognition of the existence of racial / ethnic
tension should not constitute proof of ethnic voting as the sole or even
major determinant of voting behaviour. And when evidence emerges that
appears to contradict that hypothesis, it should not be ignored, or treated
as a conundrum. Such is the approach applied to all deeply entrenched
myths, including religious ones.

I summarise below the main concerns and considerations I have so far
assembled and already published in more detail in the ethnicity and other
suites of Heretical Musings 1993 - 2003.

There is considerable ambiguity about what the concept 'Ethnic Voting'
means in the context of Guyana. The ambiguity derives from:

**The undefined (and undefinable?) character of ethnicity that permits
'ethnicity' and 'race' to be used interchangeably.** In this respect,
Guyana is often deemed to be a land of six peoples, with the 'peoples' being
described as: African; Amerindian; Chinese; East Indian; European; and
Portuguese. These categories of 'peoples' are often treated as both the
racial and the ethnic categories. How mixtures of these categories deriving
from years of miscegenation are to be categorised is quite unclear, giving
rise to an inability to unambiguously statistically stratify the electorate
ethnically by any known testable criteria. The analogy with other societies
in which tribal (cf. parts of Africa) or religious characteristics may be
clearer therefore breaks down. In the result, an elector is perhaps ethnically
whatever he / she perceives themselves to be, and this is capable of change
over time and context. In these circumstances, terms such as 'AfroGuyanese'
and 'IndoGuyanese' have meaning only to the extent that they attest to
ethnicity being a fuzzy set befuddled by degree of membership; and
therefore of limited usefulness in determining an elector's belongingness
to some ethnic category. Yet, few Guyanese will admit to not being clear
about what their ethnicity is! For instance, in the most recent census in
Guyana (September, 2002) the Statistics Bureau, despite recognising the
differences between ethnicity and race, defined the ethnic categories as:

African/Black; Amerindian; East Indian; Chinese; Mixed; Portuguese; White; Other (Specify). Their enumerators derived information by posing the question: *'To which Ethnic Group do you belong?'*, and only gave the categories if the respondent needed prompting. Under *'Other (Specify)'*, respondents may have said, for example, *'Syrian'* or *'Lebanese'*. The net result must be a set of Procrustean ethnic/racial mutually exclusive compartments into which each individual had to be fitted, or chose to fit themselves[84].

> **The undefined (and undefinable?) character of what voting along ethnic lines means.** It must be true that a voter either is or is not voting ethnically; so is it that whenever a person votes for a candidate he perceives to be of his ethnicity, he is to be deemed to be voting ethnically? And if he is not voting ethnically will he vote for a candidate of some ethnicity other than his own?

The answers to these questions must rely on an understanding of the concept of *'ethnic resonance'* in voting behaviour - a voter resonates with the voter's perception of the ethnicity of the entity for which he is voting in the same manner that an open string, or a column of air, resonates with the fundamental frequency of the musical note that has been sounded[85]. A voter 'X' votes for (resonates with) candidate 'Y' if he perceives that their ethnicity is the same.

But the concept of ethnic resonance becomes intractably fuzzy when one attempts to apply it to a political party! What constitutes the ethnicity of a political party? - a question that must be answered unambiguously if a voter is to resonate under a system of Proportional Representation with a Party List. Is it the voter-perceived ethnicity of the Party's Leader or the Party's Presidential Candidate? If it is, then does the ethnicity of a Political Party vary with the ethnicity of the Leader or of the Presidential Candidate? Or is it the preponderant ethnicity of the candidates on the Party List, regardless of the ethnicity of the Leader or of the Presidential Candidate? In any event, is the ethnicity of a Political Party mutable, or is it fixed for long periods of time?

---

84 In a survey entitled '2005 Flood Assessment of affected Population' the section 'Household Information' introduces the concept 'Family Ethnicity' and requires use of the same categorisations of the Census, but ignoring the category 'Other'. How a Chinese man married to an Amerindian woman is supposed to respond is somewhat unclear.

85 That's how operatic tenors, or sopranos, break glass tumblers.

Specifically, what is it that labels the PNCR as a Party favouring Guyanese who are ethnically African, while the PPP/C is labelled as a Party favouring Guyanese who are ethnically East Indian, despite both Parties claiming that they are multi-racial; and both parties facing criticism that they have deliberately followed policies that have militated against the welfare of the ethnic groups they supposedly favour? Can these labels be reversed, or in any way changed?

Is there no room for issues and rationality in the theory of a voter's decision-making? And if voting were not ethnically determined (whatever that means), would the result of elections be different, and therefore more desirable?

The difficulty of determining what the aggregate societal mandate of the elections has been. Here I refer (cf. the essay 'Who shall govern us?') to the different interpretations of aggregate voting behaviour if the PR formula is not used uniquely to derive that aggregate result from individual votes. To the extent that other formulae for aggregation of individual votes could lead to PNC wins from the same actual individual votes, would the supporters of the ethnic voting theories maintain their stance? It does appear to me that the truth of the ethnic voting hypothesis requires the societal aggregate result to be always a PPP 'win' for Guyana's demographic mix, so if a not unreasonable aggregation formula does not produce a PPP 'win', does ethnic voting become a mirage dependent on the choice of formula for the aggregation of individual votes? Is the situation not akin to the problem of the efficacy of prayer, or of deciding who is the best cyclist in the Tour de France?[86]

The consequent statistical difficulty (and probably impossibility) of determining whether Apan Jhaat is the major decision-making criterion in elections where the secrecy of the vote is preserved. Are we not in the realm of untestable hypotheses akin to the religious questions of the existence of God, of the efficacy of prayer, and of

---

86 The winner of the Tour de France is the cyclist who completes the arduous course in the shortest time. He earns the yellow jersey. The winner of the green jersey, however, is the cyclist who scores the most points over the various stages of the race. Which is the better cyclist? A not dissimilar puzzle relates to the question in athletics: 'Who is the fastest man?' if that question does not specify the distance over which the answer is to be considered.

similar matters; and therefore condemned to the limbo of perpetual conjecture?

It is particularly the last of these observations that convinces me that the existence of ethnic voting as a practice (as a behavioural pattern), should be treated as a powerful myth. I maintain this view even in the context of the reality of ethnic tensions in our multi ethnic society, where the instruction "Apan Jhaat" to voters is a dastardly and irresponsible instruction that has been issued. Whoever issued the instruction deserves to be condemned in this life, and in the next!

Here I describe a **myth** as **a commonly held belief that is untrue, or untestable, especially one that offers an explanation of some fact or phenomenon**. The category thus includes:

- the existence of God, Ol'higue, Baccoo;
- the efficacy of prayer;
- the Bible as the word of God;
- 'guard' rings;
- the effectiveness of obeah;
- black cats as evil omens;
- the unluckiness of Friday 13th ;
- Horoscopes;
- the efficacy of all lucky charms;
- evil eyes;
- the inherent 'inferiority' of persons of African descent;
- cannibalism;
- many prescriptions by International Financial Institutions about the road to economic prosperity; and
- the inherent 'inferiority' of women.

Some myths derive from revelation, some from faith, some from prejudice, many from plain superstition, and all from the undeniable desire to provide explanations for the universe we inhabit. For all, I suggest that experience has shown that it is dangerous to make any myth the cornerstone of our decision-making[87]. We would nevertheless be unwise to ignore the reality that myths are perceptions widely held by persons in the society; and

---

87   It is interesting that if *'the existence of God'* is treated as a myth, and we accept that myths should not be the cornerstone of decision-making, then it is remarkable that among the Constitutions of countries, Albania under the Stalinist dictator Enver Hoxa was the world's only official atheist state. The

their existence must therefore be considered and catered for in assessing persons' likely behaviour. But such considerations must not transmute the myths from the category of myths into the category of proven truth.

Opinion formers, faced with the complexities and uncertainties of life in a complex adaptive system, often become mythists, to preserve their own sanity and to maintain their position of influence as opinion formers. Hence the relevance of the quotations at the beginning of this essay.

What appears to be true is that ethnic voting in Guyana is a culturally acceptable fabrication. Its acceptability derives mainly from the same prejudices that establish ethnic stereotypes. The salient question is not why ethnic groups indulge in ethnic voting, but why each main group insists on assuming that the other main group does, and how might this cycle of ascription be broken?

Earlier, I had mentioned that despite the inherent ambiguities of the matter, few Guyanese will admit to being not clear about what their ethnicity is! We are scared to death, as individuals in a multi-ethnic society, of losing our cultural identities. We wish to preserve the richness of ethnic diversity amidst the threat of the leveling into an amorphous cultural 'greyness' that might be imposed by physical and cultural miscegenation. Our problem is somewhat the analogue of that faced by Darwin where, given the then popular assumption that heredity was a blending process, he could not explain how heredity did not lead to a convergent blending of characteristics, incurring the perils of the blend of the average, and how natural selection could work. He did not have an understanding of the concept of a unit of heredity, a 'gene' - although Gregor Mendel had hit upon it in Darwin's time!

Similarly, we do not yet have a concept of a unit of ethnic heredity. So we cling to ideas of cultural separateness while simultaneously embracing the idea of 'Guyaneseness', with great mental discomfort about how the blend leading to Guyaneseness might co-exist with the desirable rich diversity that requires unblended separateness.

Actually, the 'blending' difficulty is still firmly with us in other areas of our understanding, or lack thereof. For instance, few well educated individuals do not understand that white light shone through a prism breaks

---

Preamble of Guyana's Constitution ends with the words *'May God protect our people'* – to what effect I remain unclear!

down into the colours of the rainbow, i.e. red, orange, yellow, green, blue, indigo, and violet, and is the explanation of the rainbow. In this sense, white is the 'blending' of these colours into which it separates when shone through a prism, whether that prism be a glass prism or drops of water in the clouds. We also know, from experience with pigments, that blending red with yellow produces orange, and blue with yellow produces green; but if you blend pigments of all the colours of the rainbow what results is a greyish black. Indeed, in these days of colour printers for computers, mixtures of Cyan, Magenta, and Yellow (by overlaying dots of ink in varying proportions) produce seven basic colours: black, red, green, blue, cyan, magenta, and yellow. A mixture of Cyan, Magenta, and Yellow produces Black, often referred to as 'Composite Black'. 'Black' may therefore be thought of as the **presence** of all colours, while 'White' could be thought of as the **absence** of all colours, and vice versa! Resolving this conundrum requires some knowledge and understanding about physics of wavelengths, and the distinctions between 'Additive' and 'Subtractive' primary colours in the process we call 'blending'. An equally intriguing question is why when two musical notes are 'blended' (as in the sense of producing harmony by playing the two notes simultaneously) one **does not** get a new note, and the ear can clearly detect the two separate notes that were sounded; whereas in the case of mixing colours, one **does** get a new colour. It is perhaps apposite at this stage of my musings to recite a story I received recently on email from my daughter, who had got it in her email. Quite correctly, she guessed the story would amuse and fascinate me. What she did not know was that I would adopt it as part of my 'cautionary conjectures' about things that could happen when reliance is placed on myths. The specific myth to which the story refers is the idea that *'The Bible is the word of God'.*

The Jehovah's Witnesses have provided many like me with ample exhortation to believe. For instance, one of their tracts entitled 'Why Read the Bible?' contains the following:

"The Bible is unlike any other book - it contains loving instruction from God. (1 Thessalonians 2:13) If you apply what the Bible teaches, you will benefit greatly.......The Bible contains truths that give enlightenment. Those who gain Bible knowledge are liberated from the misconceptions that dominate the lives of millions."

The counter to this Jehovah Witness asseveration is that the Bible may be a product, not of God, but of many men who created and revised it as a historical record of chaotic and traumatic times; and it has mutated through very many translations, additions, and revisions. The net result is that there has never been a definitive version of the book called the Bible - a kind of Fax from God.

Might the truth be that both interpretations are correct? The answer given by the Catholic Truth Society appears to be 'Yes'.

The Catholic Truth Society, using the basis of the Second Vatican Council (1962 - 1965), has had its view endorsed by Pope John Paul II in text (dated 14 December 1990) on the jacket of 'The Holy Bible New Revised Standard Version'. That text includes the following: *In Sacred Scripture it is God who speaks, but he speaks 'through people and in a human fashion.' The books of the Bible 'have God as their Author', yet people who composed them are also their 'true authors'.*

Obviously, one can choose which of these statements about the Bible one wishes to believe.

Now here is the story. It is offered as a cautionary tale to all, but mostly to my deeply religious compatriots whose inveighing against the state being precluded from discriminating against anyone on the basis of 'sexual orientation', held up the passing of the amendments to the fundamental rights section of Guyana's Constitution in the first year of the new millennium:

Constitutional Amendment (proposed for the USA)
The Presidential Prayer Team is currently urging us to: "Pray for the President as he seeks wisdom on how to legally codify the definition of marriage. Pray that it will be according to Biblical principles. With many forces insisting on variant definitions of marriage, pray that God's Word and His standards will be honored by our government." Here is a proposed Constitutional Amendment to codify marriage on biblical principles:

> **A.** Marriage in the United States shall consist of a union between one man and one or more women. **(Gen 29:17-28; II Sam 3:2-5)**
> **B.** Marriage shall not impede a man's right to take concubines, in addition to his wife or wives.
> **(II Sam 5:13; I Kings 11:3; II Chron 11:21)**

C. A marriage shall be considered valid only if the wife is a virgin. If the wife is not a virgin, she shall be executed. **(Deut 22:13-21)**

D. Marriage of a believer and a non-believer shall be forbidden.
(Gen. 24:3; Num 25:1-9; Ezra 9:12; Neh10:30)

E. Since marriage is for life, neither this Constitution nor the constitution of any State, nor any state or federal law, shall be construed to permit divorce. **(Deut 22:19; Mark 10:9)**

F. If a married man dies without children, his brother shall marry the widow. If he refuses to marry his brother's widow or deliberately does not give her children, he shall pay a fine of one shoe. **(Gen. 38:6-10; Deut 25:5-10)**

Ignoring prejudices for or against 'Nike', 'Reebock', or 'Fubu' as irrelevant, let us look at what might be or has been on the basis of acceptance of the myth of *'Ethnic Voting in Guyana'*. Consider the following conjectures which, if true, indicate that the myth is malignant:

The demographically determined certainty of loss of a 'free' election by the group that is demographically disadvantaged has to be averted by the practice of rigging; and this in turn has to be responded to by counter rigging by the group that is demographically advantaged. These are the only 'rational' game theoretical responses. So a variety of appropriate electoral malpractices, generically called 'rigging', become the order of the day[88]. And the most effective rigger wins. Free elections become infected by 'fubar'[89]. Since the objective is not construction of a level playing field on which all ideas on **issues** could contend, but instead is the grand prize of being the Government, there are two predictable results. First, rigging and counter rigging would be aimed at winning the grand prize; and second, there would be no sharing of the grand prize once it has been won. Guyana does not have, and never did have a Westminster system. But even if it had, the propulsion of the society towards 'winner take all' would have occurred because of the belief in the myth of 'ethnic voting' by

---

88 If this aspect of my conjectures is accepted, then we are faced with the following puzzle: *The published results of the votes represents the actual votes cast amended by the riggers. Accordingly, no analysis of the published results can be an analysis of the unadulterated actual 'unrigged' votes.*

89 'Fubar' is the terminal state following 'snafu'. 'Snafu' means 'Situation normal, all fouled up'. 'Fubar' means 'Fucked up beyond all recognition'.

almost all contestants, and not from its Westminster genes! The society's portfolio of prejudices / stereotypes intuitively supports the correctness of the idea that each voter wishes to have leadership that ethnically looks like them (ethnic resonance). These are the same prejudices / stereotypes that underpin the assumption that ethnic groups would vote for candidates, or a group of candidates, perceived to be of their own ethnicity. The main problem is whether 'Apan Jhaat' will continue to be perceived as an evolutionarily stable strategy for winning elections in Guyana, regardless of whether there is statistical evidence that a person's vote is primarily ethnically determined. By 'evolutionarily stable' I mean a strategy which is the best one when utilised against any strategy (including itself) of one's competitors as the competition called elections is repeated in a milieu of unequal ethnic composition. My assertion is that once the myth of ethnic voting is believed, then the strategy of Apan Jhaat will be perceived to be evolutionarily stable. Many of us who believe the myth will embrace the view that in a society in which persons are being encouraged to vote along ethnic lines, manipulating electoral processes to redress demographic imbalances is a reasonable and acceptable response. Manipulation and counter manipulation of the electoral processes become entrenched practice, the battle for control of the Elections Commission by political parties cannot be eschewed (autonomy must be denied by having the Commission be a 'Budget Agency' subjected to a 'concerned Ministry' – cf. Fiscal and Management Accountability Act 2003), and issues must take a back seat in decisions about who should govern. This is a part of what causes me to declare the myth *malignant*.

A related dimension that supports my declaration of malignancy is that the myth appears to be underpinned by the following conjecture:

> The pursuit of political power in Guyana is based on competition between ethnic blocs. Each bloc is led by and spoken for by the charismatic or putatively charismatic leader of the relevant political party. Accordingly, if cooperation among Guyanese is to be achieved, there must be successful conflict resolution dialogue between mainly the leaders of the political parties related to the two largest ethnic blocs.

This conjecture appears to have been unreservedly accepted by all foreign governments and donor institutions as axiomatic. And that acceptance is in no way shaken by the empirical evidence of the persistent dialogue failure of all possible pairings of leadership: Forbes Burnham / Cheddi

Jagan; Desmond Hoyte / Cheddi Jagan; Desmond Hoyte / Janet Jagan; Desmond Hoyte / Bharrat Jagdeo; Robert Corbin / Bharrat Jagdeo. Indeed, failure is explained by the stubbornness and lack of good sense of each of the five possible pairings among six different leaders over nearly four decades; and the truth of the conjecture remains unchallenged. For as long as persistent dialogue does not take place, the conjecture is not falsified.

This lack of challenge persists even in the context of the spirit of Article 13 of the Constitution, which asserts that *'demos' must be inserted into the **process** of governance*; thereby requiring the inclusion of so-called civil society in consultation about issues, the abandonment of attempts at centrality of control, and is clearly not satisfied simply by dialogue between the putative leaders. What if political leaders do not speak for ethnically predetermined sections of the electorate on every issue; or there is an issue on which political leaders do not have settled considered opinions; or if there are pressing issues about which political leaders know little?

Also, since the myth derives from the portfolio of prejudices/stereotypes, and prejudices/stereotypes are not either eradicable or mutable in the short or medium term, then the myth itself will persist with all its malignant effects at least in the short or medium term. Accordingly, if the malignant effects are to be avoided, what has to be changed is the electoral game to which the Jhaat strategy is applied; and the change has to be one that makes the strategy no longer 'rational' or 'evolutionarily stable'.

The only change that could achieve this is one that changes the focus of the electoral process to one of 'issues' and on choosing among the solutions to the issues put forward by competitors[90]. That new focus must also be superintended by an Elections Commission that is autonomous - i.e made impervious to political influence (including financial influence).

The hope will be that, generally, voters would not argue that regardless of the issue, *'what competitors of my ethnicity say must be best'*. Surely, this is the fundamental axiom of a 'rational' electorate; but rationality may be overruled by the irrationality of prejudice since, as Seneca noted, 'the mind is slow to unlearn what it learnt early'. If this not unreasonable hope

---

90   A proposal for achieving this is contained in the essay entitled **'The Parris Electoral Process Conjecture (PEC)'** in the book **'1992- 2003 Heretical Musings about Guyana'**, published in 2004. The essay was itself written in 1998 and offered to the Constitution Reform Commission of that same year. The book can be obtained by visiting the Website: www.trafford.com

is misplaced, then one can only shrug and stoically note that a society deserves the government for which it votes and the system of governance to which it does not vibrantly object[91]; and, as the last sentence of the new Preamble of our new Constitution states, *'May God protect our people'*!

END
W. H. Parris (Aug 23, 2004)

---

91   An echo of the Bertrand Russell assertion to Sidney Webb that *'democracy has at least one merit, namely, that a Member of Parliament cannot be stupider than his constituents, for the more stupid he is, the more stupid they were to elect him.';* and that of George Bernard Shaw that *'Democracy is a device that ensures we shall be governed no better than we deserve.'*

APPENDIX # 10
Computer Keyboards

DVORAK

1	2	3	4	5	6	7	8	9	0	[	]		
`	,	.	p	y	f	g	c	r	L	/	=	\	
a	O	E	u	i	d	h	t	N	s	-			
;	q	J	k	x	b	m	w	V	z				

RIGHT (One Hand)

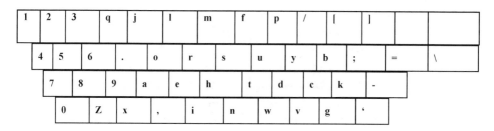

1	2	3	q	j	l	m	f	p	/	[	]	
4	5	6	.	o	r	s	u	y	b	;	=	\
7	8	9	a	e	h	t	d	c	k	-		
0	Z	x	,	i	n	w	v	g	`			

LEFT (One Hand)

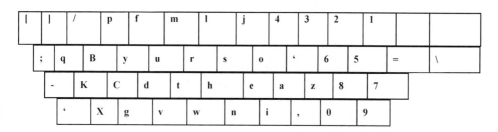

[	]	/	p	f	m	l	j	4	3	2	1	
;	q	B	y	u	r	s	o	`	6	5	=	\
-	K	C	d	t	h	e	a	z	8	7		
`	X	g	v	w	n	i	,	0	9			

Appendix # 11
Ethnicity and Race

This book is **not** about arguing the case for drawing distinctions between the concepts of 'ethnicity' and 'race'. However, it is necessary to indicate some distinctions since one should not allow the idea that the slaves did not have their own settled views of the ethnic groups to which they belonged. Donald Keith Robotham,, Professor of Anthropology, Graduate Center, City University of New York, in his contribution to the Encyclopaedia Britannica on the study of ethnicity, minority groups, and identity has made a contribution that includes the following text:

> *"Ethnicity refers to the identification of a group based on a perceived cultural distinctiveness that makes the group into a "people". This distinctiveness is believed to be expressed in language, music, values, art, styles, literature, family life, religion, ritual, food, naming, public life, and material culture. This cultural comprehensiveness - a unique set of cultural characteristics perceived as expressing themselves in commonly unique ways across the sociocultural life of a population- characterizes the concept of ethnicity. It revolves around not just a "population", a numerical entity, but a "people", a comprehensive unique cultural entity.*

> *The concept of ethnicity contrasts with that of race, which refers to the perceived unique common physical and biogenetic characteristics of a population. The criteria used to characterize a group - whether comprehensive unique cultural characteristics or biogenetic ones - determine whether the group is regarded as an ethnic or a racial group. In the late 20th century and at the turn of the 21st century, "Irish" was considered an ethnic label while 'white" was a racial one."*

The article in Encyclopaedia Britannica goes on to note that much anthropology demonstrates that identities have been and are invented and reinvented for political and other purposes.

It is in this context, that Guyanese may wish to ponder the following comments made in the book ***"Yoruba Beliefs and Sacrificial Rites"*** by Omosade Awolalu, B.D., S.T.M., Ph.D., Senior Lecturer in African Traditional Religion, University of Ibadan:

(1) [Page 45, last paragraph] The Yoruba have the habit of pouring the first drop of any drinks on the ground and of throwing some portion of food to the earth before they drink or eat in order that the spirits may drink and eat first. *(This has to do with the belief that there are powerful spirits of ancestors who are buried in the earth dwelling therein)*

(2) [Page 47, fourth paragraph] The belief that there are divine creatures living under water has led to people referring to these spirits as "Mammy-Water".

(3) Extraordinary Trees [Page 49, second paragraph] ....trees singled out as abodes of certain spirits include *Eegun (*silk cotton tree*; eriodendron orientale)*

(4) [Pages 77, 78, 79] Beliefs in magical preparations and practices.

Anyone who has grown up in an Afro-centered rural community in Guyana will be familiar with the alcohol drinking habits based on (1); with the superstitions based on (2) and (3) - water mama, silk cotton tree in the churchyard or burial ground; and with concepts and practices based on (4) of charms, guard rings, coconut brooms stood upside down, babies with protective coils or charms worn round their necks[92], waists, or wrists.   All these, unless they derive from remarkable coincidence, suggest connections with the Yoruba people who live in Nigeria and some neighbouring countries.   The relevant ethnic group classification would then be Yoruba - but not all individuals from Africa would qualify for membership of this ethnic group which constitutes one of the largest ethnic groups in West Africa! At the time of their capture and transportation to Guyana as slaves, they would have known, in a manner that neither the enslavers nor the colonisers would have known or cared what ethnic group they belonged to. The ethnic labels currently used by the Guyana Stats Bureau is simply the result of this ignorance which permits all ethnic groups from the geographical area known as Africa to be deemed to belong to one ethnic group called African / Black - a treatment not dissimilar to that given to Amerindians, regardless of the tribe to which persons belong or from which they originate.

There is another interesting circumstance related to this matter of ethnicity, race, and likely voting behaviour. I think of it as the Corentyne

---

92   For instance, **asafoetida** tied in a little bag hung on the body as trusted protection against evil spirits.

phenomenon. There, one can find several communities containing persons whose physical characteristics would lead to the casual observer, operating solely on the basis of race, categorising them as 'African/Black'; but other ethnic dimensions such as their use of language (including pronunciation and nuances), their musical and their dietary preferences, and other cultural habits, would justify their being categorised as 'East Indian'. Thus the wrapping of the package may conflict with its content. It would be most unwise to think that such a person would necessarily consider themselves as belonging to the racial group closest to their physical appearance; or that they would automatically vote against the PPP/C as a political Party. The whole concept of ethnic voting may not be relevant!

END

PART II

CONJECTURES

ELECTORAL

PARRIS

Some Important Fundamentals

There are two sets of concerns that I associate with making proposals for an electoral system that is different from the existing one, and that takes account of the weaknesses that derive from issues identified in Part I. One set of concerns has to do with the conceptual and technical difficulties associated with creating such a new system. The other set of concerns has to do with the complex of ideas mentioned in the Introduction of my book, BUNARO - the difficulties and dangers of proposing a paradigm shift, as stated by Machiavelli.

For the convenience of readers, the quote from Machiavelli is repeated here:

> *"It must be remembered that there is nothing more difficult to plan, more doubtful of success nor more dangerous to manage than the creation of a new system. For the initiator has the enmity of all who would profit by the preservation of the old institutions and merely lukewarm defenders in those who would gain by the new ones. The hesitation of the latter arises in part from the fear of their adversaries, who have the laws on their side, and in part from the general skepticism of mankind which does not really believe in an innovation until experience proves its value. So it happens that whenever his enemies have occasion to attack the innovator they do so with the passion of partisans while the others defend him sluggishly so that the innovator and his party are alike vulnerable.*
> *On this subject it is further necessary to inquire whether such innovators can rely on their own strength or must depend on others, that is, whether they must ask help of others to carry on their work or use force. In the first case they always come to a bad end and accomplish nothing but when they can depend on their own strength and are able to use force they rarely fail"*[93]

For instance, it has been alleged that Pythagoras sentenced Hippasus to death by drowning because Hippasus proved that the square root of 2

---

93 A modern testament to the likely accuracy of Machiavelli's assertions is the saga of Mikhail Gorbachev's successes and failures between 1971, when he was named a member of the Central Committee of the Communist Party of the Soviet Union, and Dec.25, 1991 when he resigned the presidency of the Soviet Union which ceased to exist that same day.

could not be expressed as a rational number, i.e. the ratio of two integers; and refused to recant. Hippasus, with logic on his side, had insisted that the concept of irrational numbers needed to be introduced into number theory as it was then understood and practiced. This contradicted the then guiding philosophy that whole numbers and fractions could explain all natural phenomena. Hippasus was a young student of Pythagoras who, though he could find no flaw in the logic that led to Hippasus' conclusion, resorted to force.

Indeed, the concept of irrational numbers became respectable only after the death of Pythagoras! Yet, quite correctly, Pythagoras has been recorded in history as a highly intelligent person, a brilliant mathematician to whom the world is deeply indebted - but the characteristics that underpin that assessment did not prevent him from drowning Hippasus[94].
This predisposition to the rejection of ideas that conflict with 'truth' established by custom and practice has surfaced even in so-called modern times. Thus, for instance, in the conceptually turbulent evolution of ideas that led to the emergence of quantum theory (in conflict with the classical ideas of Newton and Maxwell) Louis de Broglie set out ideas in his doctoral dissertation in 1924 to the University of Paris relating momentum (a particle-like property) to the wave-like property of wavelength. It was mainly the university's informal consultation with Albert Einstein, who recognised the importance of de Broglie's ideas, which averted the university's non-awarding of the degree on the basis of the heterodoxy of the notion. As things turned out, five years later in 1929, Louis de Broglie was awarded the Nobel Prize for physics!

What appears to be required for a paradigm shift is a willingness to entertain seriously a counterintuitive possibility. Generally, the greater the scope of a paradigm shift, the longer it takes for the new paradigm to be generally accepted. Willingness to entertain counter-intuitive possibilities is related to one's age and to the ideas that the education system had pumped into one's mind during its formative years. As Seneca is alleged to have noted: *The mind is slow to unlearn what it learnt early.*

The table in Appendix # 1 to this Part II gives the Age and Gender Distribution of Members of Parliament as at 20 January 2010. It shows

---

94   G.H.Hardy, in his book 'A Mathematician's Apology' has noted in a footnote to Section 13 that in the matter of the 'irrationality' of the square root of 2 the proof is traditionally ascribed to Pythagoras, and was certainly a product of his school.

that more than three-quarters of Members of Parliament are in the age range 41 to 65 years. Accordingly, the educational misrepresentations highlighted in the Articles referred to as Appendix #2 (Education -Mais) and Appendix# 3 (Education - A further Note) of this Part II, **but not reprinted there**[95], are ingrained in the mental predispositions of current Members of Parliament. The situation is therefore one in which serious revision of the existing electoral system is likely to be unpalatable to, and perhaps not understandable by, many Members of Parliament and their political parties. Accordingly, proposed revision may well tend to be perceived mainly as an activity in which political advantage is being sought; and therefore to be looked at askance. Such a perception contributes to making leadership cadres of political parties, and Members of Parliament, almost unable to appreciate the technical difficulties that inhere in the conceptualisation of an amended electoral system.

The immediately following paragraphs attempt to indicate some of the fundamental **technical** difficulties.

In Paris in 1785, the Marquis de Condorcet exposed a problem now referred to as Condorcet's paradox. The problem can be stated thus:

"Assume there are three alternatives: X, Y, Z, among which choice is to be made by free and fair voting. One-third of the voters prefer X to Y and Y to Z; one-third prefer Y to Z and Z to X; and one-third prefer Z to X and X to Y. Then X will have been preferred to Y by a majority, Y to Z by a majority, and Z to X by a majority. What should be declared as the societal decision based on these freely expressed individual preferences?"
It is tempting to think that the way out of this paradox, for clearly it must be an arithmetical trick, is to correct the imperfection in the particular system of majority voting. *Unfortunately, not only is this not a way out of the problem, **but also there is no way out!***

Kenneth J. Arrow, who was awarded the Nobel Prize in Economics in 1972, presented a paper entitled *"Public and Private Values"* to a symposium on Human Values and Economic Policy at the New York University Institute of Philosophy. In that paper he presented a proof of a very powerful generalization now referred to as *"The Impossibility Theorem"*. This theorem says that something like Condorcet's paradox characterises every

---

95   These two Articles [**Education - Mais**; and **Education- A further Note**] can be found in the publication entitled: '**1992 - 2003 Heretical Musings about Guyana**' by W.H.Parris.

voting system. More specifically, it says that there is never a way to derive societal preferences from individual preferences that can be guaranteed to satisfy the following four conditions:

(a) *the societal preferences must be transitive, i.e. if X is preferred to Y, and Y is preferred to Z, then X is preferred to Z;*
(b) *the societal preferences and the individual preferences must be restricted to the available alternatives;*
(c) *if every individual prefers X to Y, then the societal preference must be to prefer X to Y; and*
(d) *the societal preferences must not be automatically determined by any individual's preferences.*

In the listing of these conditions, (a) requires choices to be 'rational'; (b) requires the choices to be 'disciplined' in the sense that neither the society nor the individual can express preferences for choices that are not available; and (d) presumes that no 'dictatorial' behaviour is allowable by any person or group of persons. Condition (c) has an obvious appeal, in that it would be untenable to have things any other way.

If, (quite reasonably?), you are of a mind to accept (a), (b), c), and (d) as joint characteristics of 'reasonableness' in decision-making in the society, then a disturbing way of restating Arrow's theorem is to state that any decision rule based on voting **must** **make 'unreasonable' decisions at least some of the time!** It should follow that any electoral process based on the decision-rule of voting needs to be continually monitored by the organisation conducting and overseeing the voting and the analysis of the results. That monitoring should involve a transparent process to ensure that a warning signal occurs to indicate when an 'unreasonable' result **has occurred in translating expressed individual opinions into a societal opinion.** It should be realised that 'not unreasonable' results should not be presumed to be the only ones derivable from any chosen voting system! When an instance of 'unreasonableness' occurs, some statistically technically respectable procedure must be transparently deployed to derive a 'reasonable' interpretation of the societal interpretation that should be derived from the expression of the individual opinions. Appendix #5 of Part I has given real-life examples of this phenomenon.

To continue with this matter of technical difficulties, it is useful to revert to the reference above to quantum theory. This theory is based on quantum logic - a logic that amends the classical logic of Aristotle by dispensing with the Aristotelian law of the excluded middle. Thus mutually exclusive states such as those in which an object can be 'here' or 'not here', but not both, are not the only possible states. There can exist any number of other states that are superpositions of 'here' and 'not here'. This superposition principle permits the mixing of states that would in a classical way of thinking be mutually exclusive of each other.

This deviation from Aristotelian two-valued logic, and the related flirtation with 'fuzzy' as opposed to 'crisp' sets, may all sound like a peculiar counterintuitive way of thinking reserved for highfalutin mathematicians and physicists; but there is a sense in which ordinary folk are familiar with things very akin to it. Thus, for instance, the response to the casual question "How are you doing?" might well be "So-So". One interpretation of that answer is that the responder is simultaneously doing "marvellously well" (in some dimensions), "terribly badly" (in some other dimensions), and "variously okayish" (in yet others). The net result is that the responder is not uniquely in any one of the states of well-being that could be defined in a mutually exclusive framework. Indeed, the 'shades of grey' character of much of real life may be far more prevalent than we are taught to perceive intuitively than the 'black/white' framework of mutual exclusivity in classical logic.

Inherent in the Appendices of this book are many examples of our reliance on the principle of mutual exclusivity required by classical Aristotelian logic as compared with quantum logic. Indeed, this reliance co-exists with our reliance on many gadgets whose design and manufacture depend on quantum logic[96]. I am unsure how important avoiding this version of 'schizophrenia' is; but am sure that severe difficulties in the process of governance derive from our treating some aspects of our lives in accordance with the principle of mutual exclusivity.

Thus, for instance, in the matter of 'Ethnicity' we accept the Statistics Bureau's definition of mutually exclusive ethnic groups, and seek to characterise ourselves in this manner. Such characterisations lead to conundrums like those related to 'ethnic voting'; and in turn to the need to devise systems (including electoral and governance decision-making processes) to avoid whatever ill effects we apprehend derive from such behaviour by an electorate that firmly believes in the existence

---

96   I have seen an estimate that "30% of the GDP of the United States is derived from quantum-based industries: semiconductors, lasers, etc." What are the implications for so-called developing countries like Guyana?

of mutually exclusive ethnic groups, based on the "pure species" of genetics. Among my cherished observations on this matter is that Forbes Burnham could never with good political sense deny that he was ethnically 'African', nor that he was simultaneously legally Amerindian by his genealogy![97] Also, I find it quite surprising how highly intelligent persons live comfortably with, and participate actively in, a system in which an individual whose maternal grandfather is deemed to be pure African, maternal grandmother is deemed to be pure Chinese, paternal grandfather is deemed to be pure East Indian, and whose paternal grand mother is deemed to be pure Portuguese, is expected to pick one of the mutually exclusive ethnic categories supplied by the Statistics Bureau as the category to which the person belongs. I am reminded of a line in the lyrics of a song sung by Satchmo: 'My only sin was the colour of my skin'. Despite all these internal systemic contradictions, it is probably true that many individuals believe in 'ethnic characteristics', and allow it to be a significant part of the determinants of their behaviour, including voting behaviour.

It is against this background that the electoral system is used as a device to determine which political party should be responsible for governing Guyana. If one assumes that governance has to do with a cybernetic/ feedback approach to guiding the pursuit of the objectives and goals set in Articles 13, 14, and 15 of the current Constitution, then there are several criteria that our electoral process should satisfy.

For readers' convenience, the verbatim content of each of the Articles mentioned is given below:
Article 13
> *The principal objective of the political system of the State is to establish an inclusionary democracy by providing increasing opportunities for the participation of citizens, and their organisations in the management and decision-making processes of the State, with particular emphasis on those areas of decision-making that directly affect their well-being.*

Article 14
> *The goal of economic development includes the objective of creating, promoting and encouraging an economic system capable of achieving*

---

97   There is the interesting question about whether the Amerindian Act is not in conflict with the Constitution - see Appendix # 4 of this Part II, entitled 'The Act of the Amerindians'. This Appendix was written some five years ago.

and maintaining sustainable competitive advantage in the context of a global competitive environment, by fostering entrepreneurship, individual and group initiative and creativity, and strategic alliances with domestic and global business partners in the private sector.

Article 15

The goal of economic development includes the objective of laying the material basis for the greatest possible satisfaction of the people's growing material, cultural and intellectual requirements, as well as the dynamically stable development of their personality, creativity, entrepreneurial skills, and cooperative relations in a plural society. The State shall intervene to mitigate any deleterious effects of competition on individuals or groups of individuals.

These three Articles together imply a new paradigm of Government, which may be stated as follows:

The responsibilities of the entity responsible for Government are to:

(A)   Stimulate the generation of creative solutions by the community to the community's perceived problems;
(B)   Manage effectively, and support, the implementation of these solutions; and
(C)   Account to the community, in a continual way, for its stewardship in conducting the activities of (A) and (B).

This paradigm has as an integral component, the concept of "meaningful consultation", a term that is described in the provision (alteration of article 232) of the Title 10 Interpretation section of the Constitution. That section states:

"consultation" or "meaningful consultation" means the person or entity responsible for seeking consultation shall
-
(a) Identify the persons or entities to be consulted and specify to them in writing the subject of the consultation and an intended date for the decision on the subject of consultation;
(b) Ensure that each person or entity to be consulted is afforded a reasonable opportunity to express a considered opinion on the subject of the consultation; and

(c) Cause to be prepared and archived a written record of the consultation and circulate the decision to entities consulted.

Accordingly, the criteria to be satisfied by the controllers of the electoral process that is used to choose who is to govern, ought to include:

(i) **giving pride of place to** the activity of the controllers of the process **ascertaining** effectively, by statistical survey methodology, **the areas which the society deems to be the main areas affecting the well-being of individuals** comprising the society that is to be governed.

(ii) **requiring the entities** that choose to vie for the leading governance roles **to make transparent, formally well-publicised, proposals about how they intend to treat the problems** associated with these main areas.

(iii) **defining and executing** statistically technically acceptable **procedures to derive societal opinions from individually formally expressed opinions** on the proposals. These procedures should be continually monitored to ensure the currency of their technical appropriateness.

Item (ii) above implies that an entity vying to be chosen to govern should not be free to publish a manifesto directed to **its own imagined version** of the concerns of the society. Only what has been determined to be the main concerns of the society, as determined by the organisation conducting the electoral process, should form the focus of the manifesto.

I have a strong suspicion that this focus on the identification, and monitoring, of the attempts at resolution of the society's problems, as implied by Article 13 of the Constitution, must exclude the involvement of non-diplomatic post Guyanese resident outside Guyana, e.g. in Iran, or in New York; and non-resident political parties, e.g. a Guyanese political party based in Alaska, or in Canada, would not be allowed to offer themselves for election as the governing party.

It should be apparent that "Decision-making" power is intended **to remain** with the electorate. The result of National and Regional Elections should in no way divest the electorate of that power. That power is not to be handed over to any one or more political parties. The elected government has to undertake, and be held accountable for, the responsibilities described above, within a framework of relevant consultation protocols that have to be devised to accord with the meaning and intention of on-going "meaningful consultation".

Approximately a dozen years ago, I first conceptualised an Electoral process that could satisfy the conditions identified above. The following section gives that conceptualisation, from which my subsequent thinking has not suggested that I resile. That subsequent thinking includes a comment on the General Elections of 2001, which is offered in the Appendix of this Part II.

THE PARRIS ELECTORAL PROCESS CONJECTURES (PEC)

A. Introduction

Recent events have highlighted a plethora of weaknesses in Guyana's electoral process. Foremost among these weakness are three that have to do with fundamental concepts that undermine the process itself. These three are:

(a)   The vulnerability of the process in terms of its producing results that are simply a reflection of ethnic prejudice. We henceforth refer to this as *"ethnic predetermination."*

(b)   The lack of systemic assuredness that the process will produce results that satisfy some of the necessary conditions for good governance in a democracy. We henceforth refer to this as *"satisfaction of fundamental governance minima."*

(c)   The absence from the process of built-in, specific, institutionalised arrangements for each application of the electoral process to represent attempted improvements on the basis of previous applications of the process, with specific reference to (a) and (b) above. We henceforth refer to this as *"cybernetic adjustment."*

The objective should be to construct an electoral process that:

- minimises ethnic predetermination;
- satisfies and facilitates adherence to stated fundamental criteria of good governance in a democracy; and
- has built in to it a feed-back mechanism designed to allow stepwise adjustment of the process on the basis of monitoring the results of previous applications of the process, with respect to the two objectives mentioned above.

The following sections B, C, and D discuss each of the areas of weakness with a view to providing the rationale for the changes suggested in section E as minimal systemic improvements that need to be made to the electoral process. We henceforth refer to these changes and their rationale as **"PEC."**

Underpinning the whole approach of this proposal is recognition of the fact that, looked at from a statistical vantage point, an election is a special kind of opinion survey of the population defined as "the electorate." The data gathering aspects of the electoral process should therefore be made to conform to the statistical norms of good opinion survey practice, and the algorithms used to derive the population aggregates from individual choices should also be made to conform to the norms of good statistical practice. It should follow that the overseer of the electoral process, the Elections Commission, should have resident, built-in, strengths and operational competence in these matters.

As in all opinion surveys, a pivotal issue is the definition of the matter on which opinion is being sought. This paper's view on that aspect is informed by the following recitation of various rights and views contained in the declarations and guidelines quoted below from several documents published by the United Nations:

(1)   *Article 5 c) - Declaration on Social Progress and Development*

"the right of all elements of society to active participation in defining and achieving development goals."

(2)   *Article 21(3) - Universal Declaration of Human Rights*

"The will of the people shall be the basis of the authority of government; this will shall be expressed in periodic and genuine elections which shall be by universal and equal suffrage and shall be held by secret vote or by equivalent free voting procedures."

(3)   *Human Rights and Elections (Professional Training Series No.2)* *Handbook*
Last sentence of Paragraph 36.

"Without a well-informed electorate, it is impossible to guarantee that elections genuinely reflect the will of the people."

(4)   *Guidelines for Electoral Assistance, Monitoring and Observation (May 1993)*

(Questions related to) Measuring potential for an informed choice by the electorate

- has campaigning been adequate to make people understand issues and positions?
- have understandable voter education materials reached all sectors of the voting public?
- do voters in fact understand the central issues and parties?

These views, and the implied answers to the questions in (4) above, combine to colour the Paper's concept of the "empowerment" of voters for which we should strive; and to determine the main dimensions of the opinion to be surveyed in the exercise called "elections." Also, in the matter of empowerment of voters, it should be noted that the clarity of an answer is facilitated by the specificity of the question to which the answer is being given. This is true at both individual and societal levels.

B. *Ethnic Predetermination*

This area of weakness is perhaps best approached by repeating the question that I posed in my monograph *"some More of My Favourite Heresies Vol#2"* as a part of the essay entitled *"The Ethnic Problem (More Interesting Insights)."* The question was there put as follows:

> *"Assuming that we have philosophical or other reasons for objecting to the determination of which Party governs being substantially influenced by ethnic considerations, does there exist a set of changes to the current electoral system that could nullify or at least make minimal the effect of ethnicity?"*

My conjecture is that the answer to that question, though not given in the essay referred to, is "Yes."

The answer proposed by PEC is based on the truth of the following four assertions:

(i)   Ethnic bias or prejudice, whether in voting or in any other behaviour, is an endogenous characteristic of the society, not eradicable in the short or medium term.

(ii) Once the question being posed directly is: **"Who should govern us?"** the operation and effect of that bias or prejudice cannot be nullified by the use of any voting system, whether or not based on a mix of some form of proportional representation and first - past - the - post on a constituency basis.

(iii)   The **effect** of the bias or prejudice on the results of voting **can** be reduced by introducing *"rationality of choice"* into the voters' decision making process.   This observation is key to the derivation of an amended electoral process.

[The truth of this third assertion is demonstrated in the algebra and arithmetic of the essay entitled *"Red balls, Blue balls, & Ethnic Voting Patterns"* in my monograph *"some of My Favourite Heresies."* The essay is repeated as Appendix #1 of Part I of this book There it is demonstrated that if a parameter of rational choice is introduced, the actual results of the decision making process deviate significantly from those expected when pure prejudice operates.]

(iv)   An implication of (i) and (ii) above is that the rational reaction of any Party that thinks it commands an ethnic majority must be to play the "ethnicity" card if it wishes to secure the majority of votes in an electorate in which that ethnic group is in the majority.   From the point of view of contesting Parties, elections are about securing power through garnering the largest number of votes possible, and rational as opposed to moral behaviour must be presumed as this objective is pursued.

These four sets of assertions together imply that the direction in which we should look for the answer to the question posed at the beginning of this section should not be informed by any notion of finding a voting system that could eradicate ethnic bias; nor any notion that political parties can be persuaded to replace rational game-theoretic behaviour by sub-optimal moral strategies.   In this respect we should accept as accurate and apposite the observation made by Lester Thurow in his book *"The Future of Capitalism - Page 84,"* that *"What the public logically rejects, it emotively accepts. Not surprisingly, politicians use what moves the public to change their voting behaviour and don't listen to what the public tells them about their thoughts."*

It is against this background that this conjecture argues that the direction in which we should look should involve:

(a) **a reformulation of the question/s being posed to determine the answer to the matter of who should govern the country.**
[That reformulation should encourage rationality of choice, particularly about *"defining and achieving development goals"*, and the individual choices should then be aggregated to provide the societal answer to the matter of who should govern the country; so that the answer is a derived answer, itself based on a rational derivation. *The question of who should govern the country should not be posed as a direct question to the voters, no matter what the voting system used!*]

(b) **a reformulation of the algorithm used to aggregate the individual voter choices into a declared societal choice.**

Without a departure of this kind, the opinion survey called an election cannot escape being mired in ethnic polarisation; and the purpose of the election, viz. reflecting the will of the people about how they wish to be governed - the objectives they wish to have pursued, and the manner of pursuing those objectives - would not be satisfied.

C. *Satisfaction of fundamental governance minima.*

It appears that there exists currently a consensus that our society should be managed in a manner that conforms to some set of notions that it is democratic and that it is basically capitalist. No political party currently claims that it subscribes ideologically to any variant of socialism or communism. We also consensually agree to subscribe to the national motto *"One people, One nation, One destiny."*

In these circumstances it is useful to ponder the truth of the following quotation from Lester Thurow's book mentioned in Section B above.
"Unfortunately, neither capitalism nor democracy is a unifying ideology. Both are process ideologies that assert that if one follows the recommended processes one will be better off than if one does not. They have no "common good," no common goals, toward which everyone is collectively working. Both stress the individual and not the group. Workers are expected to maximize their own incomes - quitting whenever wages are higher somewhere else. Firms are expected to maximize their own profits - firing workers whenever it will raise profits. Voters are expected to vote their self-interest. Neither imposes an obligation to worry about the welfare of the other.

> *When anyone talks about societies being organic wholes, something more than the statistical summation of their individual members' wants and achievements, both capitalists and democrats assert that there is no such thing. In both, individual freedom dominates community obligations. All political or economic transactions are voluntary. If an individual does not want to vote, or buy something, that is his or her right. If citizens want to be greedy and vote their narrow self-interest at the expense of others, that is their right. In the most rigorous expressions of capitalist ethics, crime is simply another economic activity that happens to have a high price (jail) if one is caught. There is no social obligation to obey the law. There is nothing that one "ought" not to do. Duties and obligations do not exist. Only market transactions exist."*

If the electoral process that we intend to have underpin good governance is to take any account of these alleged characteristics of the high weight of "individuality" in democracy and capitalism, that process needs to find a way of adding and imposing community type considerations - about the country, and about the Region - on voter decision making. Simple reliance on democracy and capitalism is insufficient to generate the cooperation presumed by the national motto.

It is against this background that the following assertions refer to main minimum conditions that ought to be satisfied if the electoral process is to facilitate the process of good governance in our society that we wish to have characterised by democracy, capitalism, **and** our national motto. What is required is a system of governance that would allow and encourage cooperation to evolve as a persistent characteristic of decision-making and implementation.

MINIMUM GOVERNANCE CONDITIONS

(i)   The achievement of good governance requires **transparency** in the criteria that voters are being asked to use to determine who should govern the country.

(ii) In a milieu of representative democracy, those criteria should reflect **empowerment of the voters** in the sense that the criteria should be based on what voters, individually and collectively, assert are their main current concerns about:
- the country taken as a whole;
- the Region in which they live; and
- their personal circumstances.

(iii) In the context of (i) and (ii) above, **political parties** wishing to propose themselves as candidates to govern the country **should not be left free to impose their own criteria** of what is important to voters on the three dimensions mentioned in (ii). To be eligible for selection by a rational process in the interest of the electorate, **political parties** contesting the election **should be prepared to pronounce on their positions on, and proposals about, the concerns of the electorate.** The electoral process should overtly seek to ensure that this requirement is satisfied, and is made to be the main basis of voter expression of choice. The practice of contesting political parties defining the issues on which the election is to be fought, and gearing their electioneering on that basis would need to be avoided. Without such avoidance, empowerment of voters would be diminished; and *"the will of the people as the basis of the authority of government"* will not have been ascertained and reflected in the results of the elections.

(iv) An incumbent government should not be automatically allowed to remain in government if the electorate that elected it is patently dissatisfied with its performance on the dimensions of the criteria used for choosing it; and **a predetermined frequency of determination of an index of electorate dissatisfaction should be established**. Instead of the traditional N-year term of government (N=5?), there needs to be set a trigger level of persistence of electorate dissatisfaction that leads to the electoral process revisiting the question, by holding elections, of who should govern. Thus the costly exercise of holding elections will not be undertaken unless the electorate is sufficiently dissatisfied for a predetermined extended period with the performance of the government. Also, in this manner, at the very least, elections will be held often enough to ensure that governmental authority continues to reflect the will of the people - the basis of governmental legitimacy.

If any of these conditions is **not** satisfied, then there **can** and should be an honest query about the operation of good governance in a representative democracy.

D. *Cybernetic Adjustment.*

Good governance is unlikely to be achieved without an established mechanism for allowing action to be influenced by continual systematic comparison between what has actually been achieved and what had been targeted to be achieved. It is this difference between target and actual achievement that is supposed to be "fed back" into the decision making process to determine future action. No such process can occur unless there is continual monitoring to provide that "feed back." This is the essence of a cybernetic approach to management of any system.

It follows that the electoral process itself, and the actual results of that process, need to be the subjects of continual monitoring to allow the cybernetic character of good governance to manifest itself with transparency.

We therefore are well advised to commit ourselves to a regimen of systematic experimentation and change from time to time of the electoral process itself, never subscribing to the view that what we are trying to achieve is an electoral process that is perfect and good for all time and all circumstances. The core of the systemic nature of the experimentation would have to be the clear assertion of the criteria of adequacy being used to test the appropriateness of the electoral process. The institution to conduct this continual monitoring should be the Elections Commission; and it therefore has to have a continuous existence. There ought also to be a Standing Parliamentary Committee to which the Elections Commission tenders its analyses of, and consequent advice and proposals on, the functioning of the electoral process. Such an arrangement will facilitate and permit consensually agreed, stepwise, systemic improvements of the electoral process with adherence to the concept of cybernetic management

E.   The PEC

1. The conduct of all the activities mentioned below will be the responsibility of the Elections Commission, which will have to be appropriately institutionally strengthened to implement them and will have to operate as a permanent full-time institution.

2. ***The basis of voting should be made to be the expression of voter choice on specific questions.*** These questions should be determined by the ascertainment of the electorate's views on what are its relevant concerns in each of the three areas mentioned in section **C. (ii).**

3. These concerns would be ascertained through the implementation of a statistically valid opinion sample survey, where the population

being sampled would be the electorate. The sample used would be a weighted random sample, weighted to ensure representativeness of the electorate on at least the dimensions of age, gender, ethnicity, and geographical location (including but not restricted to Region). The results of the survey will be made public.

4*.   In the area of ***"the country taken as a whole,"*** the five most frequently cited issues of concern would be ascertained.

5*.   In the area of ***"the Region in which respondents live,"*** the four most frequently cited issues of concern would be ascertained for each Region.

6*.   In the area of ***"personal concerns,"*** the three most frequently cited issues of concern would be ascertained for each Region.

[* The underlying assumption is that country concerns are more complex to describe than Regional concerns, and Regional concerns are in turn more complex to describe than personal concerns. Progressively lesser numbers of dimensions are therefore used to capture the categories of concerns - the 5, 4, 3 sequence.]

7.   The opinion sample survey would simultaneously ascertain the degree of satisfaction which respondents have with the performance of the incumbent government in each of the areas mentioned in 4, 5, & 6 above; **but this part of the data of the survey will not be analysed, nor the results published prior to the election. They will, however, be analysed and published immediately after the results of the elections have been declared.**

[The reason for delaying publication is the need to avoid such publication influencing the choices exercised by voters.]

8.   The Ballot Papers would be designed to ascertain from each member of the whole electorate:

-    in the matter of ***"the country taken as a whole,"*** for each of the five most frequently expressed concerns ascertained from the survey, the answer to which of the contesting Parties is best suited to deal with it. (There would thus be five choices made, not all necessarily of the same Party).

- in the matter of *"the Region in which respondents live,"* for each of the four most frequently expressed concerns ascertained for that Region from the survey, the answer to which of the contesting Groups / Parties is best suited to deal with it. (There would thus be four choices made, not all necessarily of the same Party).

- in the matter of *"personal concerns,"* for each of the three most frequently expressed concerns ascertained for that Region from the survey, the answer to which of the contesting Parties is best suited to deal with it. (There would thus be three choices made, not all necessarily of the same Party).

(Note: On this ballot paper, the listing of the Parties & their symbols would be randomised so that the various questions will be associated with different orders of listing of the political Parties. The temptation to simply tick choices down one column that always refers to the same Party will thus be avoided.)

9. On the basis of the votes cast (i.e. the choices made), a composite score will be calculated for assignment to each Party:

- for *"the country taken as a whole,"* each Party will score from each Ballot Paper a minimum of zero and a maximum of five. The totals of the scores on the individual Ballot Papers will form the first part of the basis for determining the proportion of country-wide support which each Party gets.

- The other part of country-wide support will be determined by the results of votes on *"personal concerns."* Here each Party will score a minimum of zero and a maximum of three on each Ballot Paper. The totals of these scores on the individual Ballot Papers will form the other part of the basis for determining the proportion of country-wide support which each Party gets.

- Each Party's composite score for country-wide support will be calculated as five times their score on *"the country taken as a whole"* plus four times their score on *"personal concerns."* From each Ballot paper, each Party's composite score for country-wide support will thus range between a minimum of zero and a maximum of 37, i.e. (5x5 + 4x3). The weightings of "5" and "4" are an attempt to make "country-wide" concerns slightly more important than "personal" concerns. These composite scores will be summed over all Ballots cast in a Region to determine the proportions of "country-wide" support within each Region for each Party, and these proportions will be used in accord with LR-Hare to allocate the seats which that Region will contribute to the National Assembly.

- for each Region, each Group / Party will score from each Ballot Paper a minimum of zero and a maximum of four. The totals of the scores on the individual Ballot Papers in a Region will form the basis for determining the proportion of support which each Group / Party gets to determine the allocation of seats, using LR-Hare, on Regional councils.

10. The calculation of the scores mentioned above can easily be done through the utilisation of an appropriate database program by computer, with the proportionalities and allocations of seats being done similarly. *(The appended Table gives an hypothetical illustrative example for a Region, called Region 4, in which there are 500 voters, 14 seats to be allocated, and 10 contesting political parties).*

11. Every two years, the opinion sample survey should be redone to monitor:

    (a) whether there have been significant changes in the concerns expressed; and

    (b) the degree of satisfaction which individuals have with respect to the conduct of government and regional councils in relation to the concerns on the basis of which they were elected.

The results of these surveys will be made public.

12. Political Parties contesting the elections should be constrained in the hustings, by clearly established and published rules, to focus their comments on the issues that will be addressed on the Ballot Papers.

13. Each contesting Political Party will be required, by a date designated by the Elections Commission, to present to the Commission its manifesto detailing its proposed policies and actions related to each of the five areas of concern determined by the opinion survey for the category *"the country taken as a whole,"* and for each Region for each of the four concerns determined by the survey for the category *"the Region in which respondents live."*

14. It will be the responsibility of the Elections Commission to disseminate widely these manifestoes to the electorate.

SOME GENERAL COMMENTS

1. The focus on specific issues as a basis for voting for Parties should not only introduce "rationality of choice", and thereby dilute the effect of ethnic prejudice, but it also ought to favour the development of new parties whose manifestoes include innovative proposals for dealing with the various areas of concern. The evolution of the democratic process needs the fostering of variety of creative views to replace a polarisation around traditional parties.

2. Whichever party wins the general election and therefore accepts the responsibility to form the government, would be well advised to interpret the mandate it has been given in the light of the responses to the categories of voter concern. Thus, for instance, if voting behaviour rejected the winning party's stance on a particular concern, there would have been highlighted the need to revisit that stance in favour of the preferred alternative; and maybe ministerial responsibility for that aspect of governance might be given to a representative of the party whose proposals were preferred.

3. The introduction of compulsory publication of manifestoes, comprising specific proposals about policies and programs related to the electorate's stated areas of country and regional concern, ought to inhibit the emergence of frivolous parties. It ought also to force traditional parties to stay focused on current issues, and avoid reliance on their historical forebears whose influence from beyond the grave should therefore be minimised.

4. PEC should have an impact on the style of electioneering, thereby reducing the expenditure on flashy American-style advertising of the nature of a personality cult.

5. The "feed-back" character of PEC should serve to keep the government aware of and concerned about what the electorate thinks. It has the advantage of the government knowing that the electorate knows that the government knows what the electorate thinks about its concerns, and about the results of the government's actions in relation to those concerns.

6. The Elections Commission will be transformed into a full-time institution concerned in an on-going way with monitoring

fundamental areas of governance. It will, among other things, be in a position to pronounce on an empirical basis about whether the society is indeed escaping from its alleged predisposition to choose who governs on the basis of ethnicity. It will also be well placed to make contributions to the questions of the gender and age biases in our system of governance.

7.   For the smooth running of the country, there will have to be special legal provisions and processes established for the implementation of PEC; and also for the process of transition from a government to its successor. In the matter of transition, the analogy with gear changing in a car is a useful one. Governments need to be changed with the same smoothness that is desirable for gear changing in a car, so that elections do not represent expensive systemic hiccups or traumas to which the society is periodically subjected in its pursuit of continuous good governance. To achieve this kind of "seamless" transition there may be employed the device of a period of overlap and hand-over from a government to its successor - sprint relay style. PEC lays the basis for an electoral process that facilitates this kind of "smoothness," effecting change only when it is necessary with consequent desirable impact on the political stability of the country.

END (**PEC** *November 13, 1998)*

The following Table gives an hypothetical illustrative example for a Region, called Region 4, in which there are 500 voters, 14 seats to be allocated, and 10 contesting political parties.

A. COUNTRY-WIDE VOTER CHOICES (i.e. Best Party to Handle Area of Concern)

CONTESTING PARTIES IN REGION 4

Area of Concern	1	2	3	4	5	6	7	8	9	10	TOTAL
Inflation	300	100	50	40	10						500
Drugs & Crime	200	150	70	35		40		5			500
Racism	100	350			50						500
Infrastructure	50	200	100	70		80					500
Unemployment	20	100	50	80	50	15	60	10	75	40	500
TOTALS	670	900	270	225	110	135	60	15	75	40	

B. PERSONAL PROBLEMS CHOICES (i.e. Best Party to Handle Area of Concern)

CONTESTING PARTIES IN REGION 4

Area of Concern	1	2	3	4	5	6	7	8	9	10	TOTAL
Low Wages	200	300									500
Cost of Living	125	275	100								500
Unemployment	150	100	200	50							500
TOTALS	475	675	300	50	0	0	0	0	0	0	

C. COMPOSITE SCORES FOR SEAT ALLOCATION TO NATIONAL ASSEMBLY (5xA + 4xB)

CONTESTING PARTIES IN REGION 4 -   14   Seats

	1	2	3	4	5	6	7	8	9	10	TOTAL
Composite Score	5250	7200	2550	1325	550	675	300	75	375	200	18500
PR %	28.38%	38.92%	13.78%	7.16%	2.97%	3.65%	1.62%	0.41%	2.03%	1.08%	100.00%
Seat Allocation	*4*	*6*	*2*	*1*	*0*	*1*	*0*	*0*	*0*	*0*	*14*

Appendix #1

Age & Gender Distribution of Members of Parliament
(Government & Opposition) as at 20 January 2010

Age Min *Years*	Age Max *Years*	Mid point *Years*	Govt Males	Govt Females	Govt Totals	Opp Males	Opp Females	Opp Totals	Parl Males	Parl Females	Parl Totals
18	25	21.5	0	0	0	0	0	0	0	0	0
26	30	28	1	0	1	0	0	0	1	0	1
31	35	33	0	0	0	0	1	1	0	1	1
36	40	38	3	0	3	0	0	0	3	0	3
41	45	43	4	0	4	3	0	3	7	0	7
46	50	48	0	3	3	1	3	4	1	6	7
51	55	53	4	0	4	3	2	5	7	2	9
56	60	58	7	2	9	2	1	3	9	3	12
61	65	63	6	1	7	3	3	6	9	4	13
66	70	68	3	0	3	3	0	3	6	0	6
71	75	73	1	1	2	0	0	0	1	1	2
76	80	78	0	1	1	0	0	0	0	1	1
		Totals	29	8	37	15	10	25	44	18	62
AVG AGE		(Yrs)	54.72	59.25	55.70	56.33	53.00	55.00	55.27	55.78	55.42

Note: This listing excludes information about five MPs because their personal files are incomplete. Also, Parliament has two vacant seats.

Appendix #2
Education -Mais! (1995)

Appendix #3
Education (A Further Note) -1996

These two Articles [**Education - Mais**; and **Education- A further Note**] can be found in the publication entitled: '**1992 - 2003 Heretical Musings about Guyana**' by W.H.Parris. The publication can be obtained from Trafford Publishing at www.trafford.com

The choice has been made not to republish those articles here since they do not focus simply on our electoral processes. They are mentioned as recommended reading, however, because they highlight the fundamental fact that both the leaders and the led in Guyana[98] are the products of the system of **mis-education** that has been blessed by Guyana's officialdom for several decades.

For instance, we have been formally taught that the future is uniquely determined by the present and the past *[cf. the exam questions on the unique next term in a series whose past and present terms have been given (e.g. 1, 2, 3,4,....whose fifth term is said to be uniquely '5'), when the mathematical truth is that the next term can always be whatever you wish it to be[99]].* Also, we have been required to learn 'old' theories and have not been exposed formally to the 'new / revised' theories that have replaced / amended them, even though those revised theories underpin the manufacture and functioning of many of the gadgets (e.g. computers, cell phones, microwave ovens, aeroplanes) that we crave or need to use. Thus, for example, 'fuzzy' sets and 'quantum' theory (and their implications) remain obscure concepts to many of the individuals educated exclusively in the Guyana system of education; even though understanding the realities of the modern world, with a view to governing one's own country in a milieu of non-benign competition, requires some such basic understanding.

---

98   *cf. The implications of the age distribution (Appendix #1) of Government and Opposition members in Parliament .*

99   cf. The Laplace interpolation formula which can fit a polynomial to any sequence whatsoever.

Guyana continues to produce many persons of much learning and not much sense in relation to the realities with which governance must deal; and many Guyanese are prone to accept and pay for rubbish offered to them by local and foreign consultants and commentators who have been similarly mis-educated. The Guyana formal education system (current and past) ought not to be recommended as sufficient, and should be recognised as misleading, if it is intended to produce Guyanese needed for governance in accordance with the aspirations of independence as stated in various documents such as the Constitution.

Additionally, Guyanese, especially those of African descent, are not formally taught who they are[100], who their ancestors are, nor that they do **not** emanate from a race of nobodies *(loongera??)* characterised by primitive music (mainly drumming) and dance, and who have contributed little or nothing to the world of current scientific and other knowledge. The book *'Blacks in Science ancient and modern'*, edited by Ivan Van Sertima *(copyright 1983 by Journal of African Civilizations Ltd.,Inc. and that by 2007 had been reprinted sixteen times)*, in which some of the pivotal contributions of African civilisations to: Metallurgy; Astronomy; Mathematics[101]; Architecture and Engineering; Navigation; Agricultural Science; Medicine; and Writing Systems, are catalogued gives the lie to the idea of those civilisations being primitive, and of technology being the preserve of enlightened Europeans. Promotion of feelings of self-worth, and the eschewing of sycophantic behaviour, do not appear to be prime objectives of the Guyanese (public and private) education system, especially as it relates to people of African descent. There is no suggestion made that the enslaved were ripped from societies that ever routinely used what is now described as 'advanced' technologies in the areas mentioned in the list given above. The myth of the male African as 'the exotic savage', a libidinous genitally well endowed fellow, who 'invented nothing', and 'explored nothing', has been well preserved and transmitted for centuries by our educational system, ancient and modern; and it appears to be well set to continue to so do[102].

---

100 *cf. The previously quoted Swahili proverb: The beginning of wisdom is knowing who you are.*

101 cf. *The book Africa Counts: Number and Pattern in African Culture by Claudia Zaslavsky.*

102 cf. *The reference in the Coda of this book to the views of the celebrated and supremely influential Scottish philosopher, David Hume whom Adam Smith described as "approaching as nearly to the idea of a perfectly wise and virtuous man as perhaps the nature of human frailty will permit".*

Indeed, a deep revision of the approach to education in Guyana is required. One of the objectives of that revision should be to counteract the deleterious effects of decades of persistent mis-education of Guyanese. Also, since you almost certainly cannot teach that which you do not know, a companion objective of the revision should be the appropriate re-tooling of the teachers and the curricula, at all levels, in the current system of mis-education[103]. This kind of deep and wide revision should be treated as one of the necessary conditions for producing the people resources to pursue effective governance without the distractions of the current divisive beliefs about ethnicity. Such revision is required to ensure a severe reduction in the proportion of persons who behave, sometimes surreptitiously, like bigoted philistines[104] while occupying pivotal positions in the process of governance.

---

103 *The section"Teachers' Guide" by Ivan Van Sertima in the book 'Blacks in Science ancient and modern' gives some useful pointers to dealing with this aspect of the education process.*

104 *This phenomenon of* **'bigoted philistines'** *is not infrequently associated with material and intellectual poverty. Being* **'born too poor'** *and (because of the cultural deficiencies and other dimensions of* **mal-education***) pursuing material and social objectives to distance one's self from one's origins, or to disparage or undervalue unfamiliar cultural activities, especially in literature and music, is the unfortunate duo of cause and effect.*

CODA

I suspect that much of what has been written in this book is heretical. It flies in the face of conventional wisdom and of much of what passes for commonsense. Indeed, it often sides with the beaten servant in Molière's *Amphitryon* who observed: ***"That conflicts with common sense. But it is so, for all that."*** In embarking on the journey to deriving a new electoral system, it prefers the conclusions of logic to the destinations of fanciful flights of intuition, even while admitting the possibility of fallibility of reasoning. I have heard it said that *"Those who attempt to change others' behaviour should remember that deviation from the norm and forging ahead of one's time are the prerogatives of prophets and fools: One must be sure of his calling."* I have very little evidence that I am a prophet!

Also, I am aware of the view expressed by Ivan Van Sertima on the back cover of the book "Great Black Leaders: ancient and modern" which he edited. That view is: *'....that disaster seems to stalk anyone who challenges things as they are in the hope of transforming them into things as they should be.'* In this matter he concurs with a view that had been spelt out in more detail centuries ago by Niccolo Machiavelli in The Prince' *(written in 1513)* as follows:

> *"It must be remembered that there is nothing more difficult to plan, more doubtful of success, nor more dangerous to manage than the creation of a new system. For the initiator has the enmity of all who would profit by the preservation of the old institutions and merely lukewarm defenders in those who would gain by the new ones. The hesitation of the latter arises in part from the fear of their adversaries, who have the laws on their side, and in part from the general skepticism of mankind which does not really believe in an innovation until experience proves its value. So it happens that whenever his enemies have occasion to attack the innovator they do so with the passion of partisans while the others defend him sluggishly so that the innovator and his party are alike vulnerable.*
>
> *On this subject it is further necessary to inquire whether such innovators can rely on their own strength or must depend on others, that is, whether they must ask help of others to carry*

on their work or can use force. In the first case they always come to a bad end and accomplish nothing but when they can depend on their own strength and are able to use force they rarely fail."

I sincerely hope that in relation to the issues of Electoral Systems and Governance in Guyana, the following maxim, attributable to the Duc de La Rochefoucauld, turns out to be a false statement: **"We have not the strength to follow our reason all the way."**

Against the background of the concerns expressed above, I have nevertheless taken heart from two Articles that have come to my notice. The more recent one is a contribution to Philosophical Transactions of The Royal Society B 27 March 2009 vol.364 no. 1518755-762 on the Theme Issue Group decision making in humans and animals. The Article is entitled ***'Independence and interdependence in collective decision making: an agent-based model of nest-site choice by honeybee swarms.'*** It is the result of collaboration among: **Christian List** *[Department of Government, London School of Economics, London WC2A2AE, UK]*; **Christian Elsholtz** *[Department of Mathematics, Royal Holloway, University of London, Egham, Surrey TW20 0EX, UK]*; and **Thomas D Seeley** *[Department of Neurobiology and Behavior, Cornell University, Ithaca, NY 14853, USA]*. The freely provided Abstract of the Article reads as follows:

Condorcet's jury theorem shows that when the members of a group have noisy but interdependent information about what is best for the group as a whole, majority decisions tend to outperform dictatorial ones. When voting is supplemented by communication, however, the resulting interdependencies between decision makers can strengthen or undermine this effect: they can facilitate information pooling , but also amplify errors. We consider an intriguing non-human case of independent information pooling combined with communication: the case of nest-site choice by honeybee (Apis mellifera) swarms. It is empirically well documented that when there are different nest sites that vary in quality, the bees usually choose the best one. We develop a new agent-based model of the bees' decision process and show that its remarkable reliability stems from a particular interplay of independence and interdependence between the bees.'

An interesting observation is that there is no suggestion that the 'remarkable reliability' results from the existence of any 'virtuoso' bee leading the members of the hive.

The second Article, by **Natalie Angier**, was published on April13, 2004.in the New York Times. It is entitled **'No Time for Bullies: Baboons Retool Their Culture'**. The opening paragraph states:

> *'Sometimes it takes the great Dustbuster of fate to clear the room of bullies and bad habits. Freak cyclones helped destroy Kublai Khan's brutal Mongolian empire, for example, while the Black Death of the 14th century capsized the medieval theocracy and gave the Renaissance a chance to shine.'*

The Article refers to a study that appeared on April 13 , 2004 in the journal PloSBiology (online at www.plosbiology.org) about what is called a **'drastic temperamental and tonal shift that occurred in a troop of 62 baboons when its most belligerent members vanished from the scene.'** The cause of the vanishing was the death of the most aggressive males caused by their eating meat tainted with bovine tuberculosis while foraging at a garbage dump. The consequent change in demographics was followed by **'a cultural swing toward pacifism, a relaxing of the usually parlous baboon hierarchy, and a willingness to use affection and mutual grooming rater than threats, swipes and bites to foster a patriotic spirit.'** The Article remarks that **'the Forest Troop has maintained its genial style over two decades, even though the male survivors of the epidemic have since died or disappeared and been replaced by males from the outside.'** It may well be that the cultural retooling that took place among the troop of baboons can have an analogue in Guyana consequent on the deaths of the political leaders who were the leading figures in the two main political parties.

It is my view that developments like these will not occur in Guyana without the stimulus of serious collaborative research efforts by the University of Guyana and the Elections Commission. There is a sense in which Guyana's governance problems are not unique, as is indicated by the following references. These references are on Page 13 of the July-August 2009 edition of the Good News magazine where it quotes two articles from British publications.

One article deals with some views allegedly expressed by **Daily Mail columnist Stephen Glover** in the June 4, 2009 article entitled *"The Sad Truth is that our MPs Are Second Rate"*. Though the comments are about British MPs, the views may quite fortuitously be relevant to the Guyana situation in 2010. Those views were as follows: *"We will continue to be poorly governed no matter which party is in power. The root problem underlying all other problems is the low quality of our political class. Most MPs have little or no useful experience outside politics. Some of them are too young. Not many are intellectually distinguished. Nonetheless these people rule us. They attempt to govern us. They spend, or misspend, billions of pounds of our money. They take us to war. They make huge decisions about our lives. And they often make a muck of things"*. I am not inclined to claim that similar comments are not applicable to the Guyanese situation.

The other area of possible similarity may well be the views about what the voting public thinks about members of Parliament. The magazine claims that the June 6, 2009 editorial in the Spectator entitled "Enough Already"contains the following statements: *"British democracy is at a low ebb. Polling data shows that more than 80% of voters think that MPs [members of Parliament] put their own and their parties' interest ahead of those of the country, that three quarters do not trust MPs to tell the truth"*. Again, I do not have the courage to claim that the Guyanese voting public would not express similar views were they to be polled.

Admittedly, this book does attempt to deal with the electoral system as opposed to the wider issues of governance. But it is that system which determines who will be responsible for governing, having been chosen by the electoral process. It is also that system which defines who can / ought to put themselves up to be chosen by the electoral process.

However, the emphases which this book has sought to place on aspects such as: representativeness; the need to construct and use consultation protocols; the need to avoid approaches related to gematria in determining quantities like the number of seats to be allocated to contesting groups; and the resolution of statistical difficulties in deriving societal opinions from the votes of individuals[105]; all demand that the participants in the analyses of these topics equip themselves with appropriate tools of numeracy. The

---

105 cf. The analysis of the results of the 1992 General Elections as done in the essay *'Who Shall Govern Us?'* published in 1996 and reprinted as Appendix #5 in Part I of this book.

levels of illiteracy, innumeracy, and insouciance that currently characterise the majority of the extant leadership, and the led, in Guyana would have to be severely reduced for the research efforts to bear fruit. These levels of illiteracy, innumeracy, and insouciance determine the content of, and unjustifiable reliance on, so-called 'intuition and commonsense'; and therefore the tendency towards the paramountcy of pedestrianism and mediocrity in decision-making related to matters of governance in Guyana.

In a brief informal letter from Hugh Desmond Hoyte to the author, dated January 25, 2000, the following three sentences (which formed almost all of the content of the letter) were stated:

> 'I picked up the enclosed book, *"Principles of Electoral Reform"* at the bookstore last week.
> I have had a hurried reading of it and am amazed at the complexity of the concept of *"Representativeness"* in voting systems.
> Happy reading, if you could find the time.'

The book being referred to is **Principles of Electoral Reform** by **Michael Dummett**. The bookstore is Austin's Book Services on Church Street in Georgetown. To anyone who really knew the man Hoyte, they would read into that brief note the seriousness with which he perceived the matter, and the humility with which he admitted and sought to improve his lack of knowledge of the matter. A proper evaluation of the statement, two years later, in his Address to the PNC's 13th Biennial Congress, August 16 - 18, 2002 about 'inclusive governance' being an idea whose time has come, should benefit from this insight. Certainly, he did not mean simply that political parties should form coalitions in their pursuit of power. I wish that other leadership types would follow suit in giving a meaning to 'inclusive governance'; and that this book will serve them well in that regard.

The first paragraph of the section entitled *"Some Entrenched Myths"* in Part I of this book is as follows:

> "One of the prices we pay for not being omniscient is that, under the pressure to act in response to some stimulus, we often make assumptions that are just best guesses with varying degrees of irrationality. These guesses cover the spectrum from *'wild'* to *'carefully pondered intuitive'*. Often, the guesses are based on

what we perceive to be our experience in the context of what we understand to be accepted wisdom; but perhaps more often they are pivotally influenced by those who purport to know - the *soi-disant* experts often with international institutional anointment."

This statement is partially misleading. The prices we pay are not for not **knowing** everything. They are for not **triggering access** to all knowledge relevant to the problem with which we are trying to deal. The issue is one of the inadequacies of the vantage points we choose to use in dealing with both the definition of the problem and the search of the solution landscape.

I have recently been indulging in my 'cush-cush' habit of re-reading books - this time around in re-reading the book **'The Holographic Universe'** by Michael Talbot which was first published in 1991, and which I acquired and first read in mid 1992. That book deals with the concepts related to holograms as investigated by conceptualisers such as Karl Pribram, John von Neumann, and David Bohm. The holographic way of looking at our world provides insights into various aspects of our society, of our beliefs, and of the objectives and practice of governance such as, for instance:

- holographic vortices generating the difficulty in changing beliefs, particularly those related to ethnicity and ethnic voting;
- the reasonableness of the objectives of governance that we set, based on perceptions that we emotionally favour about matters such as what is an acceptable dynamically stable gap between 'rich' and 'poor'[106];
- holographic explanations of why 'ordinary' persons should be included in decision-making (the co-operative approach) so as to facilitate tapping into information in the implicate order[107], and to avoid persisting with the fragmentation of our world, and our search for individual virtuosos as opposed to focusing on finding

---

106 As far back as 347 BC, when Plato died aged eighty, leaving the unfinished work titled Laws, this aspect of the problem re restriction of the disparity between rich and poor was addressed. Both a minimum property level and a maximum ratio of rich to poor were considered. In the case of the latter, the maximum allowable ratio was set at 4:1.

107 A jeopardy to be persistently avoided in this attempt to access the implicate order is that of paying the price of labouring under the paramountcy of pedestrianism.

players for concerti grossi. Indeed, the solutions to life's problems (especially those of governance, given their characteristic of acausal relationships) are more akin to composing concerti grossi than of organising scores for individual virtuosos.

Another book on which my 'cush-cush' habit has recently focused is **'frontiers of complexity - The search for Order in a Chaotic World'** by Peter Coveney and Roger Highfield. That book was first published in 1995 and was read by me in 1996. It highlighted for me the possible usefulness of a formal heuristic approach to governance in Guyana - that approach which would in a recursive way inform current or proposed practice by analysis of the results of previous practice, in an application of a feedback loop pursuing stepwise improvement. We need to abandon the notion that all governments eventually end when their leader is deemed to have failed; and that the search for a new leader is a pivotal prerequisite for establishing a new government. Instead, governance of a nation should be seen as governance of a complex adaptive system. It is therefore analogous to riding a bike, or driving a car in the senses that governance persists until the preferred destination is reached, **and during the journey governance is continually dependent on feedback and foresight with accompanying real time adjustments**. *(As a youngster, I learnt by experimentation that one could not ride a bike whose handlebar had been locked into any position, including dead straight)*. Such an approach would establish a learning-by-doing path specific to the circumstances of Guyana. It would benefit from a focus on comparing the actual results of governance with predetermined desired results, as opposed to a focus on personalities competing for the kudos of being leader as is currently the preferred practice; and of the collaborative persistent pursuit of schadenfreude by the 'opposition' in relation to the 'government'. It would support the view that we should abandon several assumptions, including that:

(1) There is a 'good for all time' system of governance that we should be striving to define and implement. Recognition of the fact that we are dealing with managing a Complex Adaptive System (CAS) should make this clear.

(2) There is a length of time (e.g. 5 years?) at the end of which we should be asking whether the 'virtuoso' that we had chosen as the best leader of the government should be changed, as opposed to using a methodology of ongoing assessment as befits the management of a CAS.

(3)   The need for a change of government be determined by evidence of the failure of the incumbent government, as opposed to our assessment of the projected emerging circumstances with which we are going to have to deal.

Quite fortuitously, this book is being written around the same time that the football world cup has entered the round of 16 phase of the competition. The USA has been beaten by Ghana, Germany has defeated England, and Argentina has beaten Mexico. All this is taking place before a watchful world in **South Africa** - a place in the world with neighbours like Mozambique where 38 years ago *(actually on 16 December 1972, six years after Guyana gained independence)*, there were the massacres at Wiriyamu and Chawola, only a few miles away from Cabora Bassa. I suspect that these names mean little or nothing to most Guyanese today; and this suspicion stimulated me to do a 'cush-cush' with the book 'Wiriyamu' by Adrian Hastings. The Introduction of that book ends with an expression of hope about Mozambique[108] : *'may it be a land of freedom, an African nation not a European appendage, and may it beyond all be a compassionate society - a land in which the little people be not trampled down.'*

I think that in the matter of governance, a not dissimilar hope may be expressed today about Guyana, with the phrase *'an African'* being replaced by the phrase *'a Guyanese'*; and I hope that this book will play some part in Guyana's pursuit of that objective in my lifetime.

Of two things I am certain. One is that the changes I recommend will not take place if migration continues at its current pace, in its current directions, and with its current characteristics. In this matter I recommend highly contemplation of a bit of verse that was written by Romona Carrico on 10 June, 2010. She kindly consented to my publishing it as an Appendix to this Coda. The verse is thought provoking even though not all migrants have the same experience.

The other is that we have persisted in maintaining a system of institutionalised racism, without recognising that we have; and we continue to listen to the pious but hypocritical pronouncements of representatives of the colonisers and institutions that implemented and fostered that

---

108 A Reuters report from Maputo (published in Guyana's Stabroek News of Saturday, September 4, 2010) concerning public protests, riots, and looting over a 30% rise in the price of bread suggests that the 'hope' is not yet about to be realised.

institutionalisation. Thus, for instance, we have recently been told by a British High Commissioner that we have a *'politicized racial divide'* which we should labour to remove. But this situation was institutionalised, its underpinnings were established, by the forebears of the very people and institutions now critical of that divide[109], thereby making the High Commissioner's advice contumelious (*'eye-pass'* in Guyanese parlance).

A good idea of the history of the **'politicized racial divide'** may be gleaned from a close study of Professor Hugh Tinker's book - *A New System of Slavery, The Export of Indian Labour Overseas 1830-1920.* For instance, Chapter 4, entitled 'Setting up the New System', contains the following passage from a letter replying to one by John Gladstone, dated 4 January 1836, to Gillanders, Arbuthot & Co. asking them to provide a hundred coolies for five to seven years. The passage is: *'The Dhangurs are always spoken of as more akin to the monkey than the man. They have no religion, no education, and in their present state no wants beyond eating, drinking and sleeping: and to procure which they are willing to labour.'* Apparently this kind of information satisfied John Gladstone who arranged for the *Whitby* and the *Hesperus* to carry his coolies to Demerara. The Gladstone coolies were allocated to his estates *Vreedenhoop* and *Vriedenstein*[110].

The Guyana situation is similar to that of San Domingo as described by CLR James in his book **'The Black Jacobins'**. In Chapter II, *The Owners*, he described how the white colonists, indulging in what he described as **"elaborate tom-foolery"**:

> *'divided the offspring of white and black and intermediate shades into 128 divisions. The true Mulatto was the child of the pure black and the pure white. The child of the white and the Mulatto woman was a quarteron with 96 parts white and 32 parts black. But the quarteron could be produced by the white and the marabou in the proportion of 88 to 40, or by the white and the sacatra, in the proportion of 72 to 56 and so on*

109 Here, I refer to the political and economic beliefs, policies and practices that generated the realities of slavery, manumission, apprenticeship, and indentureship, with, inter alia, the conundrums of ethnic/racial rivalries.

110 *'10 days in August 1834, 10Days that Changed the World'* authored by Hugh 'Tommy' Payne and published in 2001 - the story of Damon, Bean and Bagot- gives interesting and important insights into the ethos of the colonial administration and its plantocracy which underpinned the generation of our racial divide.

all through the 128 varieties. But the sang-mele with 127 white parts and 1 black part was still a man of colour.'

In Guyana's case, we have adopted the brand of ethnic groupings given to us. We preserve it in our Statistical Bureau where 'ethnicity /race' is included among our *'vital'* statistics, use it in our forms for registering deaths[111], ensconce it in our textbooks, and faithfully teach it as a basis for stereotypes in our primary and secondary schools (cf.P28 of McMillan Guyana Junior Atlas, and more recently in Sunday Stabroek, Page 21A of 30 Jan, 2011)) and in our University[112].

The conceptual and empirical basis for Guyana's criticised *'political racial divide'* was laid long ago by the 'elaborate tom foolery' of our colonisers[113]. We need to abandon this conceptual and empirical platform by discontinuing the teaching of **'ethnicity'** in our educational institutions, and by not maintaining the statistical base about ethnicity in our institutions like the Statistical Bureau. The 'tom foolery' of our colonisers was designed to entrench the myths of racialism in support of their political and economic aspirations for dominance. We need to recognise that **'beliefs are like addictions and do not surrender their grip easily'.**

I have been unable to convince myself that attempts to solve improperly defined problems (especially when the improprieties are illogicalities of definition) can be useful. The degree of uselessness is not diminished by the social or other high rank of the person or institution that suggests the attempt be made. Any attempt to resolve the so-called *'ethnic problem'* in Guyana falls into this category of uselessness. The same comment can

111 Why the ethnicity of a corpse is an important statistic is an interesting question, the interest in which is surpassed perhaps only by the recent (3 December, 2010) pronouncement allegedly made by Guyana's President that Chinese nationals resident in Guyana legally for seven continuous years and more will be automatically entitled to citizenship. How about 'African' nationals, or 'East Indian' nationals?

112 However, to the best of my knowledge, 'The Black Jacobins', or any excerpt therefrom, is not required reading in either our Primary or our Secondary schools; and probably not in our University of Guyana. I believe the same comment can be made about Tommy Payne's book.

113 *For instance, the celebrated Scottish philosopher David Hume wrote in 1753 as follows: **"I am apt to suspect the Negroes.....to be naturally inferior to the white. There never was a civilized nation of any other complexion than white, nor even any individual eminent either in action or speculation. No ingenious manufactures amongst them, no arts, no sciences."*** [Essays and Treatises on Several Subjects. London,1753,vol1,p291]*

be made about all the popular variants of the problem. Accordingly, there must be few propositions sillier than that which asserts that if the so-called Ethnic Problem (which has, in 2010, historical antecedents of more than 150 years) were resolved, then Black man, Baboo, Buck man, Backra, Chinee man, Putagee, and all kinds of Dougla would live in peace and harmony in a well-governed Guyana heaven.

Also, we need to rethink the purposes, functioning, and organisation of political parties, with a view to redefining and reforming such entities, away from their European (Eastern and Western) and North American provenance, to serve the needs of **Guyana** as the prime objective, as opposed to satisfying the hegemonic aspirations of some individual or group of individuals. I am encouraged in this direction of thinking when I note the reported comments of George Lamming about political parties at the opening ceremony of the fifth Assembly of Caribbean people conference at the University of the West Indies (UWI) Cave Hill Campus on the night of Tuesday, 3 August, 2010[114]. We need to take the Lammingesque critique seriously. The furore generated by the circumstances of President Jagdeo's recent visit to Buxton (Wednesday 18 August, 2010) has also strengthened my views on the inappropriate stances of **all** our political parties in relation to the governance of individual communities.

The content of this CODA would be incomplete if I were to not include the following cautionary comments.

First, many of the issues related to the matter of improving Guyana's electoral system are conceptual issues that are not uniquely Guyanese. They have been posed as problems with voting systems, many without final resolution, repeatedly for many centuries.

---

114 Indeed, in a gallows humour sense, I am reminded of a passage from Mark Twain's 'What stumped the Bluejays' where their human characteristics are highlighted. That passage is: *"A jay hasn't got any more principle than a Congressman. A jay will lie, a jay will steal, a jay will deceive, a jay will betray; and four times out of five, a jay will go back on his solemnest promise. The sacredness of an obligation is a thing which you can't cram into no blue-jay's head.............. Yes sir, a jay is everything that a man is. A jay can cry, a jay can laugh, a jay can feel shame, a jay can reason and plan and discuss, a jay likes gossip and scandal, a jay has got a sense of humour, a jay knows when he is an ass just as well as you do - maybe better. If a jay ain't human, he better take in his sign, that's all."*

Secondly, major academic work *(here I have in mind particularly the work of Kenneth Arrow that has led to the so-called "Impossibility Theorem")* proves conclusively that we should not expect our cherished, intuitively attractive views, of democracy in action to be satisfied.

Thirdly, given the desire of politicians to be 'top dog' in a competitive milieu dealing with the acquisition of political power through some electoral system, there is the ever present possibility of strategic voting (not the crudity of stealing ballots, but the more sophisticated dishonesty of voting for persons whom one does not favour for strategic reasons to disadvantage strong competitors). The work of Allan Gibbard and Mark Satterthwaite (the Gibbard-Sattherthwaite Theorem, published in the early 1970s) demonstrates that any democratic election among at least three candidates is prone to manipulation through what might be called strategic voting. One has no way of ensuring that a voter will vote their honest opinion. If enough voters vote as though they prefer a candidate that they do not in fact so prefer, that pretense **can** influence the outcome of the elections. No electoral system can be devised to be proof against such tactical/strategic voting!

Fourthly, in addition to the three conceptual difficulties just mentioned, there is the difficulty (a real human difficulty) associated with making a choice between two equally attractive alternatives. Encountering this kind of difficulty is particularly likely when one is dealing with conjectures, since 'logic' may not provide reliable tie-breaking capabilities. Here I am referring to circumstances related to the legend of Buridan's donkey which starved to death because, standing halfway between two equally attractive stacks of grass, it could not make up its mind which one it wished to eat. Quite what we wish to do with our electoral system might well pose us problems akin to that of the dilemma of Buridan's ass.

A final comment may be useful. The following quotation is attributed to Piet Hein:
>   *"A problem worthy of attack*
>   *Proves its worth by fighting back."*

In the matter of Guyana, its electoral system, and its system of governance, there should be no doubt that this constitutes *"A problem worthy of attack";* so lets gird up our loins and prepare for the fight.
END

APPENDIX
New shores

So! We're moving on, going to de new shores!
Cyan wait, what a change!
Now ah gon be able to do all de tings ah couldn't do before
Yes! Ah gon walk de streets all hour ah de night - no fear
They ain't got no choke and rob fu me frighten

Eh eh, ah gon get me food fu cheap cheap!
Lawd, imagine, fridge always stock up with de cheese
Yu know, all them different cheese, even de ones with dem holes in dem
And de beef - me nah gat fu pressure am before me eat
Nice and sweet... yes, ah moving to de new shores...

Yu know, when yu ova deh, yu aint got fu worry bout hospital yu know!
Yu just go and is just so dem does tek care ah yu
YES! Is not like we public hospital yu know, it nice, nice
Yu get sick deh, is no worries!
Permanent vacation! Jumping up, ah moving to de new shores...

Hehe, no Miss Mavis fu mind me business!
Me can do what meh want, and nah gat fu worry bout who winda blind shaking yu know
Yeah man, me nah gat fu worry who gon come and aks me fu keep lil fish fu them,
Then seh it lil bit when they collect it back...Lawd, me moving to de new shores!

SIX MONTHS LATER...

Well I tell yu, we real stupid yu know!
Imagine, we gat paradise hay, and abee nah know da!
Ow lawd! One night in de big city, de cops come
Guns, tear gas, and what-not - some terrorist living in de next apartment
Gimme back me lil choke and robber, yeh...

A gon miss de cheap food though. But wait a minute,
Why we food gat fu be so expensive? Oh right, de IMF devalue we dollar

We not good enough fu eat foreign thing, much less enjoy foreign services
And we got fu pay de high price, cause we aint know bout value added -
How come we exporting cocoa and importing chocolate? We stupid, is
wha!

Oh gawd! Me son get sick, and we go to de dacta.
Well guess wha, de bills start fu arrive when he get betta and come back
home!
Yu know is sick ah get sick to! This expert bill and dat expert bill, lab bill,
medicine bill, all kinda bill!
Gimme back me old bruk down public hospital, yeh, at least me nah get no
bill when me come home!
And when me in de waiting room whole day waiting, is good gossip me
getting yu know...Eh, eh!

Imagine, up to now me nah know me neighbour!
No, not even de one they seh is terrorist - maybe that is why?
Me nah know, but oh lawd how ah de wish somebody de come fu borrow
lil flour,
Or offer fu look me son while I wuk de security job - YES! I was company
directa back home yu know
But de security job was all that ah coulda find on them blasted shores...

Them new shores? Them does suck blood!
Tek we life, we still developing they country fu them yu know...colonialism
done, but we still colonised...
We stupid, give them we brains, and left we paradise fu them playground
Wise up people, wise up! Is time fu build we own,
WE OWN

Romona Carrico
©10 June 2010

ABOUT THE AUTHOR

William, Haslyn, Parris (born 2 March, 1941), facilitated by two scholarships he won in 1959 – one to UCWI, Jamaica, and the other the Guiana Scholarship – obtained degrees in Mathematics (BSc Special, UCWI, Mona – 1962); Economics (BSc. Hons – 1966, LSE); and Economics specializing in Statistics (MSc -1967, LSE).

His career has encompassed the positions of Mathematics Teacher at Queen's College (1962 – 1963), Senior Economist at the Central Bank of Guyana (1967 – 1969), Chief Economist of the Central Bank of Guyana (1969 – 1971), Chief Executive Officer, Guybau and subsequently Guymine (1971 – 1981), Chairman of Guyconstruct (1976 – 1980), Chairman of the Bauxite Industry Development Company, BIDCO (1982 – 1983), Deputy Chairman of the State Planning Commission (1977 – 1983), Chairman of the State Planning Commission (1983 – 1991), and Deputy Prime Minister responsible for Planning and Development (1984 – 1991).

During the 24 year period (1967 – 1991), Mr Parris played key roles in the negotiations that led to the nationalizations of the bauxite companies Demba (1971), and Reynolds in Berbice (1975); which gave rise to Guybau, Bermine, and subsequently their merger Guymine. He lived through the systemic consequences of those nationalizations in the position of being responsible for the running of the bauxite industry as its Chief Executive Officer.

He was subsequently involved in designing divestment strategies, and in divestment negotiations, initiating those for the bauxite and sugar industries, and completing those for the national Telephone Company, and Demerara Woods Limited. He also undertook the negotiations which led to the 50/50 joint venture between Reynolds and the Government of Guyana – Aroaima Mining Company Ltd.

Early in the 1970's he became a member of the Central Executive of the then ruling People's National Congress, and continued to be a member of that Party until 1991. the more than a quarter of a century of intimate exposure to academic, public sector and private sector business activities (including being on Boards of several companies), and politics, has provided the author with interesting insights into the economic development process, both nationally and internationally (all gained at ringside or in the ring so to speak).

On 1 May, 1991, Mr. Parris demitted office as Deputy Prime Minister, having achieved 50 years and several academic and other awards such as the 'Daily Chronicle 1971 Man of the Year', the most prestigious being the national award, Cacique Crown of Honour (C.C.H.) in 1980. He opted for a private life in the private sector, and currently is a member of the Board of Omai Gold Mines Ltd.

Mr. Parris has been involved in a number of matters concerning the Constitution of Guyana. These matters have included: the negotiations leading to the Herdmanston Accord (17 Jan 1998); the Constitution Reform Commission of which he was Secretary (1999); the Oversight Committee on Constitutional Reform (1999 / 2000) as Coordinator; and as one of the Commissioners of the Guyana Elections Commission (2001) – a post he demitted on 31 July, 2006.

He has published several books, including: Bunaro (a set of essays on economic development relevant to Guyana); The Constitution of Guyana: What will it look like?; an Annotated Handbook of the 17 July 1999 Report of The Constitution Reform Commission of Guyana;1992-2003 Heretical Musings about Guyana; and Two Volumes of Ribald Tales of Guyana.